Galactic Diplomacy

Getting to Yes with ET

Galactic Diplomacy

Getting to Yes with ET

Michael E. Salla, M.A., Ph.D.

www.ExopoliticsInstitute.org
Kealakekua, Hawaii, USA

Galactic Diplomacy :
Getting to Yes with ET

Published by the Exopolitics Institute
PO Box 2199
Kealakekua, HI 96750 USA

ISBN-13: 978-0-9822902-1-7
ISBN-10: 0-9822902-1-7

Library of Congress Control Number: 2008943849

Printed in the USA

Author's Website: www.Exopolitics.Org

Publisher's Website: www.ExopoliticsInstitute.org

Contents

Table of Figures

Other Books by Michael E. Salla, Ph.D

Exposing U.S. Government Policies on Extraterrestrial Life: The Challenge of Exopolitics (Exopolitics Institute, 2009)

Exopolitics: Political Implications of the Extraterrestrial Presence (Dandelion Books, 2004)

The Hero's Journey Toward a Second American Century (Greenwood Press, 2002)

Co-Editor, *Essays on Peace* (Central Queensland University Press, 1995)

Co-Editor, *Why the Cold War Ended* (Greenwood Press, 1995)

Islamic Radicalism, Muslim Nations and the West (Indian Ocean Center for Peace Studies, 1993)

Acknowledgements

It has been four years since the publication of my last book, *Exposing US Government Policies on Extraterrestrial Life* (2009), which presented my exposé on what the U.S. government has been secretly doing on the issue of extraterrestrial visitation. For many readers, that book exposed the dark side of what has been secretly happening. I was asked "where was the positive side to extraterrestrial visitation"? What would give people hope and optimism that extraterrestrial visitation would enrich our lives, rather than limit it through the egregious activities of government, military and corporate entities? This book is my answer to those questions.

This book has been made possible by the many courageous whistleblowers and "experiencers" that have come forward to give their first hand testimonies about extraterrestrial life. Chief among them are the classic "contactee" cases that have historically been ignored by most UFO researchers, even though they ironically have the most to contribute to unraveling the mysterious behind UFOs and extraterrestrial visitation. To all these men and women, I and the world owe a profound debt of gratitude.

I have been fortunate to be able to directly interview individuals that have had direct contact or exposure to extraterrestrial visitors. These include (all U.S. based unless otherwise indicated): Wesley Bateman; Al Bielek; Dan Burisch; Alex Collier; Carlos Diaz Castro (Mexico); James Gilliland; Charles Hall, Niara Isley, Luis Fernando Mostajo Maertens (Bolivia), Preston Nichols, Hector Palacios (Mexico); Frank Stranges, members of the prepare4contact Yahoo forum, and those that chose to remain anonymous.

I am very grateful to the many whistleblowers, researchers, and colleagues from around the world that have shared with me their own testimonies, insights and/or the fruits of their own research. In particular, I wish to thank: Haktan Akdogan (Turkey); Maurizio Baiata (Italy): Stephen Bassett; Mike Bird (Canada); Art Campbell; Grant Cameron (Canada); James Courant; Kerry Cassidy; David Coote; Robert Dean (C.S.M. U.S. Army, ret.); Richard Dolan, M.A.; Robert Fleischer (Germany); Neil Freer, Neil Gould (Hong Kong); Come Carpentier de

Gourdon (India); William Hamilton, III; Hon Paul Hellyer; Richard C. Hoagland; Dr Lynne D. Kitei; Ed Komarek; Dr Scott Jones (Commander, USN ret.); Manuel Lamiroy, Lic. Juris. (South Africa); John Lear; Melinda Leslie; Dr Joe Lewels; Antonello Lupino, Laurea (Italy); Jim Marrs; Joan Ocean, M.Sc.; Jaime Maussan (Mexico); Steve Moreno; Steve Natale; Jeff Peckman; Mary Rodwell (Australia); Bill Ryan; Luca Scantamburlo (Italy); Clifford Stone (ret. U.S. Army), Wendelle Stevens (Lt. Col., USAF ret.), Victor Viggiani, M.Ed.; Dr Thomas Valone; Donald Ware (Lt. Col., USAF, ret.); Alfred Webre, J.D.; Dr Robert Wood (McDonnell Douglas); Ryan Wood; and again those who have chosen to remain anonymous.

I wish to thank George Arnold and two other librarians at American University's Main Library who provided research assistance for Chapter 2. I am also grateful to William Hamilton for permission to cite his personal notes of a 1991 interview with Sgt Charles L. Suggs. And thanks also to Clay and Shawn Pickering who helped arrange interviews with individuals with knowledge of the secret meetings between the Eisenhower administration and extraterrestrial races.

I am very grateful for Hugh Matlock who generously provided the hospitality, intellectual stimulation, editorial suggestions and research environment for completing earlier versions of several chapters in this book. My deep gratitude goes to Gesanna LahMan and Giorgio Piacenza who proof read this book and spotted numerous typographical errors. I am especially grateful to Giorgio who made many helpful editorial suggestions.

My heartfelt thanks go to Angelika S. Whitecliff without whom this book would not have been possible. She has supported the idea of Galactic Diplomacy from its inception, and contributed her own unique skills to making it more than an abstract idea. Much more importantly, over the four year period that this book has been in the making, she tirelessly supported my research with great intelligence, love and inspired advice.

Introduction

This book introduces first hand witness and whistleblower testimonies revealing that the USA, Britain, Russia and other major national governments have been secretly conducting, or known about, diplomatic relations with different extraterrestrial civilizations since at least 1952. These testimonies reveal that galactic diplomacy (aka 'exodiplomacy') with extraterrestrial visitors began with discussions over the development of thermonuclear weapons, the first of which was detonated by the Truman administration in November, 1952. Diplomatic discussions then expanded to include issues such as technology development, alien bases, extraterrestrials living on Earth, human rights, and use of earth resources. In frustration over lack of government transparency with their citizens, some extraterrestrials began contacting private citizens to inform them of the true nature of alien activities on Earth, and diplomatic relations with governments.

The above claims will immediately raise in many readers' minds the cliché, "extraordinary claims require extraordinary proof." In this book I will refer to some of the thousands of eyewitness reports, whistleblower statements, 'contactee'/'abductee' claims, radar recordings, photos, film, and released documents, that give abundant evidence that extraterrestrial life is indeed visiting Earth.[1] Is this large pool of eyewitness testimony the "extraordinary proof" needed to substantiate the "extraordinary claims" made in the above paragraph? That is something each reader has to ultimately decide. In making such a decision, however, there is a critical piece of information that I highly recommend the reader first consider.

Critical to any comprehensive inquiry on the question of visiting extraterrestrial life is evidence that the topic has the highest security classification among government agencies and military departments. In 1950, a senior Canadian official in the Department of Transportation, Wilbert Smith, travelled to Washington DC to find out what the U.S. knew about 'flying saucers'. He reported back to his superiors in a Top Secret Memorandum: "The matter is the most highly classified subject in the United States government, rating higher even than the H-bomb."[2]

An October 1969 Memorandum by US Air Force Brigadier General C.H. Bolender confirmed that UFO reports affecting national security were investigated differently, and were more highly classified than ordinary reports. Reports with no national security implications were released to the public through the official Air Force investigation, Project Blue Book, that ran from 1952 to 1969. Bolender said: "reports of unidentified flying objects which could affect national security are made in accordance with JANAP 146 or Air Force Manual 55-11, and are not part of the Blue Book system."[3] JANAP refers to a Joint Army Navy Air Publication 146 that required UFO sightings - by military and civilian pilots, and maritime personnel - be reported in a system created for "vital intelligence sightings" called CIRVIS.[4] JANAP 146c, released in 1954, made it an offense for military servicemen or civilian airline pilots to disclose information about UFO sightings that had national security implications.[5] Offenders could be prosecuted under the Espionage Act which imposed fines of up to $10,000 and ten years imprisonment. Bolender's memo confirms that UFO sightings with national security implications were automatically classified under the CIRVIS system, and could not be released to the general public unless later declassified.

In 1975, Senator Barry Goldwater - who was also a Major-General in the US Air Force reserves - commented about his own failed efforts to learn more about the UFO/flying saucer phenomenon: "I have tried in the years past to have the material collected by the Air Force to no avail. It is still classified above Top Secret."[6]

More recently, in December 2012, we have the extraordinary off-air comments by the Russian Prime Minister and former President, Dmitry Medvedev, after a television interview that each new President is given a highly classified briefing document on the topic of extraterrestrial life:

> Along with the briefcase with nuclear codes, the president of the country is given a special 'top secret' folder. This folder in its entirety contains information about aliens who visited our planet... Along with this, you are given a report of the absolutely secret special service that exercises control over aliens on the territory of our country...[7]

Introduction

Based on the preceding claims by the above public officials we can be sure of two things. First, the topic of extraterrestrial life has very high, if not the highest, security classification in the respective national security apparatuses of the world's leading nations. Highly compartmentalized national security programs have been created where access is based on stringent classification requirements well beyond the "Top Secret" given to most senior government employees and elected political representatives. Second, agreements have been made by leaders of the national security apparatus concerning extraterrestrial life. Some of these agreements, as I will show in subsequent chapters, not only concern the topic of extraterrestrial life, but directly involve extraterrestrials themselves. Some of whom, as Medvedev remarked and I discuss at length in chapter six, even reside on our planet with special national security entities monitoring them!

The idea that leaders of the national security apparatus would be audacious enough to enter into agreements concerning extraterrestrial life without telling their citizens or elected representatives is not far-fetched. A close reading of the Brookings Report delivered to the U.S. Congress in 1961 makes clear the thinking of national security experts contemplating whether or not the existence of extraterrestrial life would be announced if discovered. Titled "Proposed Studies on the Implications of Peaceful Space Activities for Human Affairs," the Brookings Report devoted several sections to discussing the public policy implications of extraterrestrial life. The Brookings Report described the potential impact of extraterrestrial life or 'artifacts' being found on nearby planetary bodies. The Report stated:

> While face-to-face meetings with it [extraterrestrial life] will not occur within the next 20 years; artifacts left at some point in time by these life forms might possibly be discovered through our space activities on the moon, Mars, or Venus.[8]

The Report described the unpredictability of societal reactions to the discovery of extraterrestrial artifacts:

> Evidences of its [extraterrestrial] existence might also be found in artifacts left on the moon or other planets. The consequences for attitudes and values are unpredictable, but would vary profoundly in different cultures and between groups within complex societies; a crucial factor would be the nature of the communication between us and the other beings.[9]

The Report also mentioned that devastating societal effects could result from contact with more technologically advanced off world societies:

> Anthropological files contain many examples of societies, sure of their place in the universe, which have disintegrated when they had to associate with previously unfamiliar societies espousing different ideas and different life ways; others that survived such an experience usually did so by paying the price of changes in values and attitudes and behavior.[10]

Of those most likely to be affected by the discovery of extraterrestrial life, the Brookings Report has a surprise:

> It has been speculated that, of all groups, scientists and engineers might be the most devastated by the discovery of relatively superior creatures, since these professions are most clearly associated with the mastery of nature, rather than with the understanding and expression of man. Advanced understanding of nature might vitiate all our theories at the very least, if not also require a culture and perhaps a brain inaccessible to earth scientists. [11]

This surprising insight helps explain why scientists have been among the most vociferous debunkers of evidence supporting the discovery of extraterrestrial life – their way of life is most threatened by such a discovery!

Most importantly, the Brookings Report went on to raise the possibility of suppressing any announcement of extraterrestrial life or artifacts for national security reasons: "How might such information, under what circumstances, be presented or withheld from the public?"[12]

If a group of objective researchers from the Brookings Institute could recommend to the U.S. Congress that revealing the existence of extraterrestrial life might lead to societal collapse, then it is not so strange that elected governments around the world have been so silent on the issue. A brave attempt was made in the late 1970s to have international governments officially examine the evidence, persuasive even three decades ago, that extraterrestrial life was something worth taking seriously.

The Prime Minister of the newly independent state of Grenada took it upon himself to get the United Nations to take the possibility of extraterrestrial life seriously. Beginning in 1977, he succeeded in his hectoring of UN members to take action. The United Nations General Assembly finally passed Decision 33/426 in December 1978 wherein it recommended:

> [T]he General Assembly invites interested Member States to take appropriate steps to coordinate on a national level scientific research and investigation into extraterrestrial life, including unidentified flying objects, and to inform the Secretary-General of the observations, research and evaluation of such activities.[13]

Unfortunately, the General Assembly Decision was never implemented, and to this day, governments are largely silent about the possibility that extraterrestrial life is visiting our world. More recently, in an October 2010 Press Conference, the Director of the UN's Office for Outer Space Affairs, Dr Mazlan Othman pointed out that a mechanism does exist within the Office of Outers Space Affairs by which the UN would coordinate an international response to the discovery of extraterrestrial life.[14]

At this point it's worth pointing out that first hand witness testimony is powerful evidence that can be presented in a court of law to persuade a jury beyond any reasonable doubt about some legal issue. It's a historic travesty that the same standards of testimonial evidence used in court rooms all over the world to determine the truth associated with legal issues, aren't used to determine the truth behind the extraterrestrial issue.

Extraterrestrial life has been discovered, and senior national security officials have been reticent to disclose this fact not only to their citizens, but to most elected representatives. While the traditional approach among UFO researchers has been to accumulate further evidence to indisputably prove the existence of UFOs and the extraterrestrial hypothesis, after seven decades of officially sanctioned deception, such an approach is no longer suitable.[15] The information age makes available the evidence of visiting extraterrestrial life at any computer terminal around the world. A new approach to the massive evidentiary pool is necessary. An approach that helps **prepare** people to a fact that governments have yet to publicly acknowledge. Extraterrestrial life has been discovered, and some advanced civilizations have been visiting our planet for *at least* seventy years.

This book prepares the reader for the fact that technologically advanced extraterrestrial life exists, and has been visiting our planet since at least the 1940's. This fact has been kept secret by a carefully orchestrated set of policies developed by national security officials with the historic support of a small select group of elected government representatives. These policies are implemented in highly classified compartmentalized programs with strict need-to-know security provisions in place.[16] This means that the vast majority of government, military and corporate officials are simply out of the loop on the extraterrestrial issue.

Not only have select governmental authorities deceived their citizens and peers about extraterrestrial life, but major governments led by the U.S. have secretly entered into direct diplomatic relations with extraterrestrial life. Most disturbing to the reader will be evidence that some major governments, principally the U.S., have entered into secret agreements with some extraterrestrial groups that have *de facto* 'treaty' status. Some of these agreements concern the acquisition and

6

development of extraterrestrial technology, and their advanced knowledge, found around the world or in outer space.

"Galactic diplomacy" – which I use as a synonym for "exodiplomacy" - is not mere speculation from the pen of futurists or science fiction writers. It is currently a highly classified national security program where a select group of authorized government, military and corporate officials, are secretly meeting to discuss extraterrestrial life and technology. In some cases, these officials are communicating directly with representatives of extraterrestrial civilizations.

The reader has basically three choices given the startling evidence that galactic diplomacy is secretly occurring. The first is to dismiss testimonial evidence of extraterrestrial life, and tacitly allow select government authorities to indefinitely continue their secret galactic diplomacy. Keeping one's head in the sand by openly debunking evidence, no matter how credible, has been the recourse of many in the scientific community up to the present. This is by no means solely due to the devastating impact on the world view of scientists and engineers of the discovery of extraterrestrial life pointed out by the Brookings Report. The 1953 Robertson Panel, secretly convened by the CIA, recommended debunking evidence of flying saucers due to national security concerns over the public's reaction.[17]

Debunkers typically raise the cliché "extraordinary claims require extraordinary proof," and proceed to establish an extraordinarily high standard for accepting any evidence as admissible on the issue of extraterrestrial life. They then proceed to debunk all evidence for alien visitors to our world on the basis that none of the testimonial evidence reaches the extraordinarily high standards required to prove "extraordinary claims." Yet, truth remains true even when one is unable to prove it. Eyewitness testimony doesn't cease to be evidence simply because a witness or whistleblower can't prove what they saw or experienced. That is especially the case when national security agencies view the topic of extraterrestrial life as highly classified, and will consequently intervene to maintain secrecy on the grounds of national security.

Later in this book (chapter seven) I will show that elements of the national security apparatus have directly intimidated witnesses and whistleblowers, and removed *hard evidence* supporting their *extraordinary claims*. We need to consider all the evidence that extraterrestrial life is visiting our world, and not dismiss it out of hand because of a cliché that is unsuitable due to a national security factor that works to maintain secrecy on the issue of alien life.

Some may argue that a debunking approach is most prudent and vehemently oppose any kind of informed public policy discussion of extraterrestrial life. Undoubtedly, some will choose to trust governments to do the right thing while the urgent economic contingencies of 21st century life soak up one's attention.

Exposing governmental agreements concerning or directly involving extraterrestrial life is the second choice before us given the evidence that galactic diplomacy is secretly occurring. Becoming active in a global process to pressure government authorities to disclose all they know about alien life and technology, will be the preferred choice of many once the evidence persuades them. This requires concerted efforts to gain access to classified files that have been carefully hidden in the national security system, and in some cases placed in private corporate archives out of reach of most governments and even military authorities.[18] *Transparency* and *accountability* will be the catchwords of the day as select government agencies slowly reveal solid evidence of extraterrestrial life, and what has transpired behind closed doors to keep this secret from the general public, the mass media and most public officials.

The third choice is the most proactive. It invites the reader to seriously contemplate becoming active in a citizen based diplomatic outreach with extraterrestrial civilizations visiting our planet. This choice will appeal to many who are disheartened by the depth of deception by select national security authorities over the existence of extraterrestrial life. Governmental authorities will lose much of the public trust when the truth is disclosed, and it will take some time to restore it. In the meantime, private citizens either acting in an individual capacity or in small groups can participate in galactic diplomacy with extraterrestrial life.

This book assists those attracted to the second and third choices over how to react to the secret galactic diplomacy or "exodiplomacy" that has been occurring. Those adopting the first choice will predictably hide behind the cliché "extraordinary claims require extraordinary proof," and ignore or systematically debunk evidence concerning extraterrestrial life. If they choose to read on, they will likely dismiss what follows as a speculative foray based on unverified claims. On the contrary, this book offers information and resources that will assist those seriously contemplating the latter two choices that galactic diplomacy is very real and something to be immediately dealt with.

Those desiring to expose secret governmental activity in diplomatic relations concerning extraterrestrial life, will be given the necessary basic information tools to hold responsible government, military and corporate officials accountable for past policies, and to ensure governmental transparency in the future. Alternatively, those desiring to become active in citizen diplomacy initiatives will be given essential information for discerning the motivations and activities of visiting extraterrestrial civilizations. This is indispensable for practicing a citizen based form of galactic diplomacy.

Getting to Yes is the title of a popular book in the field of conflict resolution that reveals how to conduct negotiations based on recognizing all the parties "needs" or "vital interests."[19] In the *Getting to Yes* negotiation model it is necessary to focus on the vital interests of a party, and avoid bargaining over 'positions'. This is because 'positions' tend to reflect a zero-sum thinking where one party wins or loses, as opposed to vital interests that can lead to win-win solutions. In "principled negotiations" all parties' vital interests are represented, and part of any negotiated outcome.

When it comes to the visitation of extraterrestrial life, testimonial evidence reveals that private citizens are a party whose vital interests in secret negotiations have not been represented at all. This indicates that secret negotiations are "unprincipled" according to the model developed in *Getting to Yes*. In order to illustrate key concepts in *Getting to Yes* and how these apply to negotiations with extraterrestrial life, I have adapted the above ideas in Figure 1.

"Getting to Yes with ET" is consequently not solely diplomatic activity secretly pursued by government, military and corporate entities from around the world, but an inalienable right that belongs to private citizens. Private citizens have a right to have their interests directly represented in any negotiations where their vital interests are involved. In the United States, this is recognized in the Constitution where diplomatic agreements require ratification by the two thirds of the U.S. Senate which directly represents the interests of private citizens.

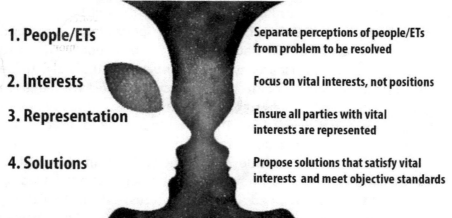

Getting to Yes with ET
BASIC STEPS IN PRINCIPLED NEGOTIATIONS

1. People/ETs — Separate perceptions of people/ETs from problem to be resolved

2. Interests — Focus on vital interests, not positions

3. Representation — Ensure all parties with vital interests are represented

4. Solutions — Propose solutions that satisfy vital interests and meet objective standards

Copyright, Michael Salla, Ph.D 2013   Adapted from Ury and Fisher, *Getting to Yes*

Figure 1. Getting to Yes with ET. Image credit: Stan Ho

Private citizens have an inherent right in being directly represented and/or participating in any decisions over who among the various extraterrestrial visitors are willing to satisfy our vital interests in any diplomatic agreements. Guaranteeing a direct role of private citizens in any agreements reached with extraterrestrial civilizations will ensure that our vital interests are met, and we properly evolve as a planetary civilization. The choice is up to you. Read on and prepare yourself for the grandest adventure of all – the journey to galactic citizenship!

INTRODUCTION - ENDNOTES

[1] For an overview of different sources of evidence for extraterrestrial life, see Michael Salla, *Exopolitics: Political Implications of the Extraterrestrial Presence* (Dandelion Books, 2004) ch. 1.

[2] "Project Magnet, http://tinyurl.com/ctmlbtb

[3] "The Bolender Memo, Oct 20, 1969," http://www.nicap.org/Bolender_Memo.htm

[4] See: http://www.cufon.org/cufon/janp1462.htm

[5] See JANAP 146C for references to security regulations and punishment under the Espionage Act, http://www.cufon.org/cufon/janp146c.htm

[6] "Goldwater UFO Files: The Highlights": http://www.presidentialufo.com/articles-a-papers/402-goldwater-ufo-files

[7] See Michael Salla, "Russian Prime Minister claims extraterrestrials live among us," http://exopolitics.org/russian-prime-minister-claims-extraterrestrials-live-among-us/

[8] Brookings Report, 215. Available online at: http://www.enterprisemission.com/images/brook-7.gif For overview go to: http://www.enterprisemission.com/brooking.html

[9] Brookings Report, 215. Available online at: http://www.enterprisemission.com/images/brook-7.gif

[10] Brookings Report, 215. Available online at: http://www.enterprisemission.com/images/brook-7.gif

[11] Brookings Report, 225. Available online at: http://www.enterprisemission.com/images/brook-9.gif

[12] Brookings Report, 215. Available online at: http://www.enterprisemission.com/images/brook-7.gif

[13] United Nations General Assembly Decision 33/426 (1978), *Resolutions and Decisions Adopted by the General Assembly during its 33rd Session* (1978-1979): A/33/45 (GAOR, 33rd Session, Suppl. No. 45. An online copy of the Decision is available at: http://www.ufoevidence.org/documents/doc902.htm

[14] See: http://www.un.org/News/briefings/docs/2010/101014_Othman.doc.htm

[15] For further discussion see Michael Salla, "Exopolitics: Discipline of Choice for Public Policy Issues Concerning Extraterrestrial life," *Exopolitics Journal*, 2:4 (July 2008): 268-83. http://exopoliticsjournal.com/vol-2-4.htm

[16] See Michael Salla, *Exposing U.S. Government Policies on Extraterrestrial Life* (Exopolitics Institute, 2009).

[17] See: "Report of the Meetings of Scientific Advisory Panel on Unidentified Flying Objects Convened by Office of Scientific Intelligence, CIA, Jan 14-18, 1953" (Released November 16, 1978) 1. Available online at: http://www.ufologie.net/htm/durantreport.htm

[18] See Michael Salla, "Obama administration to clash with corporations over UFO files," http://tinyurl.com/beahgx

[19] William Ury and Roger Fisher, *Getting to Yes: Negotiating Agreement without Giving In* (1981). More info at: http://en.wikipedia.org/wiki/Getting_to_YES

CHAPTER 1

Track Two Galactic Diplomacy: The Role of Citizen Diplomacy with Extraterrestrial Civilizations

Introduction[20]

This book will present some of the evidence that there are dozens of extraterrestrial civilizations races with different motivations interacting with or monitoring global humanity.[21] I will show that extraterrestrial motivations span a wide spectrum. At one end are 'benevolent' activities aimed at uplifting humanity towards a fuller expression of its collective potential by respecting the vital interests of individuals, communities and the biosphere. At the other end we recognize manipulative activities designed to undermine human sovereignty where the vital interests of individuals are ignored.

In chapter five I will discuss some of the extensive evidence of government entities in the U.S. and elsewhere having held meetings and having reached agreements with some extraterrestrial races. These official diplomatic meetings have been highly classified and reveal that 'galactic diplomacy' or 'exodiplomacy' at an official level has been secretly underway for almost 60 years without the knowledge of most citizens and elected representatives.[22] This has resulted in the vital interests of individuals, communities and the biosphere to be ignored.

Chapters three, four and five will give a detailed explanation of the nineteen most significant extraterrestrial civilizations interacting with humanity. They reveal the role played by national security entities in the U.S. secretly reaching agreements with some extraterrestrials, while suppressing information about these agreements, and of the existence and activities of extraterrestrial civilizations in general.

More encouraging is the evidence that a number of extraterrestrial civilizations are assisting in the evolution of human consciousness. They have been communicating with private citizens and groups that are interested in more peaceful policies at a global level. These communications and initiatives linking private citizens and groups with some extraterrestrial civilizations suggest the potential for an unofficial form of 'galactic diplomacy' to be practiced. This unofficial diplomacy complements the official form of galactic diplomacy secretly conducted by government entities.

There is also evidence that the various extraterrestrial civilizations interacting with Earth are locked into a low intensity conflict over the direction and potential of global humanity in the wider galactic community.[23] These extraterrestrial civilizations work through their respective 'human allies' in the form of global elites, national security entities, private citizens, and/or non-government organizations to promote their respective agendas. Competition involving extraterrestrial civilizations and their 'human allies' on Earth appears to mirror conflicts at a galactic level.[24] This makes the extraterrestrial rivalry over the Earth's population and resources something that has interest to the wider galactic community which apparently is monitoring events on Earth in large numbers.

'Track two' or 'citizen diplomacy' offers the opportunity for private individuals or 'citizen organizations' to open communication channels and develop agreements between nations experiencing diplomatic impasses and/or violent conflict. Citizen diplomacy has been shown to be an effective process in helping establish diplomatic relations and developing suitable confliction resolution strategies for difficult global conflicts. Extending the practice of citizen diplomacy from the global arena involving international actors, into the exopolitical arena involving different extraterrestrial civilizations is both possible and necessary. This is due to the long history of secrecy, hidden rivalries and low intensity conflicts that exist between extraterrestrial races and government agencies.

Given government secrecy over the existence of extraterrestrial civilizations; the diverse motivations, agendas and conflicts involving extraterrestrial races and various government agencies; there is an urgent need for citizen diplomacy with extraterrestrial civilizations or what might be also called *'track two galactic diplomacy'*. There is a need for private citizens to establish communications with extraterrestrial civilizations; play roles in mediating between different extraterrestrial groups and global humanity; establishing track two diplomatic relations with extraterrestrials; and assist official diplomatic relations between government agencies and extraterrestrials or what might be described as *'track one galactic diplomacy'*.

Most importantly, using the conceptual mode of principled negotiation described earlier in Ury's and Fisher's book, *Getting to Yes*, we can develop a model for "Getting to Yes with ET." When those communicating with extraterrestrials recognize the vital interests of all parties directly affected by negotiations, then we have "principled negotiations."

In this chapter I examine the key principles of 'galactic diplomacy' at the unofficial level, as a form of 'track two' or citizen diplomacy aimed at establishing contact and communications with different extraterrestrial civilizations. I will analyze the nature of diplomatic representation on Earth that might be recognized by various extraterrestrial races. Particular focus will be on the representative status of different global constituencies such as politically organized humanity, cetaceans, alleged subterranean civilizations, and the role of Earth or 'Gaia' as a self-regulating organism with vital interests. Each of these constituencies have their own vital interests that must be included in negotiations that directly impact upon them.

I also examine the need for 'track two galactic diplomacy' as a means of complementing official diplomatic relations between major nations and extraterrestrial races. Finally, I explore how national security entities are likely to respond to 'track two galactic diplomacy' between private citizens/groups with extraterrestrials in terms of four key challenges confronting the practice of this form of diplomacy:

1. the extent of private communications and interactions with extraterrestrial races;
2. the coercive resources of shadow government agencies;
3. the degree to which extraterrestrial races may manipulate citizens engaging in track two galactic diplomacy;
4. and implications of initiatives and agreements reached through track two galactic diplomacy.

Three Conventional Political Models for Representing Earth in Diplomatic Interactions with Extraterrestrial Civilizations

Traditional forms of diplomacy involve appointed officials of different national political systems officially representing their nations to promote their respective "national interests" in the face of competition from, and conflict with, other nations. We witness examples of this with ambassadors and diplomats stationed at national embassies around the world to promote their national policies. Diplomacy can be defined as: "a technique of state action, [which] is essentially a process whereby communications from one government go directly to the decision-making apparatus of another." [25] Individuals appointed to diplomatic positions are typically accountable to the executive and/or legislative branches of government of their nations. In the United States, ambassadors are nominated by the President and appointed by the U.S. Senate.

These appointed as ambassadors, or 'diplomats' in general, are consequently authorized to participate in meetings aimed at producing agreements that impact on the territories and citizens of their nations. This 'official' form of diplomacy has existed for thousands of years and examples are found in the monarchs of early kingdoms who appointed representatives to meet with foreign powers; and establish treaties with other kingdoms to promote peace, trade and/or protection of each other's citizens. In the recent era, diplomacy has increasingly been defined in terms of diplomats representing the national interests of their states which transcend moral principles or global imperatives.

According to Henry Kissinger who wrote the influential book, *Diplomacy*, international diplomacy is based upon the judicious advancement of a state's national interest above all other considerations including moral principles or global interests.[26] The concept of 'national interest' evolved from the statecraft of Cardinal Richelieu of 17th century France who was the first 'modern' leader to contend that universal morality was trumped by the pragmatic concerns of the nation state. Richelieu was Prime Minister of France from 1624-1642. He diplomatically and militarily allied Catholic France with Protestant German Princes and the Ottoman Turks against the Catholic Hapsburg Empire on the basis of France's *raison d'etat* (reason of state or 'national interest').[27] This was something that appeared to be shocking and immoral in the Christian world, but nevertheless became the official policy of France. Since the thirty years War 1618-1648, the concept of national interest has subsequently become the basis of diplomatic interactions and the chief concern of diplomats representing their nation in the global community. Morality and ethical concerns, in the centuries since Cardinal Richelieu first introduced the concept of *raison d'etat*, have increasingly played second fiddle to a state's national interest when these came into conflict.

As far as the idea of vital interests of all parties in a negotiation is concerned, we can see how national interest has historically evolved to trump the vital interests of "weaker parties" when it comes to negotiations. Put simply, diplomatic discussions that emphasize the national interests of states, the vital interests of some (typically weaker) parties impacted by the discussions are secondary.

In this book, I will discuss some of the persuasive evidence of clandestine official meetings between national governments and extraterrestrial races since at least the 1950s. In the next chapter, I will examine the most well known incident which involves President Eisenhower meeting with different delegations of extraterrestrial races in secret meetings at Edwards Air Force base and Holloman Air Force base in 1954 and 1955. These meetings led the Eisenhower administration to establish agreements with extraterrestrial civilizations based on the national interest of the U.S. There was an absence of any moral imperative to inform the general public due to the profound nature of this initial contact between extraterrestrial civilizations and a major Earth government. This policy was merely a continuation of the now well established doctrine that national interest would trump morality whenever they came into conflict. The result has been that the vital interests of US and other national citizens have been violated, at least at an individual level.

The secret agreements between extraterrestrial civilizations and the U.S. government have led to the building of joint facilities, technology exchanges and permission for limited abductions.[28] The meetings and consequent agreements established between extraterrestrial races and the U.S. government have been kept secret.

The information of these meetings and agreements continue to remain highly classified, and off limits to the most senior of elected political officials. This even includes Presidents such as Clinton and Carter who were denied access to documents detailing the extraterrestrial presence.[29] More surprising is that even senior military officers are often kept out of the loop as exemplified in the case of Vice Admiral Thomas Wilson who in 1997 served as the intelligence chief for the Joint Chiefs of Staff. Wilson was denied access to classified projects involving UFO technologies that he learned about through non-official sources.[30]

The diplomatic meetings that have occurred so far have been between different extraterrestrial civilizations and representatives from the U.S. governments. These diplomatic meetings have thus followed the traditional form of diplomatic relations where appointed officials represent the national interests of their countries in meetings with foreign powers. This indicates that diplomatic relations with extraterrestrial civilizations have proceeded despite the secrecy surrounding the existence of extraterrestrial races, and the secret contact established with the U.S. and other major world governments.

It may be assumed that the U.S. and other world governments are by default the representatives of Earth in terms of its citizens and territory in establishing diplomatic relations with extraterrestrials, but this is not something that can be taken for granted. It's very important to closely examine the question of who represents Earth in diplomatic relations with extraterrestrial civilizations. After all, we private citizens have been kept out of the loop on the reality of extraterrestrial life, does that mean we have no relevance when it comes to representing the interests of our planet with off-world visitors?

As far as 'galactic diplomacy' is concerned, the Earth may be defined, in a narrow way, as the population and territory of the third planet orbiting the sun, or Sol if we wish to identify ourselves within the Milky Way Galaxy. Thus defined, the different nation states representing the regional territories and populations on Earth collectively represent the Earth. This narrow reading of who represents the Earth, as far as galactic diplomacy is concerned, would lead to three models of diplomatic representations for the Earth.

The first would be that multilateral institutions such as the United Nations would have the necessary legitimacy and authority to represent planet Earth in diplomatic relations with extraterrestrial civilizations. Presumably, the United Nations (UN) would represent the global interests of all states rather than the national interests of any one particular state. It's worth pointing out that the United Nations directly represents the interests of its member states; and, at best, only indirectly represents the interests of the world population

Figure 2. Will the United Nations represent Earth in diplomatic negotiations with extraterrestrial life?

The second model of diplomatic representation would be that dominant global powers such as the U.S. Russia and China would represent the Earth in diplomatic meetings with extraterrestrial civilizations. The dominant powers would presumably prioritize their national interests rather than the global interests of all the nations of Earth. This appears to have been the case thus far due to the minor role played by the United Nations in dealing with the extraterrestrial presence. For example, the UN General Assembly passed a *decision* in December 1978 (Decision 33/426) to establish "an agency or a department of the United Nations for undertaking, coordinating and disseminating the results of research into unidentified flying objects and related phenomena."[31] The requested agency/department was never created and the *decision* was not acted upon. This vividly demonstrates the lack of support the United Nations has had from major powers in seriously playing a role in the UFO/extraterrestrial phenomenon.

The third representational model is a hybrid where major global powers establish diplomatic relations with extraterrestrials, cooperate among themselves, and have these relations legitimized in multilateral institutions such as the United Nations. This would enable major powers to find consensus about how to promote their respective national interests in harmony with one another, and to legitimize these through the United Nations as 'global interests'. Consequently, a narrow interpretation of who represents the Earth leads to the answer, major world governments and the multilateral institutions which they comprise and dominate.

There is however a broader definition of who represents the Earth which goes beyond the notion of geographical territory and population controlled by a national government. A definition that also goes beyond the concept of 'national interest', which has become the primary focus of diplomats advancing the welfare of their nations. This broader definition involves Earth having different constituencies that may have diplomatic standing among extraterrestrial civilizations. The vital interests of these constituencies go far beyond the concept of national interest relating to modern nations and international diplomacy.

Different Constituencies with Vital Interests that need to be Represented in Getting to Yes with ET

The first constituency is what has already been examined in terms of surface humanity that is politically organized into nation states with elected political representatives, appointed officials and/or hereditary monarchical systems. This is a constituency that undoubtedly has representational status for extraterrestrial civilizations as evidenced by the agreements which have already been reached between 'shadow government' representatives and some extraterrestrial groups as will be discussed in the next two chapters. However, such 'representative status' is not exclusive which leads to the examination of other constituencies that extraterrestrials, to varying degrees, might recognize as legitimate. After all, some extraterrestrial visitors might recognize that world politics, as presently set-up, doesn't really represent the vital interests of humanity generally, let alone the rest of sentient life on the planet.

The second constituency is the various sentient species that exhibit a high degree of intelligence that also inhabit the Earth's surface territories and oceans. In addition to humans as an intelligent sentient species, we can include cetaceans such as dolphins and whales that have exhibited a high degree of intelligence and communicative skills.[32] In analyzing Dolphin communications and intelligence, Dr Michael Hyson claims that:

> the *Cetacea* (dolphins and whales) are self-aware, fully conscious, sentient, and have their own complex language. Because they have larger brains, more available cortex, and more processing power available (because of their lives in water) the Cetacea, including the dolphins, are more intelligent than we are. [33]

Other cetacean researchers such as Dr John Lilly, Timothy Wyllie and Joan Ocean have found that dolphin/whale communications are based both on their highly complex sonar abilities and on the use of telepathic communication.[34] Consequently, the intelligence and communicative abilities of cetaceans, and other intelligent animals such as elephants that also have large brains, is something that some extraterrestrial visitors might recognize. This would give cetaceans, elephants and possibly other intelligent sentient species on Earth's surface and oceans, diplomatic standing among extraterrestrial civilizations despite the former's lack of technologically developed societies. Put simply, they each have their own vital interests that need to be considered in any negotiations that directly impact upon them.

A third constituency appears to be races of beings that inhabit Earth's subterranean realms that will be discussed in chapters three and four. These subterranean races or *intraterrestrials* have been described to be both human descendants of ancient kingdoms such as Lemuria, and a non-human race that has reptilian characteristics. Evidence from a wide range of sources including government whistleblowers, contactees and remote viewers give credence to the existence of such subterranean races that have technologies far more advanced than surface humanity. According to Brad Steiger, for example, these ancient human civilizations went underground many millennia ago:

> The Old Ones, an immensely intelligent and scientifically advanced race ... have chosen to structure their own environment under the surface of the planet and manufacture all their necessities. The Old Ones are hominid, extremely long-lived, and pre-date Homo sapiens by more than a million years.[35]

Furthermore, according to a range of whistleblower and contactee testimonies, there appears to be a group of Reptilians who are indigenous to Earth.[36] Some researchers contend that most if not all UFO reports are actually sightings of the ships of these subterranean races rather than beings from other worlds.[37] Each of these subterranean civilizations has their own vital interests that again need to be included in negotiations that directly impact upon them.

I now move to the fourth constituency which may initially come as a shock to many readers. It is based on the idea that the Earth itself can be regarded as a sentient being, or at least as a self-regulating entity, and therefore has vital interests that would be acknowledged by some extraterrestrial civilizations. The 'Gaia hypothesis' is based on the theory first promoted by a former NASA scientist, James Havelock in a 1979 book, that the Earth is a sentient being which regulates the evolution of life.[38] Havelock writes:

> I recognize that to view the Earth as if it were alive is just a convenient, but different, way of organizing the facts of the Earth. I am of course prejudiced in favor of Gaia and have filled my life for the past twenty-five years with the thought that Earth may be alive: not as the ancients saw her—a sentient Goddess with a purpose and foresight—but alive like a tree. A tree that quietly exists, never moving except to sway in the wind, yet endlessly conversing with the sunlight and the soil. Using sunlight and water and nutrient minerals to grow and change. But all done so imperceptibly, that to me the old oak tree on the green is the same as it was when I was a child.[39]

While Havelock doesn't believe Gaia's sentience is the same of the ancient Greek concept of a goddess with "purpose and foresight," his reference to Gaia as a global tree would at minimum make it sentient enough for its vital interests or needs to be considered by some extraterrestrial visitors. The Gaia hypothesis that Earth is a sentient being that exhibits consciousness and life, at least insofar as it is self-regulating, is something that we can expect some extraterrestrials might recognize. We cannot overlook the Earth itself or 'Gaia', as an important constituency in diplomatic relations with extraterrestrial civilizations insofar as it is self-regulating, and therefore has vital interests.

Consequently, the question of who represents Earth in establishing diplomatic relations with extraterrestrial civilizations is far more complex given the existence of different constituencies each of which has its own vital interests. These constituencies presumably have some standing among the various courts, councils and alliances that make up the various extraterrestrial civilizations that I will later identify are visiting the Earth.

A Comprehensive Representational Model for Diplomatic Relations with Extraterrestrial Civilizations

While it may be assumed that the question of who represents the human population of at least the Earth's surface is easy to answer, it cannot be assumed that secretly appointed officials who comprise official delegations responsible for developing agreements with extraterrestrials have the necessary legitimacy to bind all of surface humanity in unannounced "treaties". While appointed officials have *de facto* power to participate in meetings and agreements with extraterrestrial groups, I will show how these operate with great secrecy and remain unaccountable to the citizenry of different nations who remain oblivious to the existence of such meetings and agreements. Furthermore, elected political representatives are denied this information thereby raising the constitutional status of such meetings and treaties and the *de jure* authority of these.

The U.S. Constitution, for example, specifically states that all treaties to which the U.S. enters needs to be ratified by the U.S. Senate. Article II, section 2, states: "He [the President] shall have power, by and with the advice and consent of the Senate, to make treaties, provided two thirds of the Senators present concur."[40] However, this constitutional provision has been bypassed by a series of executive orders and congressional actions that make it possible for agreements to be signed and implemented without the consent of two-thirds of the Senate nor with the knowledge of the general public.[41] These extra-constitutional arrangements have dubious legal standing and while these may at most have standing for short periods such as national emergencies, it is extremely doubtful that their legal standing would be sufficient for a semi-permanent arrangement which has existed for almost 60 years. In short, the diplomatic representatives of major nations that meet and draw up agreements with extraterrestrial civilizations have dubious constitutional validity, at least in the U.S., and very likely also other democratic nations.

I identified earlier other constituencies that need to be included in the question of who represents Earth in diplomatic relations with extraterrestrial civilizations. These include cetaceans and other sentient life forms with large brains that inhabit the Earth's oceans, surface or subterranean regions, and finally the Earth itself. All species that have sentience, intelligence and the ability to communicate by telepathic or other means with extraterrestrial civilizations would have some diplomatic standing. Included among these sentient life forms are the remnants of earlier human civilizations and non-human (e.g., Reptilian) life forms that have advanced technologies and communication abilities but are based in subterranean areas. It would be reasonable to assume that sentient life forms might already have diplomatic standing among extraterrestrial civilizations.

Finally, the next important constituency we need to consider as relevant for visiting extraterrestrials is the planet itself. I will spend some time discussing this Gaia hypothesis since this offers some important insights into developing a comprehensive model for addressing the question of who speaks for planet Earth.

As mentioned earlier, the Gaia hypothesis posits that Earth is a living consciousness that displays sentience insofar as it is self-regulating. Therefore the Earth itself might be considered a viable actor in diplomatic relations with extraterrestrial races. If the Gaia hypothesis is accurate, then an important consideration is whether Gaia has an *'intelligence'* or vital interests with which individuals can choose to align themselves. Havelock's Gaia hypothesis was based on the recognition that Gaia displayed a sentience that was similar to that of a tree and displayed an organic intelligence that was dynamically connected to the ecosystem: "A tree that quietly exists, never moving except to sway in the wind, yet endlessly conversing with the sunlight and the soil." While he did not believe Gaia displayed 'purpose' in the ordinary sense we would understand intelligent life, he believed it communicated with the complex ecosystem in a way that sustained life for all.

A vivid analogy of the Gaia hypothesis is the 2008 blockbuster film Avatar. The Na'vi, the indigenous peoples of the earth-like moon Pandora, have established a means of communicating with the ecology of their world, and even with its very soul or spirit. The human hero of the movie, is told that the spirit of Pandora is only interested in establishing planetary balance or harmony - planetary balance is Pandora's vital interest. Yet he is able to communicate with her in a last desperate attempt to save the Na'vi. When the Na'vi are defeated by the human invaders in a final confrontation, Pandora itself, through its diverse animal species, awakens to defeat the humans and their technology. Pandora was thus saved by the interconnected nature of life on this fictional world, and the ability of its indigenous peoples to communicate with the Spirit of Pandora and protect its vital interests.

It would be fair to say that based on the Gaia hypothesis, the Earth has an intelligence and vital interests that can be recognized by sentient species sufficiently receptive to the subtle form of communication used by the Earth's self-regulating mechanisms. On Earth, this is often demonstrated by indigenous peoples whose lives are filled by rituals and ceremonies establishing a connection with the land, and communicating with it to establish ecological balance. Just as a simple organism has a survival mechanism that influences its behavior, so too Earth exhibits communicative tendencies with indigenous peoples aimed at maintaining planetary balance. This suggests that the Earth, like any species, has at a minimum, a communicative component which makes it self-regulating, and demonstrates some degree of intelligence that promotes the evolution of sentient life in a way that maintains planetary balance or *homeostasis* as Lovelock describes it. The intelligence and vital interests of Earth is something that sentient species can choose to align themselves with, and is a process that humanity is only beginning to fathom.

If Gaia demonstrates intelligence and communicative abilities, one may ask, who best represents her vital interests? Is it some mysterious energetic force in the center of the planet; the giant Redwood trees of the U.S. Pacific coast; the cetaceans that circumnavigate the world's oceans; the tribal elders who maintain traditional relationships with the Earth's surface, individuals and groups that do energetic work with the planet; that portion of humanity which has divided itself in terms of states and territories or even alleged advanced sentient species that inhabit the Earth's subterranean realms? It can be posited that the vital interests of Earth are represented by those life forms, human or otherwise, that align themselves with the intelligence and communications of the biosphere.

It is this possible alignment with the intelligence and vital interests of the Earth that would confer legitimacy, in the eyes of some extraterrestrial visitors, to non-official representatives of our planet's interests. Thus human or other sentient terrestrial species in alignment with the intelligence and vital interests of the Earth have diplomatic standing among extraterrestrial civilizations presumably willing to recognize the sentience of Earth, as a constituency in any negotiations affecting the whole planet.

Recognizing the Earth as a legitimate constituency in establishing diplomatic relations leads to the intriguing possibility that some portions of humanity may be more legitimate than others in representing Earth as an organic unit. Rather than diplomatic representation of Earth being something that pertains solely to different nations with their elected representatives and appointed officials, it may be that individuals or groups in alignment with the vital interests of Earth may have greater diplomatic standing for some extraterrestrial visitors. This is a revolutionary idea since it first appears odd that appointed officials of national governments would have less diplomatic standing than unappointed individuals and groups who claim alignment with the Earth's vital interests. Nevertheless, the existence of Earth itself as an important constituency would be recognized by some extraterrestrial civilizations. This raises the possibility that some individuals/groups in alignment with the vital interests of the Earth may have diplomatic standing among extraterrestrials by virtue of this alignment.

In consequence, the question of who represents the Earth has two answers. The first is a narrow restrictive answer in terms of secretly appointed officials that represent different national governments or multilateral institutions such as the United Nations. The second is far more comprehensive and involves recognition of a range of sentient life forms. Politically organized humanity is but one among several important sentient life forms and constituencies, including the planet itself. It is very likely that while extraterrestrial civilizations recognize the validity of the first form of representation, they would also give validity to the second. This means that galactic diplomacy involving the Earth and its diverse populations, life forms

27

and territories is far more open and eclectic than initially thought. This raises the possibility of non-official forms of diplomatic representation involving portions of surface humanity that speak on behalf of the vital interests of other sentient species or for the Earth itself.

Who Represents Earth's Vital Interests in Diplomatic Relations with Extraterrestrial Civilizations?

As already mentioned, the Gaia Hypothesis makes possible the existence of Earth as a sentient self-regulating entity with its own communicative abilities and intelligence that directs the way life evolves on Earth. This raises an intriguing possibility. Individuals, groups and even communities that align themselves with this intelligence or vital interests of the biosphere, and who ultimately have allegiance to Earth rather than to any nation, may have the necessary authority to represent the planet. As a corollary, such individuals also have representative status for surface humanity, which is politically organized into sovereign nations. Humans living on Earth's surface are both citizens of sovereign nations and citizens of the biosphere. This implies that both the representatives of nations and representative of the biosphere, can legitimately speak on behalf of the interests of surface humanity. In order to more easily refer to those individuals/groups/communities that align themselves with the vital interests of Earth and thus represent the biosphere, I will use the term 'Earth citizens'.

'Earth citizens' differ from the rest of humanity which is politically organized into sovereign nations, where private citizens and public officials give ultimate allegiance to a nation state as "national citizens". This suggests some tension is likely to arise as to who speaks with more authority concerning the future of Earth in diplomatic relations with extraterrestrial civilizations. Is it 'Earth citizens' in alignment with Earth's vital interests, who also respect/consult with other sentient intelligent species on Earth? Alternatively, will the final authority be the diplomatic representatives of sovereign nations who give allegiance to their nations rather than the Earth's vital interests?

The tension described above is likely to be compounded by the wide difference in resources and legitimacy between 'Earth citizens' and 'politically organized humanity' or 'national citizens'. The former has great legitimacy due to its alignment with biosphere and respect/consultation with other sentient life forms on Earth; while the latter has all the resources of the modern state to support its appointed officials in diplomatic relations with extraterrestrials. Given the telepathic nature of extraterrestrial civilizations and their expected recognition of different constituencies representing the Earth, it is highly likely that there will be tension between 'Earth citizens' and 'politically organized humanity'. The question that arises is "who speaks with more authority on behalf of Earth and of humanity in general?"

'Track Two Galactic Diplomacy'

According to former U.S. Ambassador, John MacDonald, there are a number of different forms or 'tracks' of diplomacy.[42] These are in addition to the official form which involves appointed officials who have the necessary authority to represent their nations in meetings and agreements with binding force for their governments and nations. In addition to official or 'track one' diplomacy, there is a 'track two' or 'citizen diplomacy' that involves private individuals, and 'citizen organizations'. These citizen diplomats engage in various initiatives to promote diplomatic solutions to important global problems. The term 'track two diplomacy' was coined by a former U.S. diplomat, Joseph Montville in 1981 to describe early attempts by private citizens and groups to intervene in diplomatic issues and international problems.[43] He describes track two diplomacy as: "unofficial, informal interaction between members of adversarial groups or nations with the goals of developing strategies, influencing public opinions and organizing human and material resources in ways that might help resolve the conflict."[44] In its most simple terms, track two diplomacy involves concerned individuals and/or groups intervening in diplomatic impasses or international conflicts to promote solutions and dialogue between disputing parties.

The most common approach taken by intervening third parties is to identify the vital interests or needs of the conflicting parties. The goal is to get the parties to agree to some solution that recognizes and harmonizes each's respective vital interests as far as possible. Fisher's and Ury's model of "principled negotiations" outlined in *Getting to Yes*, offers a very popular model for multitrack diplomacy.

Despite initial skepticism by the diplomatic community over the participation of private citizens and groups in international diplomacy, 'track two' or 'citizen diplomacy' has grown in significance over the last three decades, and is now recognized as a legitimate process that complements government agencies in dealing with contentious diplomatic issues and resolving global conflicts.[45] In 2002, the U.S. Department of State organized a conference on integrating 'track one' and 'track two' diplomatic initiatives which was attended by private citizens, non-government organizations and members of the diplomatic community from the U.S. and elsewhere.[46]

Individuals, groups and organizations practicing track two diplomacy have been successful in receiving government and private grants to engage in this unofficial form of diplomacy in order to complement international diplomacy and assist in resolving global conflicts.[47] For example, I received two grants from the U.S. Institute of Peace, which was created and funded by the U.S. Congress, to conduct track two initiatives to resolve the East Timor conflict.[48] I invited a group of East Timorese, and later prominent Indonesian citizens, to Washington D.C. to initiate dialogue that would produce an ongoing initiative to help promote a resolution of the East Timor conflict. In the subsequent meetings wide consultation occurred with members of the U.S. and Indonesian diplomatic community, and with the United Nations. These meetings resulted in important breakthroughs which resulted in power sharing documents that helped stimulate a diplomatic solution to the East Timor conflict.[49]

A number of private organizations regularly raise significant funds from a range of government agencies and private organizations to perform track two initiatives along similar lines to what I did in the case of East Timor. The most prominent citizen groups involved in track two diplomacy include *Search for Common Ground*, *The Institute for Multitrack Diplomacy*, and the *Institute of World Affairs*.[50]

The recognition and legitimacy given to individuals, or groups performing citizen diplomacy in international conflicts creates an important precedent when examining how diplomacy might be conducted with extraterrestrial civilizations. Individuals and groups may be expected to conduct citizen diplomacy initiatives where there is a perceived need to assist official diplomacy and/or the resolution of conflicts involving extraterrestrial civilizations. Consequently, 'track two galactic diplomacy' can be defined as *the effort by private individuals and/or citizen groups to assist in improving diplomatic relations between extraterrestrial civilizations and national governments, and/or to assist in resolving conflicts between extraterrestrials and/or national governments*. These efforts may range from individual contacts that promote dialogue and information sharing, to citizen groups working with extraterrestrials to promote government disclosure, and resolving conflict between government agencies and alien civilizations.

While any individual or group can be expected to participate in citizen diplomacy initiatives with extraterrestrial civilizations, those who are self-described 'Earth citizens', as opposed to national citizens, have special significance. This significance is due to the expected recognition given to them by extraterrestrial civilizations as representatives of Gaia and other sentient species on Earth. Consequently, individuals and groups practicing citizen diplomacy may enjoy greater legitimacy and authority among extraterrestrial civilizations. This is due to the alignment of 'Earth citizens' with the vital interests of planet, and with the aspirations of other sentient species. This alignment means that 'Earth citizens' have ultimate allegiance to the biosphere and its sentient species. Earth citizens' may thus enjoy greater status than the appointed officials representing sovereign nations, when it comes to negotiating with extraterrestrial civilizations.

Track two galactic diplomacy by 'Earth citizens' who are *de facto* Ambassadors for the Earth is an important development due to the secrecy surrounding historic meetings and agreements between some extraterrestrial civilizations and secretly appointed officials of different nations. Such citizen diplomacy initiatives can result in meetings and agreements that have legitimacy among a range of extraterrestrial civilizations, and therefore significantly impact on global affairs. A key question is how national security agencies would react to agreements or communications established by 'Earth citizens' through track two diplomacy with extraterrestrial civilizations.

National Security Reactions to Citizen Diplomacy with Extraterrestrial Civilizations

A key aspect in the secrecy over visiting extraterrestrial civilizations has been the degree to which key national security agencies in the U.S. and elsewhere, have controlled information and monopolized resources devoted to extraterrestrial affairs.[51] This control by key national security agencies suggests that the initial response by such agencies to 'track two galactic diplomacy' initiatives by Earth citizens would be regarded either with extreme suspicion or outright opposition. To a degree, the anticipated response by shadow government controllers of extraterrestrial information would parallel the initial response by foreign policy professionals and diplomatic community to the emergence of citizen diplomacy in international affairs in the early 1980's. As noted earlier, this shifted from outright skepticism and dismissal, to eventual recognition and cooperation. The response to 'citizen diplomacy' by shadow controllers of extraterrestrial affairs is likely to follow a similar pattern.

The official reaction to citizen diplomacy with extraterrestrials is likely to be influenced by four challenges:

1. The extent of private communications and interactions with extraterrestrials by 'Earth citizens'.
2. The willingness of the shadow government to use its coercive resources to suppress 'citizen diplomacy initiatives.
3. The degree to which extraterrestrial civilizations might manipulate unsuspecting humans to destabilize national security agencies for 'unfriendly' extraterrestrial agendas.
4. The implications of agreements reached through 'citizen diplomacy with extraterrestrials. I will now examine each of these challenges and how they impact on citizen diplomacy with extraterrestrials before finishing with some concluding remarks.

The Extent of Private Communications and Interactions with Extraterrestrial Races

Ever since George Adamski co-wrote, *The Flying Saucers Have Landed*, in 1954, where he detailed his extraordinary meeting with an extraterrestrial, Orthon, there has been a succession of private citizens who have claimed to have been contacted by extraterrestrial races. All describe extensive communications and interactions with the extraterrestrial visitors.[52]

Figure 3. Painting of George Adamski meeting Orthon who emerged from a spacecraft. The meeting was seen by six witnesses. This is the first documented case of "track two galactic diplomacy."

Along with Adamski – whose case along with others I will describe in detail later - some of these initial contactees included Howard Menger, Orfeo Angelucci, Paul Villa and George Van Tassel.[53] These communications and interactions with extraterrestrials varied considerably depending on the contactee. Essentially all revealed that extraterrestrials were deliberately contacting private individuals to disseminate information about the existence of extraterrestrial civilizations, and the benevolent intentions of extraterrestrials making contact.

Over the years, the list of 'contactees' has grown considerably and the more well known in the recent era include Sixto Paz Wells, Billy Meier, Carlos Diaz, Alex Collier, Enrique Castillo, Luis Fernando Mostajo and Phillip Krapf.[54] These 'contactees' have consequently given public lectures, written books, formed support groups, and communicated with key elites. The purpose was to convey information given by extraterrestrials and convincing a skeptical public of the friendly nature of these extraterrestrials. Without necessarily knowing it, these contactees were actually engaging in 'track two galactic diplomacy' insofar as they represented that portion of humanity described as 'Earth citizens' who were willing to disseminate the truth about visiting extraterrestrial life and the implications for global humanity.

National security agencies have 'publicly' treated contactees with skepticism and ridicule. In reality, the agencies paid close attention to contactees in order to simultaneously extract whatever information could be gained from the contactees. At the same time, the agencies would limit the extent to which the contactees' information would enter into the public arena. For example, Enrique Castillo was invited to Washington D.C., from his native Colombia and he was subjected to a series of tests and interviews in a secret location by officials who did not identify themselves.[55] After his meeting, he was paid a sum of money, and not officially contacted again. No news of these meetings and their conclusions were released to the general public.

Another example, reveals a more sinister aspect of the way governments interact with contactees and deal with the information they are disseminating. Alex Collier claims to have been contacted by extraterrestrials from the constellation of Andromeda. He was sharing information about his contacts through a popular website and public lectures before being visited by a team of Intelligence officials who intimidated him into silence.[56] Apparently Collier was releasing sensitive information despite the official government position that since the closure of Project Blue Book, no government agency is actively investigating the UFO/extraterrestrial phenomenon.[57] I will discuss more of this officially sanctioned interference and repression in chapter six.

Control of the mass media has been the chief vehicle by which the shadow government could limit the influence of the contactees as well as the UFO phenomenon more generally.[58] The prospect that many more private citizens might experience contact with extraterrestrials and subsequently conduct 'track two galactic diplomacy' would be of extreme concern to government agencies. Yet it appears that growth of citizen diplomacy in global politics could not be prevented and was eventually welcomed by the diplomatic community. So too the growth in 'citizen diplomacy with extraterrestrials' or 'track two galactic diplomacy' cannot be prevented and eventually will be regarded as a complement rather than a threat by those conducting 'official' or 'track one' galactic diplomacy.

The Coercive Resources of Shadow Government Agencies

National Security agencies have an abundance of coercive resources that can be used to maintain secrecy over the extraterrestrial presence. The following passage from the Special Operations Manual, a document detailing recovery procedures for extraterrestrial craft leaked to UFO researchers, describes the official secrecy policy adopted in April 1954:

> Any encounter with entities known to be of extraterrestrial origin is to be considered to be a matter of national security and therefore classified TOP SECRET. Under no circumstances is the general public or the public press to learn of the existence of these entities. The official government policy is that such creatures do not exist, and that no agency of the federal government is now engaged in any study of extraterrestrials or their artifacts. Any deviation from this stated policy is absolutely forbidden.[59]

Whistleblowers such as Master Sergeant Dan Morris outlined how key national security agencies such as the NSA would coerce individuals to maintain silence, and how these coercive mechanisms extended even up to the use of deadly force to maintain secrecy:

> The National Security Agency-the killers work in that. They're the guys that, when it becomes necessary for a problem to be removed... if you watch James Bond, they're the double-O agents, if you get my meaning. Secretary of Defense Forestall was the first real powerful, known person that was eliminated because he was going to release the information – and nobody has ever paid for that crime.[60]

With a well known history of using even deadly force to maintain secrecy over the extraterrestrial presence, it might be questioned whether such coercive methods would be used against individuals and/or organizations conducting citizen diplomacy with ETs.

The key factor here is whether national security agencies would approve the use of coercive force in the present internet era where so much information is now freely available on the internet. It appears that soft censorship techniques such as eliminating public records, limiting major media exposure, hacking websites, etc., are the preferred methods of limiting information on extraterrestrials as opposed to the use of deadly force which appeared to be more widely used in the past.[61] Nevertheless, the prospect that extraterrestrials would regard track two galactic diplomacy as providing a mandate for their activities would be of extreme concern to national security agencies. This could lead to the use of coercive measures to prevent citizen diplomacy with extraterrestrials from occurring as far as possible.

The likelihood that public disclosure of extraterrestrial presence will eventually occur, suggests that national security agencies are less and less disposed to the use of the most extreme forms of coercion. This is due to the likelihood that there will soon be some form of accounting for past actions and policy decisions. Public disclosure of the extraterrestrial presence would lead to a thorough review of past secret government and corporate actions in maintaining secrecy, and some accountability for government officials or corporate employees who enforce present policies.

How extraterrestrial groups might manipulate unsuspecting citizen diplomats

The possibility that some extraterrestrials may manipulate individuals and groups engaging in citizen diplomacy is very real. The history of the extraterrestrial presence is one where a variety of agendas and activities have been conducted in order to control humanity. There is quite likely going to be continued efforts of manipulation by some extraterrestrial groups who view humanity as a resource to be controlled and exploited.[62] The prospect that unsuspecting private individuals/groups might be used by 'unfriendly' extraterrestrial groups to undermine key national security agencies performing necessary roles in monitoring extraterrestrial races is very real. This suggests that a high degree of discernment and education about different extraterrestrial civilizations is necessary for those individuals who find themselves on the forefront of citizen diplomacy.

A case which illustrates such a possibility is that concerning former Los Angeles Time editor, Phillip Krapf, and the extraterrestrial race he describes as the Verdants. Krapf was 'involuntarily' taken into a Verdant ship where he saw a large number of civilians being subjected to a number of medical procedures.[63] Together with the nature of Krapf's 'abduction' this casts doubt on the Verdants apparent 'benevolence'. When combined with the Verdants plan to establish a capital city in the American Southwest to be called 'Genesis' whereby their selected representatives would direct global events, the possibility that Krapf and others taken into the Verdants' ship were being manipulated to bring about an extraterrestrial controlled world government looms as a strong possibility.[64] Krapf himself acknowledged the possibility that he "was duped by unscrupulous ETs."[65] He insightfully described how this may have occurred with his supposed contact experiences:

> Is it possible that memories that we are so sure of, that are so real, that actually help to define who we are, could be

counterfeit? Can they be invented or even implanted by an outside source, by aliens with sinister motives or nefarious humans – government agents or otherwise – with secret technologies that are unknown to the general population?[66]

A combination of training, public education and networking by contactees and others conducting citizen diplomacy would go a long way to preventing any manipulation by unfriendly extraterrestrial groups. This is the best safeguard to ensure the integrity of citizen diplomacy with extraterrestrials since the agendas and programs of national security agencies would not initially be viewed with much sympathy by contactees.

Contactees and others participating in citizen diplomacy are largely familiar with the long secrecy and suppression of information concerning extraterrestrials. Such individuals give very little legitimacy to the actions and concerns of national security agencies despite widespread public respect for such agencies. In particular, coercive actions by national security agencies against those active in citizen diplomacy would be strenuously opposed by those practicing or supporting this form of diplomacy. The result would succeed only in undermining the integrity of this form of diplomacy, rather than preventing it all together. Since track two galactic diplomacy is an inevitable development in human-extraterrestrial interaction, a premium needs to be placed on maintaining a high level of integrity for this form of citizen based diplomacy. This will prevent undue manipulation by 'unfriendly' extraterrestrial races, some of whom will be discussed in chapter three.

Implications of Initiatives & Agreements Reached through Citizen Diplomacy with Extraterrestrials

It is very likely that some citizen diplomacy initiatives will produce agreements with, or extend permission to, extraterrestrial groups to perform certain activities. This is especially likely to be the case where 'Earth citizens' participate and thereby carry special representative status far beyond their population numbers. Extraterrestrials may find special advantages in working with Earth citizens who might be willing to agree to initiatives or projects that positively impact on the planet. For example, in October 2003, a message allegedly from a group of extraterrestrials began circulating the internet accurately describing the exopolitical situation on Earth. They requested that 'individuals without distinction' decide whether they wanted the extraterrestrials to simply "show up".[67] The "Change the World" referendum generated great interest and an internet petition granting permission to the extraterrestrials to show up had over 12,500 signatures by April 2013.[68]

The consequences of private citizens or citizen organizations reaching agreements with extraterrestrial races or giving permission to specific extraterrestrial activities would certainly be of great concern to national security agencies. It might be expected that those individuals and/or groups initiating such agreements or granting permission would be closely monitored and even subjected to harassment by national security agencies if this threatened to have wide impact. For example, in the United States, U.S. citizens participating in communications with extraterrestrials that result in agreements of some kind, may be prosecuted under the Logan Act.

The Logan Act was first passed by the U.S. Congress in 1799, and last amended in 1994. It pertains to private citizens engaging in any unofficial diplomacy with states with whom the US is in dispute. The Logan Act states:

> Any citizen of the United States, wherever he may be, who, without authority of the United States, directly or indirectly commences or carries on any correspondence or intercourse with any foreign government or any officer or agent thereof, with intent to influence the measures or conduct of any foreign government or of any officer or agent thereof, in relation to any disputes or controversies with the United States, or to defeat the measures of the United States, shall be fined under this title or imprisoned not more than three years, or both. This section shall not abridge the right of a citizen to apply himself, or his agent, to any foreign government, or the agents thereof, for

redress of any injury which he may have sustained from such government or any of its agents or subjects.[69]

To date, no U.S. citizen has been successfully prosecuted under the Logan Act for conducting citizen diplomacy. There is however the risk that private U.S. citizens that participate in meetings with extraterrestrial visitors may be prosecuted under the Logan Act.

It can be expected that the implications of agreements reached between extraterrestrial groups and 'Earth citizens' are likely to have consequences far beyond the physical numbers of such individuals and/or citizen organizations. This creates special tension since such individuals and/or citizen organizations hold no official positions and therefore have no representative status according to national security agencies, for participating in any agreements or approving extraterrestrial activities. The representative status presumably given by extraterrestrials to by self-declared Earth citizens individuals and/or citizen organizations by virtue of their being spokespersons for Gaia and other sentient Earth species, make 'Earth citizens' an important factor to be reckoned with, in the diplomatic dialogue over the role played by extraterrestrials on Earth and the future of humanity.

Conclusion: 'Earth Citizens' and 'Track Two Galactic Diplomacy'

The term 'Earth citizen' describes a portion of humanity that gives allegiance to a wider set of constituencies on Earth rather than a national government which is more narrowly focused on its 'national interests'. An Earth citizen feels a calling to respond to what they perceive to be the best interests of Gaia as a planet, and the various sentient species that inhabit the Earth's territories, oceans and subterranean realms. As more and more humans develop such allegiances beyond purely national political loyalties and interests, and align themselves with what might be described as the vital interests of the Earth and other sentient species, Earth citizens become spokespersons for the biosphere. It can be expected that such spokespersons for the Earth would be regarded by extraterrestrials and other sentient Earth species as de facto 'Ambassadors of Gaia' and thereby carry influence far beyond their physical numbers.

Earth citizens are subsequently more likely to experience contact with extraterrestrial civilizations. Extraterrestrials view such individuals as having special significance due to their alignment with the Earth's vital interests and desire to satisfy the aspirations of other sentient species. Contact with Earth citizens gives greater legitimacy to the various activities of extraterrestrial groups that make contact with global humanity. Consequently, 'Earth citizens' are likely to find themselves engaged in citizen diplomacy initiatives. This is due to their significance as representatives of the Earth and the aspirations of all terrestrial sentient species. They would receive special attention by extraterrestrials who view Earth citizens as spokespersons and *de facto* ambassadors for Earth.

There is very likely to be a great contrast between private citizens and appointed public officials in terms of galactic diplomacy and the recognition respectively given to the latter by extraterrestrial groups. 'Track one' galactic diplomacy involves public officials who are secretly appointed by the shadow government and/or national security entities to represent the national interests of their nations and deal with the extraterrestrial presence. Officials engaging in track one galactic diplomacy have all the resources and coercive potential of the modern nation state to support their activities, and collectively claim to be the official political representatives of global humanity and of the Earth's territories. Yet, in the eyes of a number of extraterrestrial civilizations, these official diplomats enjoy less legitimacy than *earth citizens*. The latter presumably speak with greater authority due to their alignment with the Earth's vital interests and willingness to represent the vital interests of other sentient intelligent species. In short, the question of who speaks with greater authority as a representative for the planet Earth and her varied species, is something that will directly impact on the choices made by extraterrestrial civilizations to communicate and interact with different parts of global humanity.

While some agreements have been reached between shadow government representatives and some extraterrestrial civilizations, other extraterrestrials have instead chosen to contact private individuals and/or citizen groups. In some cases, these private citizens are more in alignment with the Earth's vital interests, and thus *de facto* spokespersons for the planet. This suggests future tension as more of humanity comes to develop sympathies and outlooks consistent with the global interests of the planet and all sentient species, and declaring themselves to be Earth Citizens or 'Citizens of Gaia'. This is likely to herald tension between those portions of humanity respectively aligned either with their national political institutions, or aligned with a broader set of global interests that fall under the vital interest of the Earth. National laws such as the Logan Act may come into more prominence, and used against private citizens meeting with and/or reaching agreements with extraterrestrial civilizations. Nevertheless, citizen diplomacy with extraterrestrials is an idea whose time has come, and has the potential to transform a planetary reality based on national interests that ignore the planet as an organic unity.

ENDNOTES: CHAPTER 1

[20] I am indebted to Angelika Sareighn Whitecliff for her enthusiastic support, suggestions and assistance in the completion of this chapter. I also thank Hugh Matlock for identifying some typographical errors and expression of ideas concerning the 'Voice of Gaia'. An earlier version of this chapter was originally published on GalacticDiplomacy.Com (Nov 4, 2004), and is available online at: http://web.archive.org/web/20120203205723/http://www.galacticdiplomacy.com/GD-Art-1.htm

[21] Clifford Stone claims to have witnessed a First Aid manual listing 57 different extraterrestrial species in 1979. That number has most likely risen in the intervening years. See my interview with Clifford Stone published in the *Exopolitics Journal*, 1:1 (2005) at: http://exopoliticsjournal.com/Journal-vol-1-1-Stone-pt-1.pdf

[22] See chapter two. Originally published online at: http://exopolitics.org/Study-Paper-8.htm

[23] See hapters two, first published as "A Report on the Motivations and Activities of Extraterrestrial Races – A Typology of the Most Significant Extraterrestrial Races Interacting with Humanity," *Exopolitics.org* (July 26, 2004) Available online at: http://www.exopolitics.org/Report-ET-Motivations.htm

[24] For discussion of evidence and theories concerning the mirror relationship between human and galactic conflicts, see Michael Salla, *Exopolitics: Political Implications of the Extraterrestrial Presence* (Dandelion Books, 2004) 35-42.

[25] Said, A.S., Lerche, Jr., C.O. & Lerche III, C.O. *Concepts of international politics in global perspective* (Prentice Hall, 1995). 69

[26] Kissinger, *Diplomacy* (Simon and Schuster, 1995).

[27] See Anthony Levy, *Cardinal Richelieu: And the Making of France* (Carroll & Graf Publishers, 2000).

[28] See chapter five.

[29] For discussion of how Presidents Carter and Clinton were kept out of the loop of information regarding the extraterrestrial presence, see Salla, *Exopolitics: Political Implications of the Extraterrestrial Presence*, 87-95.

[30] See Steven Greer, *Hidden Truth, Forbidden Knowledge* (Crossing Point Publications, 2006) 158. See also Richard Dolan, "The Admiral Wilson UFO Story," available online at: http://www.ufodigest.com/news/0808/wilson.html

[31] Don Berliner, "UFO Briefing Document: International Agreements and Resolutions - United Nations," available online at: http://www.ufoevidence.org/documents/doc1037.htm

[32] For a detailed online study of Dolphin intelligence see: http://tinyurl.com/b2zsg79

[33] Michael Hyson, http://tinyurl.com/b2zsg79

[34] See John Lilly, *Lilly on Dolphins: Humans of the Sea* (Doubleday, 1975); Timothy Wyllie *Dolphins Telepathy and Underwater Birthing* (Bear and Company Publishing, 1993); and Joan Ocean, *Dolphins Into the Future* (A Dolphin Connection Book, 1997).

For online information go to: www.joanocean.com

[35] Quoted in online article: http://paranormal.about.com/library/weekly/aa090400a.htm

[36] For detailed discussion of different categories of Reptilians interacting with humanity, see chapter five.

[37] See online article: http://paranormal.about.com/library/weekly/aa090400a.htm

[38] Havelock, *Gaia: a New Look at Life on Earth*"(Oxford University Press, 1979).

[39] Havelock, *Gaia: The Practical Science of Planetary Medicine*, (Gaia Books Limited, 1991) 12.

[40] For online version of the U.S. Constitution, go to: http://www.law.cornell.edu/constitution/constitution.overview.html

[41] For discussion of the evolution of decision making concerning extraterrestrial affairs, see *Exopolitics: Political Implications of the Extraterrestrial Presence*, ch. 2. Online version available at: http://exopolitics.org/Study-Paper-5.htm

[42] Louise Diamond and John W. McDonald, "*Multi-Track Diplomacy: A Systems Approach to Peace* (Kumarian Press, 1996).

[43] William D. Davidson, Joseph V. Monteville, "Foreign Policy According to Freud." In *Foreign Policy* 45 (1981): 145-157.

[44] Joseph Montville, quoted in Diana Chigas, "Track Two (Citizen) Diplomacy," available online at: http://www.beyondintractability.org/bi-essay/track2-diplomacy

[45] For online article on Track II diplomacy, see Susan Allen Nan and Andrea Strimling, "Track I - Track II Cooperation," http://www.beyondintractability.org/bi-essay/track-1-2-cooperation

[46] "Integrating Track One and Track Two Approaches to International Conflict Resolution: What's Working? What's Not? How Can We Do Better?". U.S. Department of State. , 2002-01-01. Available at: http://2001-2009.state.gov/s/p/of/proc/tr/14387.htm.

[47] For discussion of Track Two Diplomacy and a variety of initiatives, see Diana Chigas, "Track Two (Citizen) Diplomacy," available online at: http://www.beyondintractability.org/bi-essay/track2-diplomacy

[48] "Political Autonomy as a Conflict Resolution Mechanism for East Timor," Unsolicited Grants, United States Institute for Peace, USIP-042-97F (1998) sum awarded: US$44,000; "Developing and Autonomy Framework for the East Timor Conflict," Unsolicited Grants, United States Institute for Peace, USIP-068-96F (1997) sum awarded: US$29,000.

[49] A short paper was written about the significance of the first of the workshops organized by the author, see Michael Salla, "Rebuilding the 'Negotiating Middle' in Intractable Conflicts, *Private Peacemaking: USIP-Assisted Peacemaking Projects of Nonprofit Organizations: Peaceworks* No. 20 (US Institute of Peace, 1998) 1-5. Available online at: http://www.usip.org/publications/private-peacemaking .

[50] The website for the Institute of Multi-Track Diplomacy is http://www.imtd.org The website for Search for Common Ground is www.sfcg.org ; the website for the Institute of World Affairs is: http://www.iwa.org

[51] See Steven Greer, *Disclosure: Military and Government Witnesses Reveal the Greatest Secrets in Modern History,* 21-32

[52] Desmond Leslie and George Adamski, *Flying Saucers have Landed* (British Book Center, 1954).

[53] For discussion of experiences of an extensive number of contactees, see Timothy Good, *Alien Base: The Evidence for Extraterrestrial Colonization on Earth* (Harper Perennial, 1999).

[54] See Sixto Paz Wells, *The Invitation*; Gary Kinder, *Light Years: An Investigation into the Extraterrestrial Experiences of Eduard Meier* (Publisher Group West, 1987); Phillip Krapf, "The Challenge of Contact: a mainstream journalist's report on interplanetary diplomacy," (Origin Press, 2001). An online article on Carlos Diaz is available at: http://www.ufoevidence.org/documents/doc1180.htm A book by Alex Collier, *Defending Sacred Ground* is available online at: http://www.alexcollier.org/alex-collier-defending-sacred-ground-1996/ . See also Enrique Castillo Rincon, *UFOs: A Great New Dawn for Humanity* (Blue Dolphin Publishing, 1997). I have mentioned some of these cases and others in chapter four.

[55] This incident is described in Castillo, *UFO: A Great New Dawn for Humanity,* 110-20.

[56] Personal interview with Alex Collier (July, 2004).

[57] See "Unidentified Flying Objects and Air Force Project Blue Book," http://www.cufon.org/cufon/malmstrom/UFO_A.html

[58] See Terry Hansen, *The Missing Times* (Xlibris Corporation, 2001).

[59] Majestic 12 Group, "Special Operations Manual, SOM1-01 - Extraterrestrial Entities and Technology, Recovery and Disposal," April 1954 Part 2 http://www.bibliotecapleyades.net/sociopolitica/sociopol_SOM1-01.htm

[60] "Testimony of Master Sergeant Dan Morris," *Disclosure: Military and Government Witnesses Reveal the Greatest Secrets in Modern History*, ed., Steven Greer (Crossing Point Inc., 2001) 359.

[61] For discussion of the use of disinformation and other 'soft censorship' strategies used by military intelligence services, see John Maynard, "From Disinformation to Disclosure," *Surfing the Apocalypse,* http://www.surfingtheapocalypse.com/maynard.html

[62] For detailed discussion of the motivations and agendas of different extraterrestrial races, see chapters three, four and five.

[63] Phillip H. Krapf, *The Challenge of Contact* (Origin Press, 2001) xix-xx.

[64] See Krapf, *The Contact has Begun* (Hay House Publishers, 1998) 118-20.

[65] Krapf, *The Challenge of Contact* (Origin Press, 2001) xvii.

[66] Krapf, *The Challenge of Contact,* xvii.

[67] For discussion of the message and its authenticity see Michael Salla, "A Message to Humanity: A Genuine Communication from an Extraterrestrial Race?" *Exopolitical Comment #7* (11/08/03) available online at: http://exopolitics.org/ET-Intervention&Berlin-Wall.htm

[68] "We Are Ready to Change the World," http://www.petitiononline.com/readynow/petition.html

[69] 1 Stat. 613, January 30, 1799, codified at 18 U.S.C. § 953 (2004).

CHAPTER 2

Eisenhower's Secret Meetings with Extraterrestrials: Laying the Foundation for 50 years of Secret U.S.–Extraterrestrial Agreements

Introduction[70]

On the night and early hours of February 20-21, 1954, while on a 'vacation' to Palm Springs, California, President Dwight Eisenhower went missing, allegedly taken to Edwards Air force base for a secret meeting. When he showed up the next morning at a church service in Los Angeles, reporters were told that he had had emergency dental treatment the previous evening, having visited a local dentist. The dentist appeared at a function that evening and was presented as the 'dentist' who had treated Eisenhower. The missing night and morning has subsequently fueled rumors that Eisenhower was using the alleged dentist visit as a cover story for an extraordinary event. The event is possibly the most significant that any American President could have conducted: an alleged 'First Contact' meeting with extraterrestrials at Edwards Air Force base (previously Muroc Airfield).

Almost one year later on February 11, 1955, President Eisenhower was again on vacation and again experienced a sudden illness – this time a bad case of the sniffles. Again, this was a cover for Eisenhower secretly travelling to an Air Force base, this time Holloman AFB, on Air Force One to have another meeting with extraterrestrial visitors. Thus began a series of meetings with representatives of different extraterrestrial civilizations during the Eisenhower administration that concluded in a 'treaty' signing.

This chapter introduces evidence that the meeting at Edwards AFB occurred with extraterrestrials with a distinctive 'Nordic' appearance, and reveals that negotiations with these 'Nordic' extraterrestrials failed to result in an agreement. A subsequent series of meetings with representatives of a different extraterrestrial civilization dubbed the 'Tall Grays' began at Holloman AFB, and led to a 'treaty' eventually being signed. The motivations of the different extraterrestrial civilizations involved in these treaty discussions will be discussed. This chapter finally examines why these meetings and agreements have been kept secret for so long, and their implications.

Circumstantial Evidence of Eisenhower's 1954 meetings with Extraterrestrials

There is circumstantial and testimonial evidence that Eisenhower met in 1954 with extraterrestrials. This started a series of meetings culminating in the signing of a treaty with a different group of extraterrestrials associated with a later 1955 meeting. What follows are the circumstances surrounding Eisenhower's alleged winter vacation to Palm Springs, California from February 17-24, 1954.

First, on the Saturday night of February 20, President Eisenhower went missing, fueling press speculation that he had taken ill or even had died. In a hastily convened press conference, Eisenhower's Press Secretary announced that Eisenhower had lost a tooth cap while eating fried chicken and had to be rushed to a local dentist. The local dentist was introduced at an official function on Sunday February 21, as "the dentist who had treated the president".[71] William Moore's investigation of the incident concluded that the dentist's visit was being used as a cover story for Eisenhower's true whereabouts.

Second, it has been reported that President Eisenhower took a C-45 airplane from nearby Norton Air Force base to travel to Edwards AFB (earlier called Muroc Airfield). According to Bill Kirklin, an Air Force medic stationed at nearby Georgia Air Force base, an ambulance was requested to stay on duty while personnel at Norton honored the visiting President. Kirklin claims that after Eisenhower's plane landed at Norton, he immediately got on the C-45 to travel in the direction of Palmdale, California which is adjacent to Edwards AFB.[72]

Third, Edward's AFB was closed for three days during the period of Eisenhower's Palm Springs visit. Lt Col Wendelle Stevens writes:

> Mead Lane, publisher of The "Round Robin" newsletter out of San Diego, had an article on the Eisenhower visit and the Muroc events of that time, in February of 1954. He described a Los Angeles Times news reporter, getting wind of the strange goings

on at Muroc, who chartered a private airplane to take him to Muroc. That airplane was refused permission to land and was turned away because the base was closed to all air traffic. He then rented a car and drove to Muroc, to try to get in, but was turned away again at the base main gate because that base was closed. A number of researchers and former military personnel confirmed that the base was closed to all servicemen who tried to enter or leave. Events of tremendous national security must have been occurring for Edwards to be suddenly closed without any prior warning to base personnel.[73]

Another whistleblower is Bill Holden who revealed his own research into the closure of Edwards Air Force base during Eisenhower's secret 1954 visit:

Now, history says that this is where he met the ETs and that an agreement was signed between the US and the ETs. And as far as that a mothership was seen coming in, there were a number of UFOs coming in, and that the base was literally shut down for 3 days. I have been able to find that the base was shut down for 3 days. I've been able to find in civilian records, newspaper accounts, and everything else, as far as those facts were validated.[74]

Fourth, nine days later on March 1, the U.S. detonated its largest ever hydrogen bomb test at the Bikini Atoll. The Bravo Test was a 15 megaton bomb, 1000 times more powerful than the 15 kiloton atomic bomb detonation on Hiroshima.[75] Only the Soviet Union has ever exploded a hydrogen bomb more powerful. This was the first Hydrogen bomb test by the Eisenhower administration. The only preceding test on November 1, 1952 was ordered by President Truman and occurred only three days before Eisenhower was elected. Eisenhower's decision to go ahead with the Bravo test may well have been linked to his trip to California and disappearance.

According to the circumstantial evidence examined so far, we know that President Eisenhower was missing for an entire evening on

February 20, and was apparently taken from Palm Springs to Edwards Air Force base. The nature of the President's unscheduled vacation, the missing President, the dentist cover story, the Bravo test and his mysterious unconfirmed flight to Palmdale provide circumstantial evidence that the true purpose of his Palm Springs vacation was otherwise. He attended an event whose importance was such that it could not be disclosed to the general public. A meeting with extraterrestrials to discuss the upcoming Bravo test may well have been the true purpose of Eisenhower's visit to Edwards AFB in February 1954.

Testimonies Supporting Eisenhower's 1954 Meeting with Extraterrestrials

There are a number of sources alleging an extraterrestrial meeting at Edwards Air force base on February 20, 1954 that corresponded to a formal 'First Contact' event. These sources are based on testimonies of 'whistleblowers' who witnessed events, read classified documents, saw films or learned from their 'insider contacts' of such a meeting. These testimonies describe at least two separate sets of *meetings over a one-year period involving different extraterrestrial groups* meeting with President Eisenhower and/or with Eisenhower administration officials. The first of these meetings, the actual 'First Contact' event, did not lead to an agreement and the extraterrestrials were effectively spurned. The second of these meetings occurred at Holloman Air Force base in February 1955 and did culminate in an agreement. This second meeting has apparently become the basis of subsequent secret interactions with extraterrestrial civilizations involved in the 'treaty' that was signed.

The First Contact meeting involved extraterrestrials who were effectively spurned for taking a principled stand on assistance in technology and nuclear weapons secrets. We begin with the testimony of a former representative for the U.S. State of New Hampshire, who provides important testimony that Eisenhower received a briefing document that set the scene for a First Contact meeting. The document clearly suggests that Eisenhower was being prepared by his national security advisors to meet with extraterrestrials to discuss nuclear weapons development and other mutual areas of interest.

Henry W. McElroy, released a video statement recorded on May 8, 2012 in Hampton Virginia, revealing he saw a secret brief to President Eisenhower concerning extraterrestrial life.[76] McElroy, a Republican, served on various committees during his time in the New Hampshire State legislature, and is best known for sponsoring a New Gold Money bill in 2004 that aimed to restore the use of Gold and Silver coins in the Granite State.[77] He most recently ran for and won the Republican primary for State Representative to the 2008 elections but did not win re-election. In his statement, McElroy claims that the brief revealed that extraterrestrials were present in the United States, they were benevolent, and a meeting could be arranged for Eisenhower.

McElroy explains in his statement that he saw the briefing document while serving on New Hampshire's "State Federal Relations and Veterans Affairs committee." On its official webpage, at the time of writing, the committee lists 18 members and is under Democratic Party control.[78] In his official working capacity at the time, McElroy claims that he was regularly "updated on a large number of topics related to the affairs of our People, and our Nation."[79] One of the topics relates to an official one page brief to President Eisenhower written by unknown national security specialists. McElroy claims to have personally witnessed the briefing document:

> I would like to submit to our nation my personal testimony of one document related to one of these ongoing topics which I saw while in office, serving on the State Federal Relations and Veterans Affairs Committee. The document I saw was an official brief to President Eisenhower. [80]

McElroy's recollection of the contents of the briefing document are startling:

> To the best of my memory this brief was pervaded with a sense of hope, and it informed President Eisenhower of the continued presence of extraterrestrial beings here in the United States of

America. The brief seemed to indicate that a meeting between the President and some of these visitors could be arranged as appropriate if desired. [81]

According to the brief, the extraterrestrials were benevolent.

The tone of the brief indicated to me that there was no need for concern, since these visitors were in no way, causing any harm, or had any intentions, whatsoever, of causing any disruption then, or in the future. [82]

As a retired State Representative, McElroy's testimony carries weight since he is a direct eyewitness of a document seen during his official duties. His testimony supports the claims of whistleblowers that President Eisenhower secretly traveled to Air Force facilities in 1954 and 1955 to have meetings with representatives of one or more extraterrestrial civilizations.

So now I turn to the claims of whistleblowers who witnessed the alleged First Contact meeting. The son of a former Navy Commander, claimed that his father had been present at the First Contact event on February 20-21, 1954. According to Charles L. Suggs, a retired Sgt from the U.S. Marine Corps, his father Charles L. Suggs, (1909-1987) was a former Commander with the U.S. Navy, who attended the meeting at Edwards Air force base with Eisenhower.[83] Sgt Suggs recounted his father's experiences from the meeting in a 1991 interview with a prominent UFO researcher:

Charlie's father, Navy Commander Charles Suggs accompanied Pres. Ike along with others on Feb. 20th. They met and spoke with 2 white-haired Nordics that had pale blue eyes and colorless lips. The spokesman stood a number of feet away from Ike and would not let him approach any closer. A second nordic stood on the extended ramp of a bi-convex saucer that stood on tripod landing gear on the landing strip. According to Charlie, there were B-58 Hustlers on the field even though the first one did not fly officially till 1956. These visitors said they came from another solar system. They posed detailed questions about our nuclear testing. [84]

Again, it needs to be pointed out that the alleged Eisenhower extraterrestrial meeting occurred nine days before the Bravo test of a 15 megaton hydrogen bomb. It may be inferred that extraterrestrials alarmed at the consequences of the U.S. testing program, initiated the meeting with Eisenhower at Edwards Air Force base.

Another testimony from an alleged witness of the secret meeting, a former U.S. Air Force test pilot and Colonel who chose to remain anonymous allegedly due to a secrecy oath, gave the following details to a member of the British aristocracy, Lord Clancarty:

> The pilot says he was one of six people at the meeting... Five alien craft landed at the base. Two were cigar-shaped and three were saucer-shaped. The aliens looked humanlike, but not exactly.... The aliens spoke English, and supposedly informed the President that they wanted to start an "educational program" for the people of Earth...[85]

Yet another anonymous military eyewitness, a U.S. Air Force officer, revealed to former Royal Air Force pilot Desmond Leslie, that a flying saucer had landed at Edwards AFB. The witness claimed President Eisenhower was taken to it:

> ... a disc, estimated to be 100 feet in diameter, had landed on the runway on a certain day. Men returning from leave were suddenly not allowed back on the base. The disc was allegedly housed under guard in Hangar 27, and Eisenhower was taken to see it.[86]

An important point to note for later discussion is that the anonymous USAF officer referred to the base being closed to returning personnel. As mentioned earlier, that is important circumstantial evidence for highly classified activities occurring at Edwards AFB over the period in question.

The Incredible Story They Tried to Hide for 28 Years

Ike Met Space Aliens

President Dwight D. Eisenhower met with beings from outer space almost 30 years ago, a British high government official reveals.

EISENHOWER met with space aliens in 1954 and saw their advanced UFO operation.

CALIFORNIA

Figure 4. 1982 British Newspaper story on Eisenhower ET meeting

A similar account was given by an USAF Air Policeman stationed at Edwards AFB on the night President Eisenhower visited. What follows is a summary of a phone interview with his widow that supports Leslie's witness:

> Her deceased husband worked as an MP for the USAF in the 1950s and told her that he was on guard duty at a secure hangar facility at Edwards Air Force base during the evening of February 20, 1954. He said that he saw President Eisenhower who was escorted inside the Hangar. He was not aware of what occurred inside the hangar, and was under shoot-to-kill orders against any unauthorized person attempting to enter the facility. He stated that a flying saucer was stored inside the hangar.[87]

In his most recent book, *Need to Know*, British researcher Timothy Good refers to another three eyewitness accounts of flying saucers seen near and/or landing at Edwards AFB on February 20, 1954. Good writes:

> Gabriel Green, an American researcher, spoke to a military officer who claims to have witnessed the arrival of the craft at Muroc. At the time I was engaged in firing practice, under the command of a general, said the officer. "We were shooting at a number of targets when suddenly five UFOs came flying overhead. The general ordered all the batteries to fire at the craft. We did so, but our fire had no effect on them. We stopped firing and then we saw the UFOs land at one of the base's big hangars." Two other witnesses, Don Johnson and Paul Umbrello, also claim to have witnessed one of the disc-shaped craft near Muroc on the evening of 20 February.[88]

It is curious that Eisenhower would attend a meeting with extraterrestrial ambassadors whose vehicles had earlier been fired upon by base personnel. Perhaps, the general involved in artillery practice was following standing orders to shoot at UFOs and was not aware of the scheduled meeting.

More testimony comes from a Jesuit priest working within a Vatican intelligence organization, the Servizio Informazione del Vaticano (S.I.V.). Speaking confidentially in 2001 to Cristoforo Barbato, an Italian researcher, the Jesuit confirmed that President Eisenhower met with extraterrestrials at Muroc Air base in 1954. The Jesuit claims that a senior catholic bishop, Francis MacIntyre, subsequently flew to Rome to brief Pope Pius XII and that the S.I.V. was created as a consequence of Eisenhower's meeting. Barbato writes:

> According to this person the reason to establish [sic] the S.I.V. was the meeting with an Alien delegation at Muroc Air Field Base in February 1954 in presence of president Dwight Eisenhower and James Francis McIntyre, bishop of Los Angeles. After that incredible event McIntyre flew to Rome to refer everything to Pope Pius XII who decided to found the S.I.V with

the aim to get every possible information [sic] about Aliens and how they interacted with the American Government.[89]

Another Italian researcher, Luca Scantamburlo, found circumstantial evidence supporting the existence of the top secret Vatican organization S.I.V. and the 'Omega' security classification the Jesuit claimed to possess. He interviewed Barbato and discovered more information about the alleged 1954 meeting:

> The Jesuit member of the S.I.V. told Barbato that on occasion of the secret meeting at Muroc Air Field Base, in 1954, military cameramen filmed the outstanding event "with three movie cameras (16 millimeters), detached in different places, loaded with color film and working by spring engines; this last rather unconformable resolution, because it compelled every cameraman to change reel every 3 minutes, it was necessary since in the presence of the Aliens and of their spacecrafts, the electrical engines of the biggest movie cameras did not work.[90]

Don Phillips is a former Air force serviceman and employee on clandestine aviation projects. He testified to having viewed a film and seen documents describing the 1954 meeting between President Eisenhower and extraterrestrials:

> We have records from 1954 that were meetings between our own leaders of this country and ET's here in California. And, as I understand it from the written documentation, we were asked if we would allow them to be here and do research. I have read that our reply was well, how can we stop you? You are so advanced. And I will say by this camera and this sound, that it was President Eisenhower that had this meeting. [91]

Philips description of a film of the 1954 Eisenhower meeting is corroborated in the testimony of the Jesuit priest who disclosed Vatican records concerning the meeting.

Another version of Eisenhower's meeting is described by one of the most 'controversial' whistleblowers ever to have come forward to describe an extraterrestrial presence. William Cooper served on the Naval Intelligence briefing team for the Commander of the Pacific Fleet between 1970-73, and had access to highly classified documents that he had to review to fulfill his briefing duties. Cooper's military records confirm that he served in the sensitive positions he claimed.[92] This lends credence that at least some of his controversial testimony is based on the U.S. Navy's secret knowledge of UFOs and extraterrestrial life. Former military whistleblowers, Robert Dean and Daniel Salter, claim Cooper had similar access to top secret UFO material as they had respectively with the intelligence divisions of the U.S. Army and U.S. Air Force.[93] Cooper describes the background and nature of the 'First contact' with extraterrestrials as follows:

> In 1953 Astronomers discovered large objects in space which were moving toward the Earth. It was first believed that they were asteroids. Later evidence proved that the objects could only be Spaceships. Project Sigma intercepted alien radio communications. When the objects reached the Earth they took up a very high orbit around the Equator. There were several huge ships, and their actual intent was unknown. Project Sigma, and a new project, Plato, through radio communications using the computer binary language, was able to arrange a landing that resulted in face to face contact with alien beings from another planet.... Project Plato was tasked with establishing diplomatic relations with this race of space aliens.[94]

Cooper's testimony is corroborated by Donald Keyhoe who also wrote about giant spaceships tracked by the U.S. Air Force in 1953 and efforts to cover this information up:

> Since 1953 it [the USAF] had known that giant spaceships were operating near our planet. At least nine times, huge alien spacecraft had been seen or tracked in orbit, or they descended nearer the Earth for brief periods. Each time it had been an

ordeal for the [US]AF censors, as they struggled to conceal the reports or explain them away when attempts at secrecy failed.[95]

Cooper's testimony that the U.S. military succeeded in establishing communication with the giant extraterrestrial spacecraft is also supported by Keyhoe's investigations of the 1953 phenomenon. Keyhoe discussed the possible failure of USAF debunking of reports of the giant spacecraft, and the implications of a leaked article describing the true motivations of the extraterrestrial visitors:

> If the "moonlet" cover up failed, the true spaceship answer might emerge as the only alternative. If it did, this could revive a disturbing article on possible alien migration to our world.... The article had been written by a high AF Intelligence officer – Col. W.C. Odell.... it had been cleared by AF Security and Review.... According to his theory, alien beings from a dying planet were considering and surveying our world as a new home – a planet similar enough to their own so that they could survive here and perpetuate their race.[96]

Keyhoe was suggesting that Col Odell may have been leaking classified information concerning what had been learned through communications with the extraterrestrials. Cooper's claim that a highly classified radio communications program, Project Plato, had been used to establish diplomatic relations is supported by Keyhoe's testimony. Cooper goes on to describe the efforts of a different extraterrestrial group with a warning about the motivations of the extraterrestrials in the giant spacecraft orbiting the Earth who, according to Odell, wanted to establish colonies.

> In the meantime a race of human looking aliens contacted the U.S. Government. This alien group warned us against the aliens that were orbiting the Equator and offered to help us with our spiritual development. They demanded that we dismantle and destroy our nuclear weapons as the major condition. They refused to exchange technology citing that we were spiritually

unable to handle the technology which we then possessed. They believed that we would use any new technology to destroy each other. This race stated that we were on a path of self destruction and we must stop killing each other, stop polluting the Earth, stop raping the Earth's natural resources, and learn to live in harmony. These terms were met with extreme suspicion, especially the major condition of nuclear disarmament. It was believed that meeting that condition would leave us helpless in the face of an obvious alien threat. We also had nothing in history to help with the decision. Nuclear disarmament was not considered to be within the best interest of the United States. The overtures were rejected on the grounds that it would be foolish to disarm in the face of such an uncertain future. [97]

The significant point about Cooper's version is that the humanoid extraterrestrial race was not willing to enter into technology exchanges that might help weapons development, and instead was focused on spiritual development. Again, the emphasis on nuclear disarmament mentioned by the extraterrestrials is significant, due to the Bravo Hydrogen Bomb Test on March 1, 1954. Most importantly, the overtures of these extraterrestrials were turned down.

Cooper's idea of more than one extraterrestrial race interacting with the Eisenhower administration is supported by other whistleblowers such as former Master Sergeant Robert Dean. He, like Cooper, had access to top secret documents while working in the intelligence division for the Supreme Commander of a major U.S. military command. In Dean's 27 year distinguished military career, he served at the Supreme Headquarters Allied Powers Europe. He witnessed these documents while serving under the Supreme Allied Commander of Europe. Dean claimed that at least four extraterrestrial groups were known to NATO commanders in 1964: "The group at the time, there were just four that they knew of for certain and the Greys were one of those groups.[98] In chapter three I will go into more detail on Dean's knowledge of these four groups.

Another source of information on the alleged 1954 Eisenhower-extraterrestrial meeting is Gerald Light. In a letter dated April 16, 1954 to Meade Layne, then director of Borderland Sciences Research Associates (now Foundation), Light claimed he was part of a delegation of community leaders at a meeting between U.S. government officials and extraterrestrials at Edwards Air Force Base.[99] The meeting involved President Eisenhower and corresponded to his February 20 disappearance from Palm Springs. The alleged purpose of Light and others in the delegation was to test public reaction to the presence of extraterrestrials. Light, according to Meade Layne, was a "gifted and highly educated writer and lecturer", who was skilled both in clairvoyance and the occult.[100] Light described the circumstances of the meeting as follows:

> My dear friends: I have just returned from Muroc [Edwards Air Force Base]. The report is true -- devastatingly true! I made the journey in company with Franklin Allen of the Hearst papers and Edwin Nourse of Brookings Institute (Truman's erstwhile financial advisor) and Bishop MacIntyre of L.A. (confidential names for the present, please). When we were allowed to enter the restricted section (after about six hours in which we were checked on every possible item, event, incident and aspect of our personal and public lives), I had the distinct feeling that the world had come to an end with fantastic realism. For I have never seen so many human beings in a state of complete collapse and confusion, as they realized that their own world had indeed ended with such finality as to beggar description. The reality of the 'other plane' aeroforms is now and forever removed from the realms of speculation and made a rather painful part of the consciousness of every responsible scientific and political group. During my two days' visit I saw five separate and distinct types of aircraft being studied and handled by our Air Force officials -- with the assistance and permission of the Etherians!
>
> I have no words to express my reactions. It has finally happened. It is now a matter of history. President Eisenhower, as you may already know, was spirited over to Muroc one night during his visit to Palm Springs recently. And it is my conviction

that he will ignore the terrific conflict between the various 'authorities' and go directly to the people via radio and television -- if the impasse continues much longer. From what I could gather, an official statement to the country is being prepared for delivery about the middle of May.[101]

Of course no such formal announcement was made, and Light's description of his and an earlier meeting involving President Eisenhower has either been the best-kept secret of the twentieth century or the fabrication of an elderly mystic known for out-of-body experiences. The events Light describes in his meeting in terms of the panic and confusion of many of those present, the emotional impact of the alleged landing, and the tremendous difference of opinion on what to do in terms of telling the public and responding to the extraterrestrial visitors, are plausible descriptions of what may have occurred. Indeed, the psychological and emotional impact Light describes for senior national security leaders at the meeting is consistent with what could be expected for such a 'life changing event'.

A way of determining Light's claim is to examine the figures he named along with himself as part of the community delegation. Could they have been plausible candidates for such a meeting? Dr Edwin Nourse (1883-1974) was the first chairman of the Council of Economic Advisors to the President (1944-1953) and was President Truman's chief economic advisor.[102] Nourse officially retired to private life in 1953. He would certainly have been a good choice of someone who could give confidential economic advice to the Eisenhower administration about the possible economic impact of First Contact with extraterrestrials. Another of the individuals mentioned by Light was Bishop MacIntyre.

Cardinal James Francis MacIntyre was the bishop and head of the Catholic Church in Los Angeles (1948-1970) and would have been an important gauge for possible reaction from religious leaders generally, and in particular from the most influential and powerful religious institution on the planet – the Roman Catholic Church. In particular, Cardinal MacIntyre would have been a good choice as a representative for the Vatican since he was appointed the first Cardinal of the Western United States by Pope Pius XII in 1952. Cardinal MacIntyre had sufficient rank and authority to represent the Catholic Church and the religious community in a delegation of community leaders.

The fourth member of the delegation of community leaders was Franklin Winthrop Allen, a former reporter with the Hearst Newspapers Group. [103] Allen was 80 years old at the time, and author of a book instructing reporters on how to deal with Congressional Committee Hearings. He would have been a good choice for a member of the press who could maintain confidentiality.

All together the four men represented senior leaders of the religious, spiritual, economic and media communities. They were well advanced in age and status. They would certainly have been plausible choices for a community delegation that could provide confidential advice on a possible public response to a First Contact event involving extraterrestrial races. Such a selection constituted a group of 'wise men' that would have been entirely in character for the conservative nature of American society in 1954. While Light may well have contrived such a list in a fabricated account or 'out-of-body' experience as Moore implies in his analysis, there is nothing in Light's selection that eliminates the possibility that they were plausible members of such a delegation.[104] Light's letter is corroborated by Cristoforo Barbato's account of a Jesuit informer concerning the 1954 meeting. The Jesuit claimed Bishop MacIntyre traveled after the meeting to Rome to brief Pope Pius XII, who then established the top secret Vatican organization to monitor further developments.[105] The selection of this particular group of 'wise men' gives some credence to Light's claim.

There is some discrepancy in the testimonials as to which was the Air Force base at which the spurned extraterrestrials met with President Eisenhower and/or Eisenhower administration officials. Cooper claims this occurred at Homestead Air Force base in Florida rather than Edwards.[106] On the other hand Suggs, the two anonymous Air Force officers, Green's three witnesses, Lear, and Jesuit priest all claim it occurred at Edwards.

In his letter, Gerald Light pointed to a meeting at Edwards Air Force Base on February 20 that involved President Eisenhower as being intense. Light's testimony implies that the meetings at Edwards did not result in an agreement, but instead resulted in intense disagreement between Eisenhower officials. Consequently, I will conclude that Suggs, the two anonymous Air Force officers, Green's witnesses, and Jesuit priest version is more accurate, and that the 'First Contact' meeting occurred at Edwards Air force base in February 20-21, 1954. It was followed by other meetings including one at Holloman Air Force base in February 1955 to be examined later.

In conclusion, the following items all make up circumstantial evidence that a meeting with extraterrestrials occurred. The first is Eisenhower's missing night. The second is the weak 'cover story' used for Eisenhower's absence. The third are reports of the three day closure of Edwards AFB. The fourth is the timing of the 20-21 February 1954 meeting 10 days before the March 1 Bravo hydrogen bomb test.

The following is a summary of testimonial evidence that Eisenhower secretly met with a delegation of extraterrestrials.

1. We have the testimony of a former Representative to the State of New Hampshire that President Eisenhower received a briefing document to prepare him for a First Contact meeting.
2. We have the testimonies of military servicemen who claimed to have been witnesses at the event.
3. We have the testimony of the Jesuit priest and other whistleblowers leaking information observed from classified documents.
4. We have Light's description of a subsequent meeting and the composition of community leaders or 'wise men' present. All these items collectively provide circumstantial and testimonial evidence that Eisenhower was present at a meeting with extraterrestrials in February, 1954 (see Table 1 at end of this chapter).

Circumstantial Evidence of Eisenhower's 1955 meeting at Holloman Air Force Base

On February 10, 1955, President Eisenhower flew from Washington DC on Air Force One to Thomasville, Georgia for a hunting vacation. He was accompanied by a chartered plane filled with the Press. Later that afternoon, Eisenhower disappeared from Press view for the next 36 hours. James Hagerty, his press secretary, told the press that Ike and his valet were "treating a case of the sniffles..."[107] In reality, circumstantial and testimonial evidence reveal that he secretly traveled to Holloman Air Force base to meet with extraterrestrials on February 11. I begin this examination of the second extraterrestrial meeting involving Eisenhower with some of the circumstantial evidence that he did travel to Holloman AFB.

First is a 2007 interview by UFO researcher Art Campbell with a security guard of Air Force One (aka Columbine III) who confirmed that it secretly left Spence AFB on Feb 11 at 4 am with Eisenhower on board. Campbell wrote:

> Then he said .... "I do recall one trip down to south Georgia (he wasn't on this one) where there were a dozen or so going to this tiny little town." He went on to say that plane crew did not ask any questions, but they learned why the following day. About 3:00 a.m. they had gotten word that the president would be leaving in an hour. "We were always ready for this kind of thing, and sure enough, the plane left one hour later." He said about a half hour before the plane left, two Air Force cars pulled up and six agents came on board. They had apparently been booked into a nearby motel somewhere for a day or so. The other agents in the little town bustled around in their darkened vehicles, indicating that the president was there. No one noticed when the president returned late at night a day or so later, and no one ever knew he had left.[108]

More circumstantial evidence comes from Bill Kirklin who from March 1, 1954 until August 5, 1955 was stationed at Holloman Air Force base at the base hospital. He claims of having received prior notification of a visit by Eisenhower in February 1955. Kirklin wrote:

> ... we heard that the president was coming to Holloman. I knew there was going to be an honor parade for him. Captain Reiner asked me if I wanted to participate in the parade. I said, "No." He said, "Fine. You will be on duty." The Parade was scheduled for early in the morning. The day before it was to take place it was called off.[109]

At the end of the day of Eisenhower's visit, Kirklin reports that he saw Air Force One leaving the base and flying over a restricted area: "After work I was in my barracks room when I was called out to see Air Force One fly overhead. It flew over the residential area of the base. This is a NO FLYING zone for all military aircraft. Only the President could get away with it."[110]

The above is circumstantial evidence of Eisenhower meeting with extraterrestrials insofar as it indicates that he was not recuperating in Georgia as his press secretary claimed. Instead, Eisenhower was secretly over 2000 miles away at Holloman Air Force base. Various aspects of Eisenhower's actual encounter with UFOs and their occupants are revealed by several first hand witnesses.

Testimonial Evidence of Eisenhower's 1955 meeting at Holloman AFB

Kirklin claims that he heard a number of people commenting on the flying saucers that had arrived at Holloman AFB during Eisenhower's visit. He says one was his colleague, Dorsey who told him:

> Kirklin, did you see the disc hovering over the flight line?"

> ""No." I am thinking something small you hold in your hand like a discus as the only craft I knew capable of hovering were the choppers and the Navy's hovercraft. There weren't that many helicopters around Holloman. "What's it made of?" I am thinking of a wooden disc with a steel edge. "Looks like polished

stainless steel or aluminum. You know just bright metallic and shiny."

I asked, "How big is it?"

"Twenty to Thirty feet in diameter. Do you want to see it?"

"Sure. But with my luck it wouldn't be there."

Dorsey replied. "It was there when I took my wife to the Commissary and it was there when we got out thirty minutes later. Go out to the front of the hospital and take a look.[111]

If Kirklin's account of what his colleague saw is correct, then at least one flying saucer was hovering over the flight line of the base for at least 30 minutes during Eisenhower's visit. Later Kirklin went to the mess hall, and overhead the following conversation:

On the way back I followed two pilots. The one on the left was in Khakis, the one on the right in winter Blues. I followed them and listened to their conversation.

Left: " Why the Blues?"

Right: "I'm the Officer of the Day, I was at Base Ops when Air Force 1 came in. Did you see it?"

L. "Yes. It's a big bird isn't it?"

R "Yes. They landed and turned around and stayed on the active runway. We turned off the RADAR and waited."

L. "Why did you turn off the RADAR?"

R. "Because we were told to. I think the one at Roswell that came down was hit by Doppler Radar. It was one of the first installations to have it in the U.S. Anyway, they came in low over the mountains, across the Proving Grounds.

Interrupted by L. " I heard there were three and one landed at the Monument."

R "One might have stayed at the Monument. I didn't see it. I only saw two. One hovered over head like it was protecting the other one. The other one landed on the active [runway] in front of his plane. He got out of his plane and went towards it. A door opened and he went inside for forty or forty -five minutes."

L. "Could you see? Were they Grays?"

R. "1 don't know. They might have been. I couldn't see them. I didn't have binoculars." ...

L. "Do you think these were the same ones that were in Palmdale last year?"

R. "They might have been." ...

R. "It might have been. I just don't know."

L. "Did you see them when he came out?"

R. "No. They stayed inside. He shook hands with them and went back to his plane."

Importantly, the pilots reveal that Eisenhower disembarked from Air Force One and met with the extraterrestrials in one of the flying saucers at the end of the flight line for at least 45 minutes. It's also significant that the pilots refer to the Palmdale (Edwards AFB) meeting in February 1954. Perhaps most significant is the hand shakes at the end of the meeting, was this evidence that an agreement was reached? As I will shortly show, indeed this is what happened at Holloman on February 11, 1955.

Art Campbell was later contacted by the family of a base electrician who worked at Holloman and witnessed a flying saucer approach the area where Air Force One was positioned. A letter from the electrician explained what happened

> So the day the President came we went out in the truck to a job where we were replacing some wire down the flight line. ... So we heard the President's plane in the morning lining up for an approach and watched it land on the far runway. So we waited for it to taxi over to the flight line so we could see him, but we didn't hear it anymore. It had shut down somewhere out there... one of the men ... said he can see out there from that pole over there, so why don't one of us go up the pole and see where the plane is? Well I had one of my climbers on and ... started up with my back to the sun, a safety measure, which also put my back to the runway where we thought his Connie was. Connie was a nickname for the big Constellation the President flew.... A few minutes later .... I could not believe what I saw. There was this pie tin like thing coming at me about 150 feet away. I thought it was remote controlled or something. 25 to 30 feet across and I started down the pole as fast as I could go.... While I was running towards the big hangar I looked back and it had stopped and it was just sitting there.[112]

The electrician's story is very revealing since it is rare first hand testimony that Eisenhower's Air Force One had landed at the end of the flight line, and was waiting to meet up with a flying saucer.

Another direct witness concerns an airman whose plane was delayed at Holloman AFB on the morning of Eisenhower's arrival at Holloman AFB. Staff Sergeant Wykoff reveals what happened in an interview:

> We had to haul a load of stuff down there. Parts that they needed, and the runway is like this. I never seen anything like that before. And anyway as we were there we saw Air Force One come in, and we didn't know who it was. And then an officer comes around and

said you can't leave. The pilot said we have to leave. And he said well President Eisenhower is here and you can't leave the field until he's gone. And I said, you can hear it over loud speakers, but it didn't do any good. I would have liked to have seen him... We didn't have the clearance to go into the mess hall and one of the other officers, a higher ranking officer came [over] to us and said would you like to go in and eat, and listen to his speech. And most of us said yes, because I'd like to see him. I didn't get to shake his hand or anything, because I didn't have the right badge, clearance to go in, but they did let us go in at the very end and we ate and listened to his speech.[113]

Wykoff is again a rare first hand witness that Eisenhower had secretly arrived at Holloman AFB base to perform some classified activities. The classified nature of Eisenhower's activities is revealed in the following recollections by Bill Kirklin of a conversation between a Captain and Colonel at the base hospital:

After supper I saw the lights that were still on in the Flight Surgeon's Office and went over to turn them off. I saw Dr Reiner talking to a Lt. Col... The Colonel was talking: "He was at the supply hanger. I was there in the front with him and some others. I was on the stage. There was standing room only with 225 men in the hanger."

Reiner. "I heard that he was at the base theater."

Lt. Col. "He might have been. He only spoke for a few minutes. Then the base Commander spoke for about twenty minutes. He had plenty of time to go to the base theater and get back."

Dr. R. "How many did he talk to?"

Lt. C. "I was there for two sessions standing room only. 225 each time. There might have been another session but I wasn't there if he spoke then."

I asked, "Who spoke?"

Lt. Col. "The Commander in Chief"

I said, "The President ... "What did he talk about?"

Lt. Col. "It's classified."

"Confidential?"

"Higher."

"Secret?"

"Higher."

I said, "Oh."

Lt. Col. "What do you mean by 'Oh?'"

"It is none of my business. I am only cleared to secret."

Lt. Col. "I would not say that if I were you."

If Kirklin's recollection is correct, then the activities that Eisenhower was performing at Holloman AFB on February 11, 1955 were classified above Top Secret. Base personnel were taken into a large hangar and debriefed in groups of 225.

Agreement reached between Eisenhower & extraterrestrials at the 1955 Meeting

According to the testimonies examined earlier, the February 20-21, 1954 meeting at Edwards AFB was not successful. The extraterrestrials were spurned due to their refusal to enter into technology exchanges and insistence on nuclear disarmament by the U.S. and presumably other major world powers. William Cooper describes the circumstances of a subsequent agreement that was reached at Holloman after the failure of the first meeting. While Cooper has a different version of dates and times for the 1954/1955 meetings, he agrees that there were two sets of meetings involving different extraterrestrials meeting with President Eisenhower and/or Eisenhower administration officials.[114]

> Later in 1954 [actually February 11, 1955] the race of large nosed Gray Aliens which had been orbiting the Earth landed at Holloman Air Force Base. A basic agreement was reached. This race identified themselves as originating from a Planet around a red star in the Constellation of Orion which we called Betelgeuse. They stated that their planet was dying and that at some unknown future time they would no longer be able to survive there.[115]

Aside from the year, Cooper's story is consistent with the above information concerning Kirklin's and other witness accounts of Eisenhower secretly meeting with extraterrestrials at Holloman AFB. According to the pilots that Kirklin overheard, there appeared to be an agreement reached as indicated by handshakes at the end of the meeting. Cooper was therefore the first person to publicly reveal details of the first meeting between Eisenhower and extraterrestrials at Holloman AFB. Most importantly, he was the first to reveal details of the agreement that had been reached at Holloman.

Cooper explained the terms of the agreement and subsequent treaty reached with the second group of extraterrestrials as follows:

> The treaty stated that the aliens would not interfere in our affairs and we would not interfere in theirs. We would keep their presence on earth a secret. They would furnish us with advanced technology and would help us in our technological development. They would not make any treaty with any other Earth nation. They could abduct humans on a limited and periodic basis for the purpose of medical examination and monitoring of our development, with the stipulation that the humans would not be harmed, would be returned to their point

of abduction, would have no memory of the event, and that the alien nation would furnish Majesty Twelve with a list of all human contacts and abductees on a regularly scheduled basis.[116]

Another whistleblower source for a treaty having been signed is Phil Schneider, a former geological engineer who was employed by corporations contracted to build underground bases. He worked extensively on black projects involving extraterrestrials. Schneider revealed his own knowledge of the treaty in the 1954/1955 time frame as follows:

[U]nder the Eisenhower administration, the federal government decided to circumvent the Constitution of the United States and form a treaty with alien entities. It was called the ... Greada Treaty, which basically made the agreement that the aliens involved could take a few cows and test their implanting techniques on a few human beings, but that they had to give details about the people involved.[117]

Schneider's knowledge of the treaty would have come from his familiarity with a range of compartmentalized black projects and interaction with other personnel working with extraterrestrials.

Yet another whistleblower source for an agreement being signed is Michael Wolf, who claims to have served on various policy-making committees responsible for extraterrestrial affairs for twenty five years.[118] He claims that the Eisenhower administration entered into a treaty with an extraterrestrial race and that this treaty was never ratified as constitutionally required.[119]

Significantly, a number of whistleblowers argue that the treaty that was signed involved some compulsion on the part of the extraterrestrials. For example, Col Phillip Corso, a highly decorated officer who was a member in various committees serving Eisenhower's National Security Council, alluded to a treaty signed by the Eisenhower administration with extraterrestrials in his memoirs. He wrote: "We had negotiated a kind of surrender with them [extraterrestrials] as long as we couldn't fight them. They dictated the terms because they knew what we most feared was disclosure."[120] Keyhoe's observations regarding the Air Force's desperate attempt to debunk the huge spacecraft sighted in 1953, point to this being the disclosure event exploited by the extraterrestrials. Corso's claim of a 'negotiated surrender' suggests that he was not happy with the agreement or 'treaty' subsequently reached with the extraterrestrials.

Charles Hall was a former weather observer for the U.S. Air Force from 1963 to 1967. He was stationed at Nellis Air Force Base's Indian Spring facility where he claims he frequently witnessed extraterrestrials called the "Tall Whites" regularly meeting with senior military leaders. He says that a secret underground base was built at Indian Springs to house the extraterrestrials and their advanced interstellar ships. Rumors of the extraterrestrials at Nellis AFB date back to the mid-1950s suggesting agreements were reached during the Eisenhower administration. Confirmation has been found for some of Hall's claims concerning anomalous events at the weather ranges, including government funding for a secret underground base at Indian Springs.[121]

Hall explained the legalistic way in which agreements with the Tall White extraterrestrials are interpreted in this response to an interview question about why he was chosen to liaise with them:

> … the decision to send me, and no one else, out to the ranges, was made by a committee of individuals that included the Tall Whites as well as high ranking USAF Generals and other high ranking members of the U.S. Government. The Tall Whites are very meticulous about keeping their agreements and expect the U.S. Government to be equally meticulous about keeping its agreements as well. If I were victimized or threatened by anyone, The Tall Whites would interpret that to mean that the U.S. Government could not be trusted to keep its agreements. The consequences would be enormous.[122]

Hall's testimony is significant since it reveals that extraterrestrials are supplied a number of resources including basing rights in exchange for technological assistance to the USAF. This has been secretly formalized by officials in the Pentagon and other key government agencies in one or more undisclosed agreements arising out of face to face meetings between national security officials and the Tall Whites.

Conclusion

Examination of evidence presented in this chapter by whistleblower or witness testimonies raise a major challenge in reaching any firm conclusions over the alleged 'First Contact' meeting between President Eisenhower and extraterrestrials. The testimonies of whistleblowers/witnesses appear sincere, positively motivated and plausible. Yet they are plagued by controversy, allegations of fraud, inconsistency and other irregularities. Due to an official secrecy policy adopted towards extraterrestrial life and a CIA sanctioned policy of debunking, we may never know the full truth behind whistleblower/witness claims. It may nevertheless be concluded that some if not most of the controversy surrounding these individuals has been caused by military-intelligence agencies intent on discrediting whistleblower or witness testimonies.[123]

While there continues to be uncertainty in the controversy surrounding whistleblower testimonies and the role of military-intelligence agencies in generating this controversy, the bulk of evidence points to a 'First Contact' meeting having occurred during Eisenhower's Palm Spring vacation on February 20-21, 1954 (see Table 1 for a summary). The testimonies suggest that the President was given a briefing document to prepare him for the First Contact meeting. The extraterrestrials in the First Contact event, a race of tall 'Nordic' extraterrestrials, that were friendly according to the briefing document McElroy read, were spurned due to their reluctance to provide advanced technology in an agreement. A subsequent meeting at Holloman AFB on February 11, 1955 resulted in an agreement with a different set of extraterrestrials, commonly described the 'Tall Grays', who did not have the same reluctance in exchanging extraterrestrial technology as part of an agreement.

Next year we will witness the 60th anniversary of a First Contact meeting between the U.S. and an extraterrestrial race on February 20, 1954, we must do so with wonder at the awesome nature of this occasion.[124] At the same time, we must do whatever necessary to make public the full details of the meeting, and the apparent spurning of what appears to be a principled extraterrestrial race that rejected technology transfers while dangerous weapons programs were in place in the U.S. and elsewhere on the planet. The subsequent meeting and agreement reached at Holloman AFB on February 11, 1955 with an extraterrestrial race willing to trade technology in exchange for 'limited medical experiments' with civilians will surely go down in history as a deeply significant event whose effects continues to reverberate through human society. Finally, we must be alert to the mounting evidence that while a treaty was signed soon after the 1955 Holloman AFB meeting, it may well have been with the 'wrong extraterrestrials'. This will adversely impact on humanity if not dealt with in a transparent and truthful manner, with full accountability.

The following two chapters will discuss in detail the different groups of extraterrestrial visitors that have been respectively involved in meetings/agreements with clandestine government agencies, and those involved in more friendly direct interactions with private citizens.

Table 1. Evidence for Eisenhower ET 1954 & 1955 Meetings

Circumstantial Evidence

- Eisenhower takes unscheduled one week vacation in Palm Springs, CA – Feb 17-24
- Eisenhower goes missing on evening of Feb 20
- Eisenhower secretly taken by plane to Palmdale which is adjacent to Edwards AFB
- Fake Cover Story Used to Cover Absence.
- Edwards AFB closed for three day period during Ike's Palm Springs visit
- Bravo Hydrogen Bomb Test Occurs 9 nine days after alleged meeting with ETs concerning nuclear weapons at Edwards.
- Security guard reveals in interview that Air Force One secretly left Spence AFB on the morning of Feb 11, 1955.
- Bill Kirklin aware of scheduled honor parade for Eisenhower during his secret visit to Holloman AFB.
- Kirkin sees Air Force One (Columbine) departing from Holloman AFB in the late afternoon of Feb 11, 1955

Direct Witnesses of meeting or documents

- Henry McElroy, Jr, a former N.H. State Representative saw a Briefing Document for a First Contact Meeting
- Charles Suggs, Navy Commander sees Eisenhower meeting with two Nordic ETs at Edwards AFB
- Lord Clancarty reveals whistle-blower testimony that Eisenhower meets with 'humanlike' ETs from five space craft at Edwards AFB
- Desmond Leslie reveals testimony of anonymous USAF officer who witnessed flying saucer landing at Edwards, base closure and Ike taken to see it.
- Widow of USAF MP says he was on guard duty at hangar with flying saucer inside when he saw Eisenhower arrive at Edwards AFB
- George Green refers to three witnesses of artillery fire upon five UFOs that later landed at Edwards AFB
- Gerald Light reports on Feb 20 meeting and of five spacecraft being studied at Edwards AFB.
- Bill Kirklin is told and overhears testimony concerning Eisenhower's visit and meeting with extraterrestrial at Holloman AFB.
- Base electrician sees Air Force One land at Holloman AFB and appear to wait for an arriving flying saucer

- Staff Sergeant Wykoff sees Eisenhower give speech at Holloman AFB in Feb 1955.

Whistleblowers revealing documents, films or supporting facts

- Jesuit Priest discloses 1954 meeting, existence of a film, Cardinal MacIntyre's involvement & Vatican response.
- Don Philips, sees documents and film of 1954 meeting
- William Cooper confirms 1954/1955 meetings based on US Navy documents.
- Phil Schneider aware of a Greada treaty with extraterrestrials that dates from 1954/55 period.
- Charles Hall aware of agreements with extraterrestrials that can be dated back to mid-1950s.

ENDNOTES – CHAPTER 2

[70] An Earlier version of this chapter was originally published as "Eisenhower's 1954 Meeting With Extraterrestrials: The Fiftieth Anniversary of First Contact?" *Exopolitics.Org* (February 12, 2004).

[71] William Moore, "UFO's: Exploring the ET Phenomenon," *Gazette* (Hollywood, CA., March 29, 1989). Available online at:
http://www.ufoevidence.org/documents/doc856.htm

[72] Bill Kirklin, "Ike and UFO's," *Exopolitics Journal*, available at
http://exopoliticsjournal.com/vol-2/vol-2-1-Exp-Ike.htm

[73] Private email sent to author on February 6, 2009.

[74] Transcript of Project Camelot, "Air Force One and the Alien Connection: A Video Interview with Bill Holden," June 2007,
http://www.bibliotecapleyades.net/vida_alien/alien_zetareticuli03.htm

[75] For description of the U.S. Nuclear Testing program at the Bikini Islands, Jane Dibblin, *Day of Two Suns: Us Nuclear Testing and the Pacific Islanders* (New Amsterdam Books, 2002).

[76] Available online at http://www.youtube.com/watch?v=NNV8-k5UvpY. Transcript available at McElroy's former website: http://tinyurl.com/bzlu74x

[77] "New gold money bill introduced in N.H. General Court,"
http://www.newswithviews.com/NWVexclusive/exclusive55.htm

[78] See
http://www.gencourt.state.nh.us/house/committees/committeedetails.aspx?code=H25

[79] Available online at http://www.youtube.com/watch?v=NNV8-k5UvpY. Transcript available at McElroy's former website: http://tinyurl.com/bzlu74x

[80] Available online at http://www.youtube.com/watch?v=NNV8-k5UvpY. Transcript available at McElroy's former website: http://tinyurl.com/bzlu74x

[81] Available online at http://www.youtube.com/watch?v=NNV8-k5UvpY. Transcript available at McElroy's former website: http://tinyurl.com/bzlu74x

[82] Available online at http://www.youtube.com/watch?v=NNV8-k5UvpY. Transcript available at McElroy's former website: http://tinyurl.com/bzlu74x

[83] Personal notes from William Hamilton from a 1991 interview with Sgt Suggs. See also William Hamilton, *Project Aquarius: The Story of An Aquarian Scientist* (Authorhouse, 2005) 85-86.

[84] Personal notes supplied by William Hamilton of a 1991 interview with Commander Suggs' son, Sgt Charles Suggs, Jr. See also, Bill Hamilton, *Project Aquarius: The Story of An Aquarian Scientist* (Authorhouse, 2005) 85.

[85] Cited in Timothy Good, *Alien Contact: Top-Secret UFO Files Revealed* (William Morrow and Co., 1993) 75

[86] Timothy Good, *Need to Know: UFOs, the Military and Intelligence* (Pegasus Books, 2007) 208.

[87] My summary of a phone interview conducted in February 2004

88 Timothy Good, *Need to Know,* 208.
89 Christoforo Barbato, "Vatican and UFO: Secretum Omega,"
http://www.ufodigest.com/secretum.html
90 Luca Scantamburlo, "Planet X and the "JESUIT FOOTAGE" Classified
"SECRETUM OMEGA." First Indirect Confirmation!"
http://www.ufodigest.com/news/1106/jesuitfootage.html
91 "Testimony of Don Phillips," *Disclosure,* ed., Stephen Greer (Crossing Point, 2001)
379
92 William Cooper, *Behold A Pale Horse* (Light Technology Publishing, 1991) 381-96.
93 Salter, *Life With a Cosmos Clearance* (Light Technology Publishing, 2003) 8. See
also Robert Dean Interview, "Command Sergeant Major Robert Dean, NATO's Secret
UFO Assessment & Setting the Record Straight" *Exopolitics Journal* (April 2006) 213-
232). Available online at: http://www.exopoliticsjournal.com/Journal-vol-1-3-Dean.pdf
94 Cooper, "Origin, Identity, and Purpose of MJ-12," in *Behold A Pale Horse,* 201-202
. Online version available at:
http://www.bibliotecapleyades.net/sociopolitica/esp_sociopol_mj12_1.htm
95 Donald Keyhoe, *Aliens from Space: The Real Story of Unidentified Flying Objects*
(Doubleday and Co., 1973) 129-30.
96 Keyhoe, *Aliens from Space:*131.
97 Cooper, "Origin, Identity, and Purpose of MJ-12," in *Behold A Pale Horse,* 201-202
. Online version available at:
http://www.bibliotecapleyades.net/sociopolitica/esp_sociopol_mj12_1.htm
98 21st Century Radio's Hieronimus & Co. "Transcript of Interview with Bob Dean,
March 24, 1996," http://www.ufoevidence.org/documents/doc1156.htm
99 The letter is reprinted in Timothy Good, *Alien Contact,* 275.
100 John Spencer, "Light, Gerald," *The UFO Encyclopedia: Inexplicable Sightings,
Alien Abductions, Close Encounters, Brilliant Hoaxes* (Avon Books, 1991) 188.
101 "A Covenant With Death by Bill Cooper," http://www.alienshift.com/id40.html
Also in William Cooper, *Behold a Pale Horse* (Light Technology Publishing 1991),
203.
102 For biographical details on "Edwin G. Nourse, Ph.D. (1883-1974)" go to:
http://en.wikipedia.org/wiki/Edwin_Griswold_Nourse
103 Franklin Winthrop Allen was author of *Instructions for Reporters for Hearings
Before the Interstate Commerce Committee* (Dispatch Press, 1918).
104 See William Moore, "UFO's: Exploring the ET Phenomenon,"
http://www.ufoevidence.org/documents/doc856.htm
105 See Cristoforo Barbato, "Vatican and UFO: Secretum Omega,"
http://www.ufodigest.com/secretum.html
106 Milton William Cooper, "Origin, Identity, and Purpose of MJ-12,"
http://www.bibliotecapleyades.net/sociopolitica/esp_sociopol_mj12_1.htm . See also
Cooper, *Behold A Pale Horse,* 202.
107 Cited by Art Campbell, http://www.ufocrashbook.com/eisenhower.html
108 See Art Campbell, http://www.ufocrashbook.com/eisenhower.html
109 Bill Kirklin is the author of "Ike and UFOs," that was published anonymously in the
Exopolitics Journal 2:1 (2007): http://exopoliticsjournal.com/vol-2/vol-2-1-Exp-

Ike.htm Kirklin's says he was told about Ike's visit in late February, this is likely a minor mistake on his part since the visit occurred on February 11, 1955.

[110] Kirklin,"Ike and UFOs:" http://exopoliticsjournal.com/vol-2/vol-2-1-Exp-Ike.htm

[111] Kirklin,"Ike and UFOs:" http://exopoliticsjournal.com/vol-2/vol-2-1-Exp-Ike.htm

[112] Transcript of electrician's family letter – recorded by Art Campbell and played on Jerry Pippin Show - 6/23/08. Available online at: http://www.ipodshows.net/Archives_3rd_quarter_2008.htm

[113] Transcript of Staff Sgt Wykoff interviewed by Art Campbell and played on Jerry Pippin Show - 6/23/08. Available online at: http://www.ipodshows.net/Archives_3rd_quarter_2008.htm

[114] Milton William Cooper, "Origin, Identity, and Purpose of MJ-12," http://www.bibliotecapleyades.net/sociopolitica/esp_sociopol_mj12_1.htm

[115] Milton William Cooper, "Origin, Identity, and Purpose of MJ-12," http://www.bibliotecapleyades.net/sociopolitica/esp_sociopol_mj12_1.htm

[116] Milton William Cooper, "Origin, Identity, and Purpose of MJ-12," in *Behold a Pale Horse,* 203-04. Also available at: http://www.bibliotecapleyades.net/sociopolitica/esp_sociopol_mj12_1.htm

[117] Phil Schneider, "MUFON Conference Presentation, 1995," available online at: http://web.archive.org/web/20000926021403/http://www.anomalous-images.com//text/schneid.html

[118] See Chris Stoner, 'The Revelations of Dr Michael Wolf on the UFO Cover Up and ET Reality," (October 2000) http://web.archive.org/web/20010105221200/http://www3.mistral.co.uk/futurepositive/mdrwolf.htm

[119] See Richard Boylan, "Official Within MJ-12 UFO-Secrecy Management Group Reveals Insider Secrets," http://www.drboylan.com/wolfdoc2.html

[120] Phillip Corso, *The Day After Roswell* (Pocket Books, 1997) 292.

[121] See Michael Salla, "Further Investigations of Charles Hall and Tall Whites at Nellis Air Force Base: The David Coote Interviews," http://exopolitics.org/Exo-Comment-36.htm

[122] "Charles Hall and the Tall Whites: Another perception of the extraterrestrial phenomenon and the Area 51," http://karmapolis.be/pipeline/interview_hall_uk.htm

[123] For description of the disinformation tactics used by military intelligence agencies, see an interview with John Maynard, "From Disinformation to Disclosure," *Surfing the Apocalypse,* http://www.surfingtheapocalypse.com/maynard.html

[124] For an article on the 50th anniversary of the Eisenhower-Extraterrestrial meeting, see Peter Carlson, "Ike and Alien Ambassadors - The Whole Tooth About Eisenhower's Extraterrestrial Encounter," *Washington Post* (Feb 18, 2004)

CHAPTER 3

First Contact: Encounters with Intraterrestrials and Solarians

Introduction: A diversity of extraterrestrial life visiting our world

We now know that President Eisenhower met with extraterrestrial ambassadors in at least two official First Contact meetings in 1954 and 1955 at Air Force bases. These involved two different extraterrestrial civilizations. This naturally raises questions of precisely how many extraterrestrial civilizations are visiting our world, and are they meeting with private citizens as well as public officials? Thankfully there is abundant evidence that answers these questions. The evidence will show that first contact has not merely involved extraterrestrials meeting with public officials in the USA and other nations. There are an extensive number of extraterrestrial visitors known to be currently interacting with Earth and the human population: both public officials and private citizens.

A leaked 1954 "Majestic document", referred to two extraterrestrial civilizations visiting Earth.[125] A 1964 classified NATO document referred to four extraterrestrial civilizations visiting Earth.[126] A 1977 Congressional Research Service Report described between two to six advanced extraterrestrial civilizations in the galaxy.[127] Finally, a classified First Aid manual for injured extraterrestrial biological entities was claimed to contain medical information for 57 different extraterrestrial species known to the covert U.S. military teams in 1979.[128] From this pool of extraterrestrial civilizations, a number are more active than others in interacting with humanity, and can be claimed to have the most significance for human evolution and sovereignty. The extensive number of reports and testimonies concerning different extraterrestrial visitors indicates that the motivations and activities of extraterrestrial civilizations vary greatly, and an idea of these motivations can be distilled from close examination of these reports and testimonies.

The most compelling testimonies on the different extraterrestrial civilizations comes from *'whistleblowers'* who served for long periods in the military and/or corporations participating in 'black projects'; and also *'experiencers'* who have had direct physical contact with extraterrestrials and communicated with them. The latter includes both *'contactees'* in the classic sense of those who have voluntarily interacted with extraterrestrial civilizations, and *'abductees'* who have done so involuntarily.[129] I will first refer to some of the main sources of information for different extraterrestrial civilizations operating on Earth, then describe their motivations and activities using available sources.

There is some debate over the accuracy of the information provided by the whistleblowers and experiencers presented in this and the next two chapters. I have argued elsewhere that 'whistleblowers' and 'experiencers' provide the strongest evidentiary sources for the extraterrestrial phenomenon.[130] Such individuals have first-hand experiences concerning extraterrestrials and associated activities of shadow government entities. They are all eyewitness accounts that would be considered in any court of law or Congressional inquiry.

What helps greatly in supporting the reliability of the information provided by 'whistleblowers' and 'experiencers' is the consistency and coherence of the testimonies; the evidence provided by them; and ultimately the credibility of the individuals involved. Consequently, this chapter focuses mainly on the testimony of a select number of 'whistleblowers' and 'experiencers' whose consistency, coherence and credibility suggest they are providing reliable information on the motivations and activities of different extraterrestrial civilizations.

Whistleblower and Documentary Evidence of Multiple Extraterrestrial Civilizations Visiting Earth

A leaked 1954 document describes the covert procedures for the recovery of crashed extraterrestrial vehicles (ETV) or UFOs. Titled SOM1-01 (Special Operations Manual), it referred to two types of extraterrestrial biological entities that might be found at ETV/UFO crash sites. Section 10 from the SOM1-01 says:

Examination of remains recovered from wreckage of UFOBs [ETV] indicates that Extraterrestrial Biological Entities may be classified into two distinct categories as follows:

a. *EBE Type I*. These entities are humanoid and might be mistaken for human beings of the Oriental race if seen from a distance. They are bi-pedal, 5-5 feet 4 [sic] inches in height and weigh 80-100 pounds. Proportionally they are similar to humans, although the cranium is somewhat larger and more rounded....

b. *EBE Type II*. These entities are humanoid but differ from Type 1 in many respects. They are bi-pedal, 3 feet 5 inches – 4 feet 2 inches in height and weigh 25-50 pounds. Proportionally, the head is much larger than humans or Type 1 EBEs, the cranium being much larger and elongated.[131]

The SOM document, if genuine, shows the earliest known effort to categorize the different extraterrestrial civilizations visiting Earth. Another official document was revealed to exist by Master Sergeant Bob Dean. He had a twenty seven year military career and at one time during his service worked in military intelligence at the Supreme Headquarters of the Allied Powers in Europe (SHAPE) from 1963 to 1967. His distinguished service record gives him great credibility in claiming to have witnessed classified information during his military service. During his SHAPE assignment he claimed he was instructed to read a detailed study of the activities of UFOs/ETs and how they might impact on Soviet-NATO relations which was published in 1964 with the title: "An Assessment: An Evaluation of a Possible Military Threat to Allied Forces in Europe."[132] In an interview, Dean described four extraterrestrial races listed in 'The Assessment' as follows:

The group at the time, there were just four that they knew of for certain and the Greys were one of those groups. There was a group that looked exactly like we do.... These people looked so much like us they could sit next to you on a plane or in a restaurant and you'd never know the difference.... Two other groups, there was a very large group, I say large, they were 6-8 maybe sometimes 9 feet tall and they were humanoid, but they were very pale, very white, didn't have any hair on their bodies at all. And then there was another group that had sort of a reptilian quality to them. We had encountered them, military people and police officers all over the world have run into these guys. They had vertical pupils in their eyes and their skin seemed to have a quality very much like what you find on the stomach of a lizard. So those were the four they knew of in 1964. But I've been told by friends that are still active in military service that it's well over a dozen by now.[133]

Another whistleblower describing different extraterrestrial civilizations discussed in government documents is Daniel Sheehan. He claims he witnessed a classified Congressional Research Service Report on extraterrestrial intelligence submitted to President Carter in 1977. Sheehan said:

The first report on extraterrestrial intelligence stated the Congressional Research Service of the official United States Congressional Library, in its official report to the President, through the House of Representatives Science and Technology Committee, concludes that there are from two to six highly intelligent, highly technologically developed civilizations in our own galaxy over and above our own.[134]

Yet another whistleblower describing different extraterrestrial civilizations discussed in government documents is Clifford Stone. He claims that due to his work in elite UFO crash retrieval teams, he was given access to a First Aid manual listing different extraterrestrial races. He described the manual in a 2005 interview:

That information was from a little publication that they had ... actually a little thick booklet, a loose leaf notebook type situation [1000 pages]. But the intent of cataloguing the different species was so that they could render the best first aid they could in identifying which species they had at any given location.[135]

In this and the following two chapters, I describe the extraterrestrial civilizations most commonly referred to in the UFO and exopolitics literature. These appear to have most strategic significance for the evolution and sovereignty of humanity, and impact significantly on a range of systemic global problems. Shortly, I will separate extraterrestrial civilizations on the basis of their belonging to one of either two major groups interacting with humanity – those intervening with humans on a voluntary basis and those doing so involuntarily. This helps us clearly separate between those extraterrestrials that recognize the importance of respecting the vital interests of humanity at the individual, societal and global levels, and those which don't.

This and the following chapter examine individual encounters with a group of extraterrestrials and highly evolved terrestrials hidden on Earth, that appear most interested in establishing First Contact with humanity. The main goal of these meetings with private citizens is to raise public awareness of extraterrestrial life and of galactic society. The main effect of these First Contact meetings has been to raise confidence among members of the general public and government/military officials that extraterrestrials can assist humanity in its evolution as a planetary culture where our vital interests are respected.

These First Contact extraterrestrial civilizations were the first reported cases of humans meeting with extraterrestrials, and chronologically are vitally important for understanding the true history of interaction between humanity and alien life over the last six decades spanning the atomic age. The First Contact extraterrestrials are outside the web of clandestine agreements between some extraterrestrial groups and 'shadow governments'/national security agencies described in chapter two – I will go into greater detail in chapter five.

Most 'contactees' report "First Contact" extraterrestrials to be friendly to humanity insofar as they respect our vital interests or needs at the individual, societal and global levels. This suggests a more ethical approach to the challenges confronting humanity as it prepares for the truth about visiting extraterrestrial life and challenges posed by advanced alien technology. It is this group of extraterrestrials that may prove to be the key in solving systemic global problems caused by those aliens working with the 'shadow government' and participating in "unprincipled negotiations" where humanity's vital interests are ignored in key areas.

Chapter five examines a grouping of extraterrestrial civilizations with whom 'shadow governments' responsible for extraterrestrial affairs have reached agreements and even collaborated in joint projects.[136] The extensive set of interlocking agreements between these races and the 'shadow government' in the U.S. and elsewhere suggests the existence of a Military-Industrial-Extraterrestrial Complex of interests. The Military-Industrial-Extraterrestrial Complex (MIEC) of interests currently controls most information concerning extraterrestrial life; and dominates government institutions around the planet, financial interests, the mass media, and is responsible for systemic global problems. [137]

While extraterrestrials belonging to the MIEC do perform a type of First Contact, strictly interpreted as the first time an individual meets with extraterrestrials, these meetings are involuntary and widely referred to as "abductions". By definition, abductions involved a violation of the vital interests of individuals. Consequently, we can distinguish between two broad groupings of extraterrestrials interacting with humanity. I will refer to off-world visitors and evolved indigenous entities hidden on Earth who meet with private citizens in a mutually voluntary manner as *First Contact extraterrestrials*. Those extraterrestrials who meet with humans in an involuntary manner, as permitted under clandestine agreements with secret government agencies, will be described as *MIEC extraterrestrials*.

Distinguishing between extraterrestrial groups in this way helps bring to prominence the complex ethical-legal-political dimensions in understanding how different extraterrestrial races choose to cooperate or not with the Military-Industrial-Extraterrestrial Complex . For example, is a race of extraterrestrials 'unfriendly' if it chooses to become part of a Military-Industrial-Extraterrestrial Complex; thereby sharing technology with national security agencies, in the guise of 'mutually beneficial projects' that lead to secrecy, human rights violations and damage to the global environment as a result of policies by the 'shadow government'? Likewise, is a race of extraterrestrials 'friendly' if it refuses to be co-opted into a Military-Industrial-Extraterrestrial Complex, thereby choosing to play a mainly observer role as a majority of the human race is exploited by human elites and extraterrestrials associated with them? While a prima facie argument can be made to answer 'yes' to both questions, this should not disguise the deeper ethical-legal-political issues that emerge through the existence of a Military-Industrial-Extraterrestrial Complex and related interactions.

Understanding the motivations and activities of the most significant extraterrestrial civilizations will help greatly in answering the above questions. This will also help private individuals respond adequately to the dilemma over which extraterrestrial races contribute to global problems confronting humanity, and which extraterrestrial races can be worked with for the evolution and vital interests of humanity.

Understanding the Different Ways Extraterrestrials Interact with humanity

We know from the second chapter that at President Eisenhower's initial "First Contact" meeting on February 20, 1954, he met with a delegation of 'human looking' extraterrestrial civilizations. The meeting proved to be an unsuccessful effort to reach an agreement on the US's thermonuclear nuclear weapons program. The apparent stumbling block was that these extraterrestrial races were not willing to provide technology that might be used by the military-industrial interests that dominated the Eisenhower administration and set the tone for subsequent extraterrestrial – human dialogue. The principled opposition of this group of extraterrestrials to being co-opted into an emerging Military-Industrial-Extraterrestrial Complex (MIEC) marks an important indicator of extraterrestrial groups outside the web of interlocking interests that make up the MIEC in the U.S. and elsewhere on the planet.

This category of extraterrestrial civilizations is primarily 'human' and can easily integrate into human society since many are indistinguishable from the rest of humanity. According to Robert Dean, this greatly concerned NATO commanders who thought these extraterrestrials could easily infiltrate military and political institutions, and pose a security threat.[138] These races are described to be from both within our own solar system, and star systems such as Lyra, Vega, Pleiades, Sirius, Procyon, Tau Ceti, Ummo, Andromeda and Arcturus. Many of these extraterrestrial civilizations have allegedly provided genetic material for the seeding of humanity on Earth.[139]

A number of researchers and 'contactees' refer to historical evidence that various extraterrestrial races are humanity's ancestors. In chapter five, I will discuss Zecharia Sitchin's views concerning the Anunnaki as the creators of modern humans, homo sapiens 300,000 years ago. Dr Arthur Horn, a former professor of biological anthropology, argues that humanity is descended not just from the Anunnaki but from a number of extraterrestrial civilizations who inserted their own genetic material to speed up human evolution.[140] He identifies a number of gaps in "the Darwinian-anthropological version of primate and human evolution" and argues that these are most likely places where extraterrestrials intervened.[141] He calls these "ET Inception Group' interventions and argues they occurred at the following evolutionary leaps in primate and human evolution:

1. The appearance of advanced primates 40 million years ago.
2. The appearance of the first member of the human biological family in Africa, Australopithecines or Hominidae [great apes] four million years ago.
3. The development of Homo habilis [handy man] about two and a half million years ago.
4. The development of Homo erectus [upright man] around 1.8 million years ago.
5. The development of Homo sapiens [knowing man] around 300,000 years ago.[142]

Stewart Swerdlow was involuntarily recruited as a child into covert government projects based at Montauk, Long Island, New York, that reverse engineered various extraterrestrial technologies. He claims that in the covert program he learned about a number of different extraterrestrial civilizations that have intervened to speed up humanity's evolution.

> While the Reptilians were the first colonists on Earth, they were not the only ones who interfered with human development on this planet. In all there are twelve other groups who donated DNA to the production of the [human] experiment. Add the Reptilians to the twelve groups, resulting in human beings with a genetic mixture of 13 different strains.[143]

I will discuss evidence of Reptilian extraterrestrials in chapter five, but it is important to emphasize Swerdlow's revelation that we have at least twelve different extraterrestrial civilizations that have contributed to human DNA. According to Alex Collier, whose contact experiences I will discuss in the next chapter, there is a total of 22 extraterrestrial races have provided genetic material for the 'human experiment'. These include Reptilian, Gray and Anunnaki races described earlier as well as those races in this second group to be examined which he describes as 'benevolent':

> That we, as a product of extraterrestrial genetic manipulation, are possessors of a vast gene pool consisting of many different racial memory banks, also consisting of at least 22 different races. Because of our genetic heritage, and because we are spirit, the benevolent extraterrestrial races actually view us as being royalty.[144]

As a result of this genetic linkage, the extraterrestrials in this group outside of the MIEC apparently view humanity in much the way a protective parent might view an adolescent son/daughter in a dangerous environment.[145] The vital interests of races in this category are to ensure that global humanity evolves in a responsible way without endangering both itself and the greater galactic community of which it is part.

There are two parts to this grouping of extraterrestrials. The first are more correctly described as *'intraterrestrials'* that have historically inhabited the Earth's subterranean dwellings. They are commonly described as remnants of an ancient human civilization that followed a separate evolutionary path to surface humanity. The second are *extraterrestrials* that have 'off-world' origins. Some have human features and can easily intermingle with the rest of humanity without being identified. These extraterrestrials are described as coming both from within our solar system and also outside of it.

Extraterrestrials outside of the network of agreements making up the Military Industrial Extraterrestrial Complex (MIEC) differ in terms of their hands-on experience with humanity and the biosphere. There are three main forms of interaction occurring here which are primarily beneficial for human evolution insofar as the vital interests of individuals, societies and the biosphere are concerned. I distinguish these from the interaction occurring through agreements with the MIEC which I will describe in chapter five as not beneficial insofar as they result from "unprincipled negotiations". I will describe the latter as a further type of intervention making a total of four types of intervention that helps distinguish all the different extraterrestrials I describe in this and the following two chapters.

There is much evidence in terms of whistleblower/contactee testimonies, photographs, films and reliable witnesses to substantiate the existence of Intervention Type A, B, and D extraterrestrials. Extraterrestrials performing Intervention Type C are much harder to get reliable information on. Discussion of them requires citing esoteric sources such as remote viewing or telepathic communications.[146] While I will concentrate on physical evidence substantiating the intervention of extraterrestrial groups outside of the MIEC, I will on limited occasions use esoteric sources to describe Intervention Type C extraterrestrials.

Table 2. Extraterrestrial Intervention Types

Intervention Type	Description
Intervention Type A	Extraterrestrials establish 'ground teams' and Earth bases with members integrating into human society for monitoring and influencing humanity's evolution. Vital interests of individuals are respected.
Intervention Type B	Extraterrestrials physically contact individuals, share information, take individuals into their ships to witness advanced technologies, and/or take individuals to extraterrestrial bases or societies. Vital interests of individuals are respected.
Intervention Type C	Extraterrestrials intervene to protect the planet's biosphere, and/or esoterically communicate with individuals collaborating in projects related to human evolution. Vital interests of individuals are respected.
Intervention Type D	Extraterrestrials establish technology exchange agreements with covert government entities and/or gain permission for genetic 'upgrade' programs, and basing rights. Vital interests of individuals are NOT respected.

Intraterrestrials

The subterranean *'intraterrestrials'* are described to be remnants of previous human civilizations on the Earth's surface such as Lemuria and Atlantis. Ancient records confirm the existence of earlier civilizations that had achieved impressive technological breakthroughs but underwent cataclysmic events. Plato for example gave a detailed account of the last days of the continent Atlantis prior to its destruction describing the advanced nature of its society, architecture and resources.[147] The idea is plausible that remnants of these civilizations were able to escape the surface destruction and relocate to the relevant safety of subterranean areas. The idea of habitable subterranean regions was recorded in works by Plato, Dante and other authors since antiquity.

Figure 5. Hollow Earth according to William Reed, Phantom of the Poles, 1906

In 1692, the English Astronomer, Sir Edmond Halley, proposed a detailed scientific theory of the inner Earth being a series of concentric shells that could support life.[148] In 1818, an enterprising American Infantry Captain, John Cleves Symmes, took Halley's theory to heart and proposed an expedition to the poles where he reasoned the main passage ways to the hollow Earth must lie. He issued the following circular:

TO ALL THE WORLD ... I declare that the earth is hollow, habitable within; containing a number of solid concentric spheres; one within the other, and it is open at the poles twelve or sixteen degrees. I pledge my life in support of this truth, and am ready to explore the hollow if the world will support and aid me in the undertaking.[149]

Unfortunately, the resources and technology did not exist to launch the expedition Symmes desired until early into the twentieth century.

The idea of advanced underground civilizations was popularized by Edward Bulyer Lytton in 1870 with the publication of *Vril: the Power of the Coming Race*. His description of an advanced underground civilization that could be traced to ancient Atlantis was accepted by many as accurate. What fascinated many was the description of *Vril* force used as a psychic ability to control advanced technology. There have been subsequently many published books giving accounts of alleged physical visits or psychic journeys to these subterranean civilizations that used advanced technologies. Many of these stories involve individuals making journeys through hidden underground passages where they mysteriously encounter *intraterrestrial* beings.[150] One of these involved a Swede, Olaf Jansen, who claims to have traveled into the hollow Earth and spent two years completing his long journey. He returned to face ridicule and imprisonment in a mental asylum for his incredible story. Just before his death in 1908, Jansen told his story to Willis George Emerson who claimed:

> ... the old man told him just before he died that the place was inhabited by a race of fair-skinned giants. The men were all twelve feet tall and the women a couple of feet shorter. Both sexes wore embroidered tunics and sandals on their feet. They were mild-tempered, dignified and lived for over five hundred years. According to Jansen they also possessed a mysterious power, much greater than electricity, which they used to drive their machinery and equipment.[151]

Jansen's story gives credence to Bulwyer's account of an underground civilization that uses advanced technology through a mysterious Vril force. As impressive the stories and theories of a hollow earth are, they would remain largely speculation if it were not for the exploits of one of world's most famous polar explorers, Rear Admiral Richard Byrd.

In 1926, Richard Byrd embarked on the first of his famous flights over the polar regions. His log entry for what he saw over the North Pole presaged what he was later to discover:

> Time and direction became topsy-turvy as we neared the Pole ... and here and there, instead of the pressing together of the ice-fields, there was a separation leaving a water-lead showing greenish-blue against the white of the snow. Once, for a moment, I mistook a distant, vague, low-lying cloud formation, for *the mountain peaks of a far away land* [italics added].[152]

Byrd's discovery of a greenish-blue water-lead was a surprise, and his intriguing reference to a far away land hinted at what he would later discover. Byrd's success led to him being promoted to Rear Admiral and significant finances for further polar expeditions. In 1929 he led an expedition to the South Pole and once again flew over one of the Earth's pole. He described His first 1929 flight is well known and described in his books, less well known is a second flight, the existence of which was quickly removed from official records. According to F.A. Giannini's book, *World Beyond the Poles* (1959) a newsreel showing what was discovered on *both* flights appeared in 1929:

> That year a newsreel could be seen in America's cinemas which described *both* flights. It also showed newspaper photographs of 'the land beyond the pole with its mountains, trees, rivers and a large animal identified as a mammoth'. Today this newsreel apparently does not exist, although hundreds of people remember viewing it.[153]

Intrigued by this reference to a missing newsreel of Byrd's second Antarctic flight, Alec Maclellan sought to confirm the existence of this newsreel and received the following letter from Miss Dorothy E. Graffin of New York:

> Re: Admiral Byrd's flights to the South Pole and what he saw in the interior of the Earth at the South Pole. Nobody ever mentions the documentary film which Byrd took on this flight and was shown in motion picture theatres throughout the United States soon after Byrd's return home. My sister and I saw this in White Plains, New York. Byrd narrated the film himself and exclaimed in wonder as he approached a warm water lake surrounded by conifers with a large animal moving among the trees...[154]

Byrd's discovery of warm water lakes, conifers and a large animal at the South Pole had the effect that this information, though initially released, was eventually removed from the public realm.

Startling testimony for the existence of subterranean civilizations came from Admiral Byrd soon after the completion of his naval expedition to the Antarctic region after the Second World War in early 1947. Operation Highjump began in December 1946 and comprised a fleet of Navy warships, an aircraft carrier and almost 5000 men. It was scheduled to last six to eight months. There was speculation that Byrd's actual mission was to lead a secret military expedition to find any Nazi bases hidden in the Antarctic. Subsequent casualties and setbacks led to the abrupt end of the expedition in February. Admiral Byrd then spoke at press conferences in South America of "many fatalities" and that the U.S. "would be attacked by flying objects which could fly from pole to pole at incredible speeds."[155]

At the conclusion of Highjump, Byrd commented about his impending trip to the Arctic where he hinted of a polar passageway to a Hollow Earth: "I'd like to see that land beyond the [North] Pole. That area beyond the Pole is the center of the Great Unknown."[156] Byrd's use of the word "beyond" is significant here. He was not referring to land "across" or on the other side of the North Pole. This territory had already been well mapped out by Artic explorers. Some of it extended across international boundaries into adjacent countries such as Russia, Finland, Greenland, Canada and Iceland. After his February 1947 flight to the Artic, Byrd proceeded to give a number of press statements that his plane flew 1700 miles 'beyond' the Pole exploring this "Great

Unknown." He also claimed to have witnessed mountain covered forests. Hollow Earth researcher Ray Palmer had this to say about Byrd's comment:

> What land was it? Look at your map. Calculate the distance from all the known lands ... (Siberia, Spitzbergen, Alaska, Canada, Finland, Norway, Greenland and Iceland). A good portion of them are well within the 1,700 mile range. But none of them are within 200 miles of the Pole. Byrd flew over no known land. He himself called it the great unknown.... He should have seen nothing but ice-covered ocean, or at the very most, partially open ocean. Instead he was over *mountains covered with forest.*[157]

What follows next is subject to great controversy but is consistent with what was sighted on his earlier polar expeditions, the suppression of information of his second 1929 Antarctic flight, and events associated with Operation Highjump.

In his posthumously published 'diaries', Byrd gives a detailed description of one of the ancient subterranean civilizations he encountered during his February 1947 flight over the North Pole. He claims that he was taken into the subterranean dwelling of an advanced race with Nordic physical characteristics. He was shown some of the wondrous technology of this society and also met the leader of this advanced subterranean race who allegedly said:

> 'We have let you enter here because you are of noble character and well-known on the Surface World, Admiral' ... you are in the domain of the Arianni, the Inner World of the Earth.... Admiral, I shall tell you why you have been summoned here. Our interest rightly begins just after your race exploded the first atomic bombs over Hiroshima and Nagasaki, Japan. It was at that alarming time we sent our flying machines, the "Flugelrads", to your surface world to investigate what your race had done.... You see, we have never interfered before in your race's wars, and barbarity, but now we must, for you have learned to tamper with a certain power that is not for man, namely, that of

atomic energy. Our emissaries have already delivered messages to the powers of your world, and yet they do not heed. Now you have been chosen to be witness here that our world does exist. You see, our Culture and Science is many thousands of years beyond your race, Admiral.'[158]

A significant feature from his encounter was the concern expressed by the alleged *intraterrestrial* over the use of atomic weapons. Byrd was always ready to communicate candidly to the press as evidenced from his remarks concerning fatalities and a new enemy that could fly from Pole to Pole at the end of Operation Highjump. However, after his February Arctic flight he was subjected to stringent debriefing and told to remain quiet on all he had witnessed. He wrote the following in his diary for 11 March 1947:

> I have just attended a debriefing and passed on my log. I am now detained for several hours and interviewed by the military and a medical team. It was an ordeal. I am placed under strict control of the international security provisions of the United States of America. I am ordered to remain silent in regard to all that I have seen. Incredible I am reminded that I am a military man and that I must obey orders.[159]

Byrd subsequently remained out of the public eye until his last Polar mission in 1956. This time he led an expedition to the Antarctic that he claimed would be "the most important expedition in the history of the world."[160] A radio announcement on January 13, 1956 said: "On January 13, members of the United States expedition penetrated a land extent 2,300 miles beyond the Pole."[161] Upon his return to the U.S. Byrd claimed: "The present expedition has opened up a vast new land."[162] Byrd's press statements appear confusing if he was just referring to the Antarctic region 2300 miles 'across' the Pole which by 1956 was well known. His reference to a land "2,300 miles beyond the Pole" was referring to a "vast new land" that justified Byrd's belief in the world historic importance of his expedition.

While there continues to be controversy over the veracity of Admiral Byrd's posthumously published diaries, they are consistent with the facts surrounding Byrd's Polar expeditions and final years. His report of "unknown lands" beyond the Poles, missing 1929 newsreel of vegetation and life at the South Pole, 1947 report of a new enemy that could fly from Pole to Pole, his encounter with advanced civilization when flowing over the Arctic in February 1947, and his silencing suggest he encountered *intraterrestrials*.

Admiral Byrd's experiences give credence to supporters of the Hollow Earth theory, and to the idea that advanced subterranean civilizations exist populated by *intraterrestrials*. These ancient civilizations have been described as Agharta, Shamballa, and Telos and have had a number of authors describing direct personal experiences with *intraterrestrials*.[163] One Norwegian told the following remarkable story:

> I lived near the Arctic Circle in Norway. One summer my friend and I made up our minds to take a boat trip together, and go as far as we could into the north country... At the end of one month we had traveled far into the north, beyond the Pole and into a strange new country.... We sailed further and further into this fantastic country, fantastic because everything was huge in size... Plants are big, trees gigantic and finally we came to GIANTS... They were dwelling in homes and towns, just as we do on the Earth's surface. And they used a type of electrical conveyance like a mono-rail car, to transport people.... We stayed with the giants for one year, enjoying their companionship as much as they enjoyed knowing us. We observed many strange and unusual things during our visit with these remarkable people, and were continually amazed at their scientific progress and inventions.[164]

As in the Olaf Jansen story, 12 foot giants that have advanced technologies are said to inhabit these underground civilizations. Byrd's Polar expeditions and his public announcements help confirm that the subterranean regions of the Earth possess vast territories inhabited by *intraterrestrials*. They possess flying vehicles that can fly "from Pole to Pole" very rapidly as candidly confirmed by Byrd in 1947 before being muzzled for national security issues.

The intraterrestrials appear to be descendants of ancient civilizations that escaped cataclysmic events on the surface. Some are described as giant Nordic looking, while others have a more Asiatic appearance. They seem very concerned about humanity's use of destructive nuclear technologies, and have an evident self-interest that such technologies are not used irresponsibly.

The manner of *intraterrestrials* interaction with humans suggests they primarily perform Intervention Type B activities; i.e., they take individuals into their ships and/or allow individuals to visit their subterranean cities. The *intraterrestrials* have knowledge about humanity's ancient history, records of violent geological events, and of natural resources for maintaining health and longevity. They also have knowledge of developing psychic abilities or Vril Force that can be used for controlling advanced technologies. The *intraterrestrials* can assist surface humanity with learning its ancient Earth history, restoring human longevity, developing psychic abilities to use advanced technology, protecting the environment and ending militarism.

'Off World' Extraterrestrials

According to Robert Dean, many 'off-world' extraterrestrials appear to be indistinguishable from humans. Many consider this group of extraterrestrials to be 'benevolent' as described by 'contactees' such as George Adamski, Orfeo Angelucci, George Van Tassell, Howard Menger, Paul Villa, Billy Meier and Alex Collier.[165] Each explains the nature of their voluntary interactions with these human looking extraterrestrials. These contactees often provide physical evidence in the form of photographs, film and/or witnesses of their contacts with extraterrestrial races. The most extensive documentation and physical evidence was provided by George Adamski, Howard Menger, Sixto Paz Wells and Eduard 'Billy' Meier. Each provided much physical evidence for investigators that continue to support their cases. Off world human extraterrestrial races appear to have different 'specialties' as a result of unique histories and planetary migrations due to galactic upheavals and conflicts. It is worth exploring the main activities of each race to understand how they either currently interact with humanity or how they may better interact with humanity to address global problems.

Solarians

The term 'Solarian' will be used to describe extraterrestrial civilizations from within our solar system. The main planets in our solar system that have extraterrestrial civilizations, according to contactee testimonies, include: Venus, Mars, Jupiter, Saturn and several of these planets' moons. This appears surprising given the extreme weather conditions on the surface of these planets. The formation of planets, however, has been argued to follow a similar process to that of Earth. That is one where a thick crust is gradually formed out of interstellar gases while the interior is largely hollow with a small interior sun. The center of mass lies in the thick crust which means that gravity keeps objects and life safely anchored to either side of the crust. Hollow Earth research Marshall Gardner elaborates on how this occurred on other planets:

> When we say that the Earth is a hollow body with polar openings and an interior sun, we back up the statement by referring to nebulas in many stages of evolution in which the gradual forming of the outer envelope of the future planet and the interior sun, and even the beginnings of the polar openings, are all clearly visible in their different stages. Then we point to the actual construction of the planets, Mars, Venus and Mercury, and we show just what the polar openings are like. We show that they are not just ice caps, because direct light has been seen to come from them. And then we demonstrate conclusively that the Earth, like Mars and other planets, has its polar openings, too.[166]

If the formation of planets does follow the model suggested by supporters of the Hollow Earth theory, then it is reasonable to conclude that the interior of these planets may be suitable for life. Shielded from the weather extremes on the planet's surface, and warmed by a small interior sun, life on these planets may support flourishing life and civilizations. As strange as this may first appear to the reader, it's worth remembering that Admiral Byrd's comments about flying into "unknown lands" totaling over 4000 miles *beyond* both Poles, gives support to the Hollow Earth theory. Also Byrd's references to a potential new enemy with "flying objects which could fly from pole to pole at incredible speeds" suggests the advanced technology of the intraterrestrials.[167] Byrd's subsequent muzzling tells us that evidence of a hollow Earth and the presence of technologically advanced intraterrestrial civilizations is a highly classified secret. Denied this revolutionary information, the scientific community has been unable to progress beyond the conventional scientific model of the Earth being a solid ball with a molten core.

The Hollow Earth theory and supporting evidence indicates that it is scientifically possible for the interior sections of many planets and moons in our solar system to support life. This makes plausible the claims of contactees concerning meetings with extraterrestrials from planets in our solar system. The most surprising case involves meetings with extraterrestrials from Venus.

George Adamski first came into public prominence for spectacular photos of UFOs around the moon using his telescope. His photos of large cylindrical UFOs and lights around the moon became well known. Adamski, however, shot into public prominence with his famous Desert Center meeting with an extraterrestrial from Venus. Acting upon a telepathic communication, Adamski and six companions traveled through California to the Desert Center with a rendezvous with flying saucers. Adamski and his companions then all saw the following:

> Riding high, and without sound, there was a gigantic cigar-shaped silvery ship, without wings or appendages of any kind. Slowly, almost as if it was drifting, it came in our direction, then seemed to stop, hovering motionless... At first glance it looked like a fuselage, of a very large ship with the sun's rays reflecting brightly from its unpainted side, at an altitude and angle where wings might not be noticeable.[168]

Five US Air Force planes came onto the scene trying to intercept the large cigar-shaped craft. Both the craft and planes departed the scene. Then another craft emerged as Adamski explains: "My attention was attracted by a flash in the sky and almost instantly a beautiful small craft appeared to be drifting through a saddle between two mountain peaks and settling silently into one of the coves about a half a mile from me."[169] After two Air Force jets roared overhead, Adamski saw someone standing in the direction from where the craft landed.

> As I approached him a strange feeling came over me and I became cautious. At the same time I looked round to reassure myself that we were both in full sight of my companions. Outwardly, there was no reason for this feeling, for the man looked like any other man, and I could see he was somewhat smaller than I and considerably younger.... He took four steps toward me, bringing us within arm's length of each other. Now, for the first time, I fully realized that I was in the presence of a man from space – a human being from another world! [170]

Adamski learned that the extraterrestrial's name was Orthon and that he came from Venus. He told Adamski that extraterrestrials from several planets in the solar system were visiting the earth. In subsequent encounters, Adamski learned that several of Orthon's companions were from Mars and Saturn. Orthon said his main purpose for the meeting was to discuss the dangers of nuclear weapons and how they could easily lead to the destruction of life on the planet. Adamski's meeting occurred on November 20, 1952, less than three weeks after the U.S. tested its first Hydrogen bomb on November 1. The timing of Orthon's meeting with Adamski suggests he hoped it would influence public opinion against further testing or use of nuclear weapons. The implication was that earlier efforts to communicate with government authorities had failed.

Adamski's entire experience was witnessed by his six companions who signed affidavits confirming Adamski's version of events. In fact, four of the witnesses immediately reported what had happened to a nearby newspaper, the *Phoenix Gazette*, that published a story on November 24 featuring photos and sketches. The Desert Center encounter was among those of Adamski's claims regarding extraterrestrial contact that, according to veteran UFO researcher Timothy Good, were "accurately reported," and "sensible and verifiable".[171]

Another contactee case discussing Solarians is Howard Menger. Like Adamski, Menger claims to have had a physical contact experiences with extraterrestrials from different planets from our solar system. During the Second World War while stationed in Hawaii, Menger claims to have met with a Venusian who traveled here in a technologically advanced space vehicle.[172] In 1953, he claims that he went to a secret location to rendezvous with extraterrestrials. There he was met by two Martian men who told him he was not the only person they were working with:

> Previous contacts had mentioned I was not the only one working with them. Now they further confirmed this, giving me actual names of people I eventually met and recognized. Not only were they contacting people in the east, but other sections of the country as well: I remember they specifically mentioned California, New Mexico and Arizona.[173]

Menger claims that he eventually took on the role of helping different extraterrestrial visitors from Venus, Mars and Saturn prepare for brief periods where they would integrate among the Earth population. He said life on Earth affected the physiological processes of various Solarian visitors: "The men, particularly the Venusians, had unusually fair skin, without hair on their arms or face, and had no need to shave. After three months on Earth, however, they became hairy and grew beards."[174]

Menger described the efforts of the Solarians to help elevate the consciousness of humanity through adopting spiritual truths. He described the courses he created where the Solarians recommended various forms of meditation and spiritual reflection. The Solarians also recommended more nutritious diets using fruits and vegetables. They gave Menger a potato grown on the moon whose protein content was measured to be 15%., five times more protein than Earth potatoes.[175] The Solarians also assisted in the development of more environmentally sustainable technologies. They helped Menger create his own free energy motor. Finally, the Solarians attempted to warn Menger of the dangers posed by some extraterrestrials that had sinister purposes and were manipulating senior governmental leaders. Menger said one Solarian told him: "there is a very powerful group on this planet, which possesses tremendous knowledge of technology, psychology and most unfortunate of all, advanced brain therapy. They are using certain key people in the governments of your world."[176]

Menger's contact experiences and UFO sightings are supported by independent witnesses, photographs, film and even scientific analysis of an alleged potato taken from the moon. A well respected UFO investigator, Timothy Good, conducted an independent investigation of Menger and concluded that some of his extraterrestrial contact experiences and photographs/films were genuine:

> ...some of the evidence suggests that he did indeed have encounters with apparent extraterrestrials, some of which were observed by credible witnesses. And regarding the photographic and cine film evidence ... my feeling is that *some* of it is genuine.[177]

A good idea of the role played by the Solarians in assisting the development of human evolution, is the contactee case of Frank Stranges. A respected Evangelical Minister, Stranges claims to have met a Venusian at the Pentagon in December 1959. Stranges' encounter began with an alleged picture of an extraterrestrial taken at a function held at Howard Menger's home by respected UFO researcher August Roberts. The photo was allegedly of a Venusian called Valiant Thor, with two companions. Stranges claims that after showing the picture at a meeting, he was given the opportunity to meet with Valiant Thor. Stranges was then taken to a secure area in the Pentagon to meet him.

Stranges claims that Thor told him that he had been a guest of the US government for three years from 1957 and was about to depart. Thor claims to have spoken with President Eisenhower and other senior officials in the U.S. political and military system. Thor's message was a spiritual one that humanity's military capacities had outstripped its ethical development. Stranges elaborates:

> He told me he had been here nearly three years and would depart in just a few months. Claiming that he would not use force to speak with men in authority in America, he was happy to consult with them at their invitation. He further stated that thus far only a few men in Washington knew of his existence in the Pentagon. And few leaders had availed themselves of his advice during these past three years.[178]

Figure 6. Picture of Valian Thor, on right, with two companions. Credit. Adam Roberts.

Stranges claims to have subsequently met Thor after his departure from the Pentagon. He was told that Thor's primary mission had now changed as a result of the failure of his efforts to persuade U.S. and world leaders to change their military policies. Thor's mission was based on the following five principles:

1. To mingle with and become as Earth people
2. To work and labor in Earth Enterprises
3. To help those who encounter possible threat or danger while striving for world peace
4. To give them advice and guidance
5. To entrust with superior knowledge those who have proven themselves
6. Divulge the essence of their mission to the collective national leaders of Earth, *only when the time is right.*[179]

Significantly, a former civil engineer and whistleblower discussed in chapter two, Phil Schneider, claims that Valiant Thor was real, and that he had a photo of him standing next to his father who worked on classified government projects.[180] Unfortunately, soon after coming out publicly with his testimony and evidence in 1995, Schneider died in highly unusual circumstances in January 1996.

Another contactee who has met and traveled with Solarians is Luis Fernando Mostaja from Bolivia. Luis is an architect from Bolivia. I met Luis at the Earth Transformation conference in Hawaii in May 2008 that I co-organized.[181] He struck me as very sincere and professional in narrating his experiences. Luis is a highly educated professional who put his credibility and career on the line by going public about his extraterrestrial contact experiences. Together with supporting witness testimony, I have a high degree of confidence that he is narrating actual physical events as they occurred to him. Luis claims that he was transported by teleportation device aboard a space vehicle that appeared near Lake Titicaca, to a subterranean city on Venus where he met with extraterrestrials there:

Immediately the starry night of the Andes began to transform itself into a magical valley. The sky had multi-colored forms. Immediately to my right, a being, with beautiful characteristics, said, "Don't worry. You are here because the time has arrived for you to corroborate everything that I have told you before. My name is E'tel. During your time with us here we're going to tell you about part of your mission, and the purpose of my presence with you." Then he started to speak about what he was observing in the sky. It was the reaction of the clouds that surround Venus. It is known as the *solar rain*. That is what was producing the multi-colored sky. On this planet, Earth, there is something similar to that – the Aurora Borealis. He said that their life on Venus is subterranean. When a civilization is more evolved they don't build above ground but mainly subterranean. And there is an explanation for that.[182]

Finally, we have the case of Sixto Paz Wells, Peru's most famous contactee. Wells began his experiences in 1974 and wrote about them in his first book, *The Invitation*.[183] According to Wells, the extraterrestrials that contacted him have their main base on Ganymede, one of the moons of Jupiter. They typically began a contact experience with an invitation conveyed by automatic writing that gives instructions on where to travel and when to meet. The extraterrestrials have emphasized spiritual growth and human evolution in making contact events possible for a wider group of people. Wells became famous in the Spanish speaking world when a prominent Spanish journalist, J.J. Benitez, wrote a story about Wells contact experiences supported by startling photographs of UFOs in the Chilca Desert, Peru.

The testimonies of the various contactees discussed so far, Adamski, Menger, Stranges, Mostajo and Wells all point to a group of extraterrestrials originating from planets within our solar system. The Solarians (comprising Venusians, Martians, Saturnians, and others) appear to focus their energies on contacting private citizens. This is due to senior government officials not responding positively to the Solarians' requests. The manner of Solarians' interaction with humans suggests they perform Intervention Type A, B and C activities; i.e., they have 'ground teams' on Earth's surface, take individuals on their ships, and pass on esoteric belief systems emphasizing spiritual growth and evolution. The Solarians appear to be focused on assisting the evolution of human consciousness, discouraging the use of destructive military technologies, advising political leaders, helping introduce new technologies, developing greater respect for all sentient life and warning of the dangers posed by some extraterrestrial visitors. Most importantly, the Solarians respect the vital interests of individuals, nations and the biosphere. This means that they are extraterrestrials that we can conduct "principled negotiations" with as outlined in *Getting to Yes!*[184]

ENDNOTES CHAPTER 3

[125] The Special Operations Manual is available in Robert Wood and Ryan Wood, *The Majestic Documents* (Wood and Wood Enterprises, 1998) 6. Available online at: http://www.bibliotecapleyades.net/sociopolitica/sociopol_som1-01.htm

[126] See Bob Hieronimus, "Transcript of Interview with Bob Dean, March 24, 1996," published online at: http://www.ufoevidence.org/documents/doc1156.htm

[127] Grant Cameron, "President Carter, Daniel Sheehan, and Donald Menzel : The Congressional Research Service UFO Studies for President Jimmy Carter," available online at: http://www.presidentialufo.com/jimmy-carter/98-the-marcia-smith-story-the-presidents-ufo-study

[128] Clifford Stone claims to have first witnessed this medical manual in 1979. See Michael Salla, "Twenty Two Years of Covert Service in Elite UFO Crash Retrieval Teams: Exclusive Interview with Sergeant Clifford Stone," *Exopolitics Journal* 1:2 (2006). Available online at: http://exopoliticsjournal.com/Journal-vol-1-2-Stone-pt-2.pdf See also Paola Harris, *Connecting the Dates ... Making Sense of the UFO Phenomenon* (Wildflower Press, 2003) 76.

[129] For discussion of contactee and abductee distinction, see Timothy Good, *Alien Base: The Evidence for Extraterrestrial Colonization on Earth* (Avon Books, 1998) 1-2.

[130] For a detailed study of seven different categories of evidentiary sources for the extraterrestrial presence, and ranking for their reliability, see Michael Salla, *Exopolitics: Political Implications of the Extraterrestrial Presence* (Dandelion Books, 2004) ch. 1. An earlier version of this chapter is available online at: http://exopolitics.org/Study-Paper1.htm

[131] Robert Wood and Ryan Wood, *The Majestic Documents*, 6. Available online at: http://www.bibliotecapleyades.net/sociopolitica/sociopol_som1-01.htm

[132] Bob Hieronimus, "Transcript of Interview with Bob Dean, March 24, 1996," published online at: http://www.ufoevidence.org/documents/doc1156.htm

[133] Bob Hieronimus, "Transcript of Interview with Bob Dean, March 24, 1996," published online at: http://www.ufoevidence.org/documents/doc1156.htm

[134] Grant Cameron, "President Carter, Daniel Sheehan, and Donald Menzel : The Congressional Research Service UFO Studies for President Jimmy Carter," available online at: http://www.presidentialufo.com/jimmy-carter/98-the-marcia-smith-story-the-presidents-ufo-study

[135] See Michael Salla, "Twenty Two Years of Covert Service in Elite UFO Crash Retrieval Teams: Exclusive Interview with Sergeant Clifford Stone," *Exopolitics Journal* 1:2 (2006). Available online at: http://exopoliticsjournal.com/Journal-vol-1-2-Stone-pt-2.pdf

[136] For description of how this 'shadow government' has evolved in the US, see Salla, Exopolitics: *Political Implications of the Extraterrestrial Presence*, ch. 2.

[137] See Salla, Exopolitics: *Political Implications of the Extraterrestrial Presence,* chs. 2

& 3.

[138] See Bob Hieronimus, "Transcript of Interview with Bob Dean, March 24, 1996," published online at: http://www.ufoevidence.org/documents/doc1156.htm

[139] See Alex Collier, "More on The Sirians," *Defending Sacred Ground,* (Leading Edge Research Group, 1996), ch 5, http://www.alexcollier.org/alex-collier-defending-sacred-ground-1996.pdf ; George Andrews, *Extra-terrestrial Friends and Foes* (Illuminet Press, 1993); and "Billy Meier Interview," (November 20, 1988) available at: http://tinyurl.com/autaucu . For a short description of a number of star systems with celestial data, and some information of the extraterrestrial races claimed to originate from these, see http://tinyurl.com/akwkjb7

[140] Arthur Horn, *Humanity's Extraterrestrial Origins,* 80-94.

[141] Arthur Horn, *Humanity's Extraterrestrial Origins,* 75.

[142] Data for these different intervention points are from Arthur Horn, *Humanity's Extraterrestrial Origins,* 75-78.

[143] Swerdlow, *Blue Blood, True Blood,* 31.

[144] Collier, "The ET Global Connection: A Lecture by Alex Collier," Defending Sacred Ground, ch. 1. Available online at: http://www.alexcollier.org/alex-collier-defending-sacred-ground-1996.pdf

[145] For discussion of the different ways extraterrestrials perceive humanity, see Michael Salla, *Exopolitics: Political Implications of the Extraterrestrial Presence,* 153-69.

[146] For discussion of remote viewing and telepathic communications with extraterrestrials as reliable sources of information see Michael Salla, *Exopolitics: Political Implications of the Extraterrestrial Presence* (Dandelion Books, 2004), ch. 1. An online version is available at: http://exopolitics.org/Study-Paper1.htm

[147] Plato discussed the social organization, architecture and resources of Atlantis in 'Timaeus' and 'Critias'.

[148] Edmund Halley, "An Account of the Cause of the Change of the Variation of the Magnetic Needle: With an Hypothesis of the Structure of the Internal Parts of the Earth," *Philosophical Transactions* (Royal Society of London, 1692).

[149] Quoted in Alec Maclellan, *The Hollow Earth Enigma* (Souvenir Press, 1999) 45-46.

[150] For some of these accounts, see Raymond Bernard, *Hollow Earth* (Lyle Stuart, 1969), Timothy Green Beckley *Subterranean Worlds Inside Earth* (Inner Light, 1992).

[151] Alec Maclellan, *The Hollow Earth Enigma,* 168.

[152] Quoted in Alec Maclellan, *The Hollow Earth Enigma,* 104.

[153] Quoted in Alec Maclellan, *The Hollow Earth Enigma,* 106.

[154] Maclellan, *The Hollow Earth Enigma,* 107.

[155] Flying Object comment cited in an interview of Admiral Byrd by Lee van Atta, "On Board the Mount Olympus on the High Seas" *El Mercurio,* (Santiago, Chile, March 5, 1947). 'Fatalities' comment also cited in "The Antarctic Enigma," http://www.bibliotecapleyades.net/tierra_hueca/esp_tierra_hueca_6c.htm

[156] Quoted in Alec Maclellan, *The Hollow Earth Enigma,* 108.

[157] Quoted in Raymond Bernard, *The Hollow Earth: The Greatest Geographical Discovery in History* (University Books, 1969) 39.

[158] Richard Byrd, *The Missing Diary of Admiral Richard Byrd* (Inner Light Publications, 1992). Admiral Byrd's Diary is available online at, http://www.v-j-

enterprises.com/byrdiar.html

[159] Quoted in Alec Maclellan, *The Hollow Earth Enigma*, 111.

[160] Quoted in Raymond Bernard, *The Hollow Earth*, 33.

[161] Raymond Bernard, *The Hollow Earth*, 32.

[162] Raymond Bernard, *The Hollow Earth*, 33.

[163] See Alec MacLeod, *The Lost World of Agharti: The Mystery of Vril Power* (Souvenir Press, 1997); and Dianne Robbins, *Telos: The Call Goes Out from the Hollow Earth and the Underground Cities* (Onelight.com Publishing, 2001)

[164] Raymond Bernard, The *Hollow Earth*, 53-55.

[165] See for example, George Adamski, *Inside the Flying Saucers*, available online at: http://www.thenewearth.org/InsideTheSpaceShips.html For discussion of experiences of an extensive number of contactees, see Timothy Good, *Alien Base: The Evidence for Extraterrestrial Colonization on Earth.*

[166] Quoted in Maclellan, *The Hollow Earth Enigma,* 176-77.

[167] Flying Object comment cited in an interview of Admiral Byrd by Lee van Atta, "On Board the Mount Olympus on the High Seas" *El Mercurio*, (Santiago, Chile, March 5, 1947). 'Fatalities' comment also cited in "The Antarctic Enigma," http://www.bibliotecapleyades.net/tierra_hueca/esp_tierra_hueca_6c.htm

[168] Quoted in Timothy Good, *Alien Base: The Evidence for Extraterrestrial Colonization of Earth* (Avon Books, 1998) 102.

[169] Quoted in Timothy Good, *Alien Base*, 103.

[170] Quoted in Timothy Good, *Alien Base*, 103-104.

[171] Quoted in Timothy Good, *Alien Base*, 154-55.

[172] Howard Menger, *From Outer Space*, 42.

[173] Howard Menger, *From Outer Space*, 60.

[174] Howard Menger, *From Outer Space*, 66.

[175] Howard Menger, *From Outer Space*, 132.

[176] Howard Menger, *From Outer Space*, 137.

[177] Timothy Good, *Alien Base*, 194-95.

[178] Frank Stranges, *Stranger at the Pentagon*, Fifth Revised Edition (1997): 39-40.

[179] Frank Stranges, *Stranger at the Pentagon*, 47.

[180] Online discussion of Phil Schneider's claims regarding Valiant Thor available at: http://www.illuminati-news.com/philip-schneider.htm

[181] For information about the series of Earth Transformation conferences I co-organized from 2006-2011, visit: www.EarthTransformation.com

[182] Luis Fernando Mostajo Maertens, "Extraterrestrial Guides: The Great White Brotherhood in the Andes & Lake Titicaca," http://exopoliticsjournal.com/vol-2/vol-2-4-Fernando.htm

[183] The English version of Wells book, *The Invitation* is available online at: http://www.amazon.com/Invitation-Sixto-Pas/dp/1887472290

[184] Ury and Fisher, *Getting to Yes.*

CHAPTER 4

First Contact: the Galactic Community introduces itself to humanity

We now examine the available first hand testimonial evidence of extraterrestrials visiting our world whose origin is from outside our solar system. It's worth repeating that the first contact experiences between humanity and extraterrestrial life involved extraterrestrials that introduced themselves to humans – whether private citizens or government/military officials – in a respectful voluntary manner. Importantly, they recognized humanity's interests at the individual, societal and global levels. The "First Contact" extraterrestrials, were the first to make contact with our world since the dawn of the atomic age, and have been here ever since. To begin this examination of visiting extraterrestrials from outside our solar system, it is appropriate to begin with our nearest galactic neighbor – the triple star system of Alpha Centauri.

Alpha Centaurians

An extraterrestrial civilization claiming to be playing a significant role in human affairs is from the Alpha Centauri star system. It is about 4.4 light years away and actually comprises three stars, Alpha Centuari, Beta Centauri and Proxima Centauri. Aside from the Solarian planets, the planets in the Alpha Centauri star systems are our closest neighbors. It is therefore not surprising that there is much evidence that the Alpha Centaurians are playing a prominent role in human affairs.

The most compelling testimony supporting the presence of the Alpha Centaurians is Elizabeth Klarer from South Africa. During the Second World War she worked for both South African and British military intelligence and was stationed in London. She claims that one of her roles was to report on UFOs and extraterrestrial contact. Klarer says that she was given this unique assignment within the military intelligence community due to a number of UFO sightings and anomalous experiences from her youth. She told the story of how 'the

Chief' a senior Intelligence official in Britain's MI6 recruited her for this special assignment. 'The Chief' began by telling her:

> Some time back I received a dispatch from South Africa stating that you had both [Klarer & her husband] reported the sighting of an unidentified flying object, which paced your DH aircraft while flying over Drakensberg, the Chief quietly said.[185]

Klarer then told the Chief about her childhood experiences and he said:

> 'It is as I suspected', the Chief remarked. 'Our planet is under close surveillance by an alien but highly advanced civilization from outer space.' He paused for a moment, looking at me intently. 'And you my dear, seem to be dedicated to this. You know what to look for, you are not afraid, and I can think of no one more qualified. Besides, you have intuition and imagination, which is very important in this advanced research. Will you do it for us?'[186]

The Chief then continued to highlight her suitability for this assignment by referring to her extrasensory abilities.

> 'This research may take you many years,' he went on. 'Therefore, every detail of information must be given me, no matter how fantastic. We are dealing with a fantastic realization, and I want you to use your powers of extrasensory perception and follow up any hunches you may have. This extraordinary ability you are so liberally endowed with can be of tremendous value to us.'[187]

Upon Klarer's transfer from London to her native South Africa, the 'Chief' once advised her of the importance of her mission: "Find that spaceship at all costs. It could mean the salvation of our planet — and our race." [188] She claims to have then spent the next few years improving her extrasensory abilities and developing her telepathic abilities so she could communicate with the extraterrestrial visitors:

Being aware of their presence in our skies, I practiced telepathy with horses, dogs and cats, and even with plants, machines or anything with the electric spark of life.... [E]ventually I was able to communicate with the man who came in the spaceship from beyond our solar system. As time went on through the years of preparation the telepathic link became stronger and stronger ...[189]

In the early 1950's Klarer's efforts were successful and she was physically contacted by extraterrestrials from Alpha Centauri. She was then taken regularly into their ships and given information about their culture, technology and spiritual philosophy. The Alpha Centaurians said that they were originally from Venus but left due to the unstable nature of the sun. They claimed that the triple star system of Alpha Centauri was more stable and that they had established colonies on seven planets revolving around Proxima Centauri. [190]

She then spoke about the increasing military threat posed to the Alpha Centaurians in visiting the Earth:

Earth's authorities have shown an aggressive reaction to our approach, giving orders to their Air Forces to shoot us down, and as that is impossible, to ram our spaceships with their own craft to bring the spaceship to ground. In this way, they could hope to find access to our superior technology, which of course, is all they want. Under these circumstances we do not contact heads of government or military authorities. [191]

The most controversial aspect of her testimony is that she had a child fathered by Akon and that she then spent four months on Meton in 1956 giving birth to their son, Ayling. She spent four months on Meton, giving a detailed overview of Alpha Centauri's civilization, its advanced technology, and how it harmoniously blends in with the planetary environment.

Klarer says that the British and the South African defense establishment monitored her interactions with the Alpha Centaurians, and 'protected' her from other nations/groups that wanted the information. For example, she described a kidnap attempt during her pregnancy by the Soviet government that wanted her child so they could use it to gain information on extraterrestrial technologies. She says that for safety reasons, the child from her extraterrestrial union remained on Meton.

Figure 7. Drawing of Akon. From Beyond The Light Barrier with permission of **New Vision Publishing**

Klarer's story sounds incredible yet there is much evidence supporting her. She did work with British and South African military intelligence thereby making plausible her conversation with an unnamed British intelligence 'chief'. Her links with the British military intelligence community and the interest of its members in extraterrestrial civilizations is illustrated in the preface of her book. Major Aubrey Fielding from the British Intelligence Corps (ret.) wrote:

> These pages tell through personal experience, of an advanced civilization in outer space, a civilization that has already found the secrets of space propulsion.... Purely imaginary, one might say, until one reads the immense amount of scientific and technical explanation given by the author.[192]

Klarer also provided photographic evidence to support her testimony, and the names of witnesses who saw the ships used by the Alpha Centaurians to visit her. She impressed audiences around the world with her detailed descriptions of the Alpha Centaurians and their technology. A book describing her experiences was eventually published in 1980.[193]

Klarer's description of the Alpha Centaurians gives a vivid account of how technology can be wisely used to benefit both humanity and the ecosystem. The Alpha Centaurians were argued to be benevolent and genuinely desiring to assist humanity in dealing with its evolution.

There are other independent sources for the existence on extraterrestrials from Alpha Centauri. A physicist from Livermore laboratories who worked on classified government projects consented to give an interview on information concerning extraterrestrials. Like many government scientists, he is dissatisfied with the non-disclosure policy of government authorities and decided to become a whistleblower. While maintaining public anonymity, he did provide documentation to his interviewers to prove his scientific background.[194] Arthur Neumann first used the pseudonym 'Henry Deacon' to describe a number of populated worlds in the Alpha Centauri system:

> Alpha Centauri and Promixa Centauri are close together. Alpha Centauri has a solar system very much like ours, but it's older. The planets are in stable orbits. There are three inhabited planets, the second, third and fourth. No, wait, the fifth, I think. Second, third and fifth.[195]

When asked if he had come across this information in the course of his work, Deacon replied:

> Yes. This is known. It's comparatively easy to get there, less than five light years away, and that's, you know, it's right next door to us. The... people... there are very human-like. They're not Grays, they're like us. The human form is very common in the universe.

Deacon's revelation is startling corroboration for Klarer's testimony that human-looking extraterrestrials inhabit Alpha Centauri, that a number of worlds are populated, and that travel there and back is relatively easy.

There have been others who have come forward to disclose the existence of visitors from Alpha Centauri. An alleged former employee of the covert Montauk and Philadelphia projects, Al Bielek, discussed a number of extraterrestrials including the Alpha Centaurians. Bielek's testimony is one of the most bizarre and controversial cases in UFO research. Yet his testimony is consistent, and according to a UFO investigator, John Quinn, Bielek, he is very credible and there is much evidence to support his claims.[196] The Alpha Centaurians, according to Bielek, provide sanctuary and protection to humans that desire assistance in dealing with the repressive polices of the shadow government. He argues that they will transport endangered humans to the Alpha Centauri star system so they are not 'eliminated' for their opposition to government policy.[197] Other sources describing Alpha Centaurians visiting the Earth are Sixto Paz Wells, Stewart Swerdlow and Alex Collier.[198] There are also a number of esoteric sources claiming that Alpha Centaurians are visiting Earth and describing their activities.[199]

The main activity of the Alpha Centaurians can described as promoting cultural relations between humanity and the Alpha Centaurians, respect for the environment, promoting social justice and human freedom, and the responsible use of advanced technology. The Alpha Centaurians belong to the Intervention Type B category of extraterrestrials; they have contact experiences with individuals, and take them on board their ships and to their home world. The Global solutions that can be promoted by the Alpha Centaurians include social justice and freedom at a global level, creating "zones of peace" or peace sanctuaries, human rights and sustainable development.

Lyra

It is appropriate to discuss extraterrestrial races further away than our immediate neighbors from our solar system and Alpha Centauri with the constellation of Lyra. Lyra is a small constellation whose nearest stars are approximately 25 light years away. Lyra is adjacent to the Draco constellation. Its brightest star is Vega. Lyra has been described as the source for the spread of human civilization in the Milky Way galaxy. On April 18, 2013 NASA announced the discovery of two habitable exoplanets in the Star System Kepler 62 which is located 1200 light years away deep in the constellation Lyra. The two exoplanets where found orbiting a star two-thirds smaller and one-fifth as bright as our sun. Kepler 62 is seven billion years old, making significantly older than our sun. It is possible that ancient life could have evolved on these worlds.[200]

Stewart Swerdlow learned about Lyra being the source of human life in this Galaxy through his experiences at the highly classified Montauk project. He described the Lyran's ancient origin and descent into a fragmented society in a hostile environment:

Approximately, 5 billion years ago, Angelic-like beings entered into the Milky Way galaxy and attempted to experience life in a physical universe. These Angelic beings who entered into this physical plane quickly became both physical and non-physical simultaneously.... Over the 4 billion linear years that these beings existed in this galaxy, they occupied a star system known

119

as Lyra. This location can be considered the birthplace, or homeland, to all humanoid beings in this galaxy.... At Montauk, we were told that physical beings from another parallel universe entered into this reality and were "guests" of the Lyrans.... Because the Lyrans were never completely physical, they did not develop weapons. This left them quite vulnerable. Now trapped in the physical dimension, they could no longer use their minds to create whatever they needed. Instead they had to rely on their bodies to do the work.... Over linear time, now in a physical state, the Lyran society became fragmented.[201]

One of the first 'contactees' to describe extraterrestrials from Lyra was Billy Meier. His claims of meeting Pleiadians/Plejarans from 1975 are supported with some of the most spectacular photographic and film evidence ever supplied by a contactee. There are also independent witnesses and physical evidence of extraterrestrial vehicles that support his claims. Independent investigations by a number of researchers found Meier's evidence was not fabricated, and lent significant support for his testimony of extraterrestrial contact. [202] Due to the amount of physical evidence provided over several decades, Meier has gained much credibility. The consistency of his testimony and accumulated evidence suggest that he has genuinely met and communicated with extraterrestrial visitors. Meier was told by his Pleiadian [Plejaran] contacts of the star system of Lyra and its human inhabitants:

The "Swiss" Plejarans have described their ancient ancestry, and consequently ours, as originating (before the Plejades) in a far sun-system in a star group near what we now know as the Ring Nebula of Lyra, for which we have called them Lyrans in the same manner as we refer to the human beings from what we call the Pleiades. These early Lyrans in their numerous migrations in their great Space Arks went to many other star systems and found suitable habitations, and put down colonies, such of which flourished and eventually launched their own space travelers.[203]

Meier further reported of a physical contact with a Lyran ship in 1977 where the Lyrans described their world and the other star systems with whom they cooperated.[204]

Another 'contactee' with information on the Lyrans is Alex Collier. Collier claims to be a 'contactee' with a race of Nordic looking humans from the constellation of Andromeda. He has had a number of contact experiences since his childhood; this developed over the years as he was given more and more information by his Andromedan contacts. Collier has given face to face interviews with veteran UFO researcher Paola Harris who has had the opportunity to examine the evidence supporting his testimony and concludes he is credible.[205] I also have analyzed Alex Collier's information, and personally interviewed him a number of times since September 2005. I have witnessed some physical evidence he has provided to support his testimony. I have also spoken with a direct witness verifying various aspects of Collier's contact experiences.[206] My conclusion from my investigation of Alex Collier is that he is very credible and most likely a genuine extraterrestrial 'contactee'.

Collier describes the start of the Lyran civilization as revealed to him by extraterrestrials from Andromeda:

> Based on the age of the Suns and the planets in our galaxy, it was decided that the human life form was to be created in the Lyran system. The human race lived there for approximately 40 million years, evolving. The orientation of the human race in Lyra was agricultural in nature. Apparently, we were very plentiful and abundant, and lived in peace. [207]

Another source of information on Lyra comes from the telepathic communications of Lyssa Royal. While telepathy remains a controversial as a source of accurate information, there is much evidence that this is the standard communication model used by extraterrestrials. Both a number of contactees and whistleblowers have spoken about telepathic communications with extraterrestrials in highly classified government projects. One whistleblower, Dan Sherman claims he was trained to telepathically communicate with extraterrestrials through "Project Preserve Destiny", which embedded within the National Security Agency.[208] Another whistleblower, Clifford Stone, claims he was employed in "Project Bluefly" and was tasked as a telepathic communicator with any extraterrestrials found at UFO crash locations.[209]

In my view, telepathic communications do not have the same evidentiary value or accuracy as whistleblower or contactee testimonies.[210] Nevertheless, information gained from telepathic communication can be a helpful secondary source to help confirm or elaborate upon whistleblower/contactee testimonies. I will therefore use those sources of telepathic communication that I consider most credible. One of these is Lyssa Royal who has written a book elaborating upon the Lyra constellation as the cradle of human civilization in the Milky Way Galaxy. Her information corresponds closely with Swerdlow's claims of beings incarnating from higher dimensional planes into physical reality, she writes:

> The Founders are the energetic grandparents of the human race. It was their desire to manifest different dimensional aspects of themselves…. Their first action was to begin making the plans necessary to spread life throughout the Lyran system. Planets were chosen within the Lyran star group to house these new races…. The Founders fragmented themselves further in order to release the consciousness necessary to incarnate on these planets…. As these groups evolved and achieved space travel, they exposed themselves to the development of other planetary groups in the area.[211]

The Lyrans possess Nordic features and correspond closely to the 'Elohim' described in religious traditions both on Earth and around the galaxy. Due to the Lyrans' role in the genesis of the human presence in the galaxy, the Lyrans can understandably be argued to have the most detailed understanding of human origins and galactic history. They can be described as the 'Galactic historians' for the human species. It can be inferred that the Lyrans help in disseminating the truth about the evolution of human races in the galaxy, and have a deep understanding of galactic human culture and of the 'human spirit'.

This is elaborated upon in the following telepathic communication from a source, H.M., that I have personally interviewed and found to be consistent, coherent and credible:

> Those from Lyra have an affinity for origins and ancient histories. So they would be useful to you to understand the past in order to transform it. As you understand your past and your origins you may be able in consciousness to go back, pattern by pattern, peel off the layers of the onion, and find your true nature. They would be excellent guides in this process, this psychological process for humanity, of understanding its motivations and its history and how it came to be.[212]

In conclusion, the manner of Lyrans interaction with humans suggests they are Intervention Type C 'extraterrestrials'; they have a largely hands off approach and use esoteric communications to assist human evolution. The Lyrans' main activities are in disseminating the unique history of the human race in the galaxy, and assisting in understanding human motivations and potentials. The global solutions the Lyrans provide include accurate information about human history, understanding galactic history, discovery of the human essence, diplomacy and conflict resolution, and global education.

Vega

According to Billy Meier, another race of extraterrestrials that physically contacted him were from the Vega star system within the constellation of Lyra.[213] The Vegans were a darker or 'blue' skinned group of humans, and were likely the 'blue race' of advanced humans mentioned in various Vedic texts, and from whom the Hindu gods Vishnu and Krishna derived.[214] The Brazilian contactee, Jefferson Souza, claims that he met the Vegans of Lyra, who he described as looking very similar to natives of India.[215] According to Alex Collier, Vega was the first star system in Lyra to be populated by humans.[216]

In addition to the Nordic looking humans from Lyra, the Vegans played an important colonizing role throughout the Galaxy.

> The first extraterrestrials who came to Earth were ... humans from worlds that exist within another dimension in the area of the Lyra and Vega systems. The first Lyrans, together with the Vegans, came to Earth initially 22 million years ago. Their stay here was very brief and they continued their travels to other star clusters and planets. Their history is largely obscure, even though assault groups occasionally continued to return to Earth. Approximately 389,000 years ago, several million Lyrans and Vegans again left their native worlds, entered our order of space and time in this dimension, and came to Earth where they mingled with the Earthlings. [217]

Significantly, the results of the Vegans and Lyrans interbreeding with humans paralleled events described in the Book of Enoch wherein the 'Nephilim' intermarried with humans and produced a race of giants that eventually died off.[218] Meier describes these events as follows:

> They procreated in the normal manner and through the manipulation of genes by genetic engineers. The results of the genetic engineering produced beings that were part human, part animal, and included giants, titans, and other creatures. In the course of hundreds and thousands of years these creatures were displaced once again, and eventually died out because they could not reproduce or because conditions for their life forms proved fatal for them.[219]

Further paralleling events described in the Book of Enoch where the leaders of the Nephilim were punished for their activities on Earth, Meier describes how the ringleaders of the Vegans and Lyrans were responsible for numerous transgressions against the native peoples of Earth and other worlds:

The many millions of Lyrans and Vegans, who had left their native worlds, were headed by 144,207 leaders and sub-leaders, etc., who reigned over their followers in a rather hierarchic manner. The leaders also transferred this behavior to Earth humans with whom they had intermingled in the past to create human descendants of various types. These 144,207 leaders and their subordinates were, indeed, the ringleaders who were essentially responsible for the misdeeds, false teachings, and false religions which were absorbed and imitated by humans on Earth. Not everything the leaders brought to Earth was evil, false, or criminal, however; many valuable items and ideas were presented to the Earthlings with regard to crafts, professions, philosophies, ways of thinking, medicine, technology, and many other things. [220]

According to Lyssa Royal, the Vegans and Lyrans were strategic competitors when it came to the colonizing of other worlds. This competition could be traced to the polarized ways each race viewed its role in the expansion of the human species:

> The first group to develop as a specific non-Lyran species was the Vegan civilization. They formed a highly distinctive philosophy and spiritual orientation and began to isolate themselves from the Lyran races.... As time passed, friction grew between the people of the Lyran races and the Vegan civilizations.... Polarization continued to grow exponentially as they grappled with their relationship between their civilization and themselves.[221]

Royal claims that the Vegans and Lyrans tried to resolve their growing conflicts by integrating their respective qualities in a variety of ways. This led to the creation of a third civilization that merged their respective qualities.[222] While not always successful, this indicates that the Vegans have experience in galactic diplomacy and conflict resolution.

According to Meier, the Vegans returning to Earth in the present era, are attempting to assist humanity, atone for past mistakes and to assist Vegan starseeds.[223] The manner of the Vegans interaction with humans suggests they are Intervention Type C 'extraterrestrials'; they have a largely hands off approach and use esoteric communications to assist human evolution. Like the Lyrans, the global solutions the Vegans provide include accurate information about human history and the Vegan heritage, understanding galactic history, discovery of the human essence, diplomacy and conflict resolution, and global education.

Pleiadians

The Pleiades is a young constellation of hot blue stars 440 light years distant from Earth. Due to its relatively young age of 100 million years, it is thought that this is not long enough for life to have naturally evolved in the Pleiades. However, according to a number of contactees, extraterrestrials fleeing instability in the Lyran constellation found the Pleiades suitable for habitation. Due to their advanced technology, they were able to terraform various planets to build flourishing civilizations throughout the Pleiades. Due to its young age, the Pleiades would not have advanced indigenous life on it and therefore would be an ideal shelter for those escaping planetary upheavals elsewhere in the galaxy.

Billy Meier described how the Pleiadians, descendents of the Nordic looking Lyrans, migrated between a number of star systems before finally settling in the Pleiades constellation:

The ancient history of the early Pleiadian ancestors in another home sun system was also described and how they came to travel to the Pleiades. A much earlier migration to this solar system is also described and how and why it failed. The one third survivors of the Pleiadian ancestors' original planet, after its devastation, evolved a new technology, and designed and built the great-spacer evacuation arks in just 900 years, and began to launch them everywhere for many hundreds of years more. The extraterrestrials visiting Switzerland are the descendants of one of those space arks which occupied one of the three planets engineered for human habitation, in one of the sun-systems in what we call the Pleiades today. They have experienced great gains and great losses many times over since that time. In a very real sense, we are descendants of their earliest colonists attempting to settle in this solar system, together with an assortment of aborigines and human exiles from a number of places.[224]

The particular star system from which Meier's Pleiadians originate is Taygeta and the main planet is Erra.[225] The Pleiadians from Taygeta identified Meier as one of their chosen 'representatives' with a mission to bring the truth of the extraterrestrial presence to humanity.[226] Semjase, the Pleiadian female who made contact with Meier, described the Pleiadians as follows:

> We are neither guardians of Earth beings nor God-sent angels or similar. Many persons suggest we are watching over Earth and her beings and would control their fates. This is not true, because we only perform a self-selected mission which has nothing to do with supervising or regulating Earth fates. Thus it is wrong to expose us as superterrestrial messengers and guardians. [227]

The Pleiadians identified a key aspect of their mission is to warn humanity of negative extraterrestrials:

> 33. There are also different life forms that have acquired much knowledge and have freed themselves from their environment. They travel through space and occasionally come to Earth.
> 34. Many of them are rather unpleasant creatures and live in a type of barbarism that frequently is nearly as bad as the terrestrials.
> 35. You should be aware of them because they often attack and destroy everything that gets in their way.
> 36. Many times they have even destroyed whole planets or forced their inhabitants into bondage.
> 37. It is one of our missions to warn the people on Earth of these creatures.

38. Let this be known to the Earth people because the time is approaching when a conflict with these degenerate human creatures becomes unavoidable.[228]

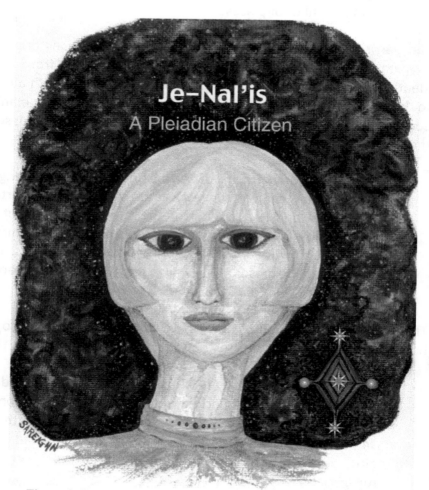

Figure 8. Drawing of Pleiadian. Credit: Sareighn

According to Collier, the Pleiadians are involved in armed skirmishes with Gray extraterrestrials in the solar system and other systems such as Sirius B.[229] Other key aspects of the Pleiadian mission according to Meier, are to assist in the uplift of human consciousness and to promote the unity of religion. [230] Significantly, Meier's Pleiadians were dismissive of the claims of many other contactees such as Adamski, and thereby implied exclusivity in relating the truths and dynamics of visiting extraterrestrials.[231] Interestingly, Collier claimed that some Pleiadians groups such as those from Alcyone operate with 'hidden agendas', while those from Taygeta (e.g., Meier's Pleiadians) are described as genuinely assisting humanity.[232] Swerdlow claims that there are 16 different extraterrestrial groups located in the Pleiades.[233]

Despite the possible 'hidden agenda' of some Pleiadians, most testimony and evidence points to Pleiadians in general having positive interactions with humans, and that they do much to assist in the elevation of human consciousness and assisting humanity in finding freedom from regressive extraterrestrials influence.[234] The manner of the Pleiadians interaction with humans suggests they are Intervention Type B 'extraterrestrials' in so far as they have physical contacts with humans, and take them on their ships to witness advanced technologies and gain further information. In conclusion, the main activity of the Pleiadians appears to be helping humanity find freedom from oppressive structures through education and consciousness raising. The Pleiadians can assist in find global solutions such as universal human rights, participatory democratic systems, the evolution of human consciousness and global education.

Procyon

According to veteran UFO researcher George Andrews, one of the space colonies spawned by the Lyrans was established on planets in the Rigel solar system in the Orion Constellation. At some point in its history, Rigel with its Nordic population underwent a destructive civil war and was taken over by Grays. Andrews gained this information from a contactee's testimony concerning a Nordic extraterrestrial from the star system of Procyon called Khyla. Khyla revealed much information about the Rigelians, Procyons and Grays to the contactee whose information was consistent with other sources and Andrews concluded was credible.[235] The contactee described Khyla as follows:

> Khyla looked like a tall handsome human, slender but muscular, masculine yet ethereal. He appeared either naturally or artificially to have black around his eyes, almost like kohl [coal]. His face was close to exquisite, but definitely masculine. He had a gaunt face with high cheekbones and piercing cobalt-blue eyes. He had fine blond hair that was almost shoulder-length. He had a muscular neck. His skin was pale flesh color, with a whitish overtone. It is hard to gauge his exact height because of the circumstances under which our encounter occurred, but it was somewhere between six and seven feet.[236]

Andrews writes about the history of Rigel as revealed by Khyla to the contactee:

> The ancestors of the short Grays were once tall Blonds. The Great War took place…. Before the great war, Rigel was a vast empire, which had been the source of most galactic seeding. All Rigelians were tall Blonds. A colony had already been established on Procyon. The Great War was a civil war of Rigelians versus Rigelians, and lasted the equivalent of three Earth centuries. A group of Rigelians who realized that the Great War was about to break out took off for the Procyon colony in crude, clandestinely built ships. … They were the only Rigelians to escape the cataclysmic devastation. All those who had remained on Rigel were transformed into short Grays.[237]

It appears that Rigel underwent a planet wide nuclear war and environmental collapse that led to life in underground shelters. It is very unlikely that the transformation of Nordic Rigelians involved them becoming 'short Grays' whose genetic material is generally accepted as inferior to human races such as the Nordics. The genetic mutation process would have taken much longer than the three centuries mentioned. It is more likely that the surviving Rigelian Nordics were incorporated into a planet wide genetic hybridization program by 'short Grays' from a star system such as Zeta Reticulum who had covertly infiltrated and undermined Rigel prior to and/or during the Great War on Rigel. The short Grays most likely succeeded in genetically engineering the 'tall Grays' or 'Tall Whites' using genetic material from the Nordic survivors who were too weak to resist the Gray hybridization agenda. These Rigelian 'Tall Grays/Whites' subsequently play a key role in diplomatic initiatives by the Grays and serve as a genetic model for new human-Gray hybrid races that allegedly represent the best of both species.

Most of the Rigelians who fled their planet traveled to the star system of Procyon to restart their civilization. Stewart Swerdlow also claims that those inhabiting Procyon are refugees from devastating wars in Lyran constellation. He says however that they came directly from Lyra, after a destructive war between the Lyrans and Draco Reptilians.[238] Swerdlow's and Andrew's research indicates that Procyon has been used as a safe haven for human refugees from a number of destructive stellar conflicts.

Procyon is a binary star system about 11.4 light years from Earth, and it was apparently the fourth planet in this system on which the Rigelians established their new colony.[239] According to Andrews, the colony of Procyon flourished until it became embroiled in sinister effort by the Grays that now populated Rigel to subvert Procyon. Khyla described the process adopted by the Grays in their subversion of Procyon:

> The Grays began to visit us, first a few as ambassadors, then as specialists in various domains where their expertise could be useful to us, as participants in different programs that involved mutual collaboration, and finally as tourists. What had begun as a trickle became a flood, as they came in ever-increasing numbers, slowly but surely infiltrating our society at all levels, penetrating even the most secret of our elite power groups.... Just as on your planet they began by unobtrusively gaining control over key members of the CIA and KGB through techniques unknown to them, such as telepathic hypnosis that

manipulates the reptilian levels of the brain, so on Procyon through the same techniques ... they established a kind of telepathic hypnotic control over our leaders. Over our leaders and over almost all of us, because it was as if we were under a spell that was leading us to our doom, as if we were being programmed by a type of ritual black magic that we did not realize existed.[240]

Figure 9. An Aldebaran (Nordic) Male. Credit: Andulairah Shah

Khyla went on to describe the eventual take over of Procyon by the Grays and the enslavement of most Procyons who did not escape. Using advanced time travel technology which involved 'multidimensional consciousness', something which the Grays apparently could not duplicate due to their degraded genetic bodies, a significant number of Procyons were able to escape and began a liberation war from the 'remote corridors of time'. Significantly, the Procyons describe how some of their resistance techniques would be relevant to the situation on Earth:

> ... it would be suicidal to attempt to fight the Grays directly with the weapons now at your disposal. One must be rational in attempting to fight back, and understand the proper way to proceed. Your own consciousness is the most potent weapon that is available to you at the present time. The most effective way to fight the Grays is to change the level of your consciousness from linear thinking to multi-dimensional awareness.... They have the technology to throw your planet out of orbit, but there is one key ability that you have and they do not have: the ability to hold in mind imagery that inspires an individual to realize his or her direct personal connection to the source of all that is... That is your key to victory.[241]

According to Alex Collier, the Procyons have recently liberated their world from Gray influence and he describes the Procyons as currently "gung ho" when it comes to dealing with the Grays.[242]

In conclusion, the Procyons main activity is in effectively resisting the extraterrestrial subversion by developing a 'multidimensional consciousness', using mind imagery to protect oneself from extraterrestrial mind control, and monitoring unfriendly extraterrestrial activity. The manner of the Procyons interaction with humans suggests they are Intervention Type B 'extraterrestrials'; they have physical contacts with individuals to warn them of the dangers posed by the MIEC and help develop strategies to counter the influence of the Grays. The global solutions that the Procyons can assist in include exposing extraterrestrial subversion, helping end global secrecy of the extraterrestrial presence, promoting multidimensional consciousness, deprogramming mind control, promoting universal human rights, and developing the internet and global communication.

Tau Cetians

Other human populated worlds are apparently the star systems of Tau Ceti and Epsilon Eridani. Tau Ceti is a star system very similar to Earth's and is almost 12 light years away. UFO researcher, Frank Crawford, interviewed a number of individuals who had physical contact with the Tau Cetians.[243] The first and most significant was an alleged whistleblower who participated in crash retrievals of UFOs; a live occupant was captured and interrogated by U.S. national security officials from a crash near Phoenix, Arizona in 1961. 'Oscar', the pseudonym used by the whistleblower, described to Frank Crawford the origins of the captured extraterrestrial who was nicknamed 'Hank':

> It was later confirmed by Hank that the stars of origin of his people were Tau Ceti and Epsilon Eridani. In later sessions Oscar discussed some reasons for the presence of the aliens. He said the[y] do not like the situation with some of the small grey aliens. He corrected us when we used the term 'grey' and said that they are actually white. The Tau Cetians feel that the abductions being carried out by some of the Greys are a great injustice to humanity. 'They are a parasitic race that has and is preying on human civilizations throughout the universe, Oscar relayed. He added that our government's involvement with the grays is very dangerous and out of control....The Tau Cetians have been preyed upon by these aliens before and they are working with other races and communities that were also victims.... (Oscar) wants people to know that if they are contacted by the Tau Cetians (humans such as he described) to not be afraid because they are here to help.[244]

The revelations by 'Hank' suggest that the Tau Cetians are present to help deal with the covert strategies and activities of the Grays. They in particular are very concerned about the nature of the agreements reached with them by the U.S. 'shadow government', and in helping individual 'abductees'. Stewart Swerdlow describes the Tau Cetians as implacably opposed to the activities of the Grays.[245]

According to 'Oscar' the Tau Cetian, 'Hank', was tortured and that this nearly caused an incident with other Tau Cetians who wanted to militarily intervene on behalf of their captured colleague.[246] John Lear also included information concerning a captured Tau Cetian and his torture in his "Disclosure Briefing".[247] The events described by Oscar are consistent with the main activity of the Tau Cetians as described in the following telepathic communication from H.M.: "One of the races is from Tau Ceti. They're specialists in intrigue and determining motivations of cloaked societies. They understand the ways that subterfuge can cripple a system. So they would be excellent contacts for undercover work."[248]

A second individual claiming to have had physical contact with Tau Cetians was Jill Waldport who described to Frank Crawford how she had been contacted by two sets of extraterrestrials, the Grays and a human looking race that attempted to help her in dealing with the Grays:

> Jill informed me that the aliens told her they didn't like what some of the aliens were doing to her without her consent. They had come to help her learn how to overcome the DECEPTIONS of the Grays and to protect herself. They explained that she needed to psychically build a shield around herself, like a brick wall, when they came for her. This would help keep her from being deceived by their MIND TRICKS. She tried it the next time the Grey's came to her and it 'seemed' to work.[249]

Crawford then revealed how Jill described the origins of the benevolent extraterrestrials as Tau Cetians:

> At this point the correlation counter in my mind was working overtime, so I decided to go for gold and ask her if they told her where they were from. Believe it or not she replied, 'Tau Seat-eye, does that make any sense?' Later I mentioned to Oscar that

I was investigating a case that involved intense interaction with Grays and Tau Cetians showing up to help. He asked where the case was from and I told him near Springfield, Illinois. He rattled off a very accurate description of Jill and said he was aware that she had been contacted. [250]

Finally, we have the extraordinary case of Jerry Wills, a noted explorer and energy healer who claims that he also met with extraterrestrials from Tau Ceti who were very tall, nearly 7 foot in height and were Caucasian looking humans. Incredibly, Wills says that they told him that he was one of them, and was dropped off as a baby in a secret program to help elevate human consciousness and society.[251] Wills was adopted by a human family, and found out late in life that he was in fact adopted. Wills has displayed unusual abilities all his life, and came to public prominence through his energy healing sessions with people that was covered by major news networks in the USA.[252] More recently, he has conducted expeditions into remote areas of Peru to find evidence of humanity's extraterrestrial origins. The main evidence that Wills has supporting his story is his unusual abilities and his own height, at 6′ 8″ tall, it is not hard to believe that he could be the off spring of a tall extraterrestrial civilization.

In conclusion, the Tau Cetians main activities lies in raising awareness of how to deal with the subversion of societies by extraterrestrial races, identifying corrupt elites and institutions, uplifting human consciousness, developing strategies for negating advanced mind control techniques, and uncovering humanity's ancient origins. The activities of the Procyons interaction with humans suggests they are Intervention Type B 'extraterrestrials'; they have physical contacts with individuals to warn them of the dangers posed by the MIEC. The global solutions they can assist in include exposing government/financial corruption and elite manipulation, monitoring extraterrestrial infiltration, deprogramming mind control and implant removal, promoting multidimensional consciousness, diplomacy and conflict resolution.

Andromedans

Andromeda is a constellation of stars that is 44 light years away. The famous Andromeda or M31 galaxy which is 2.5 million light years away can be seen through the Andromeda constellation. The first reference to extraterrestrials from Andromeda came from a tenured professor in the medical school at the University of Mexico. Also a senior member of Mexico's Instituto Nacional de Energia Nuclear (National Institute for Nuclear Energy), he used the pseudonym of 'Prof Hernandez' to release his amazing story. Prof Hernandez worked with a Mexican journalist, Zitha Rodriguez who investigated his case and eventually published the notes of his contact meetings.[253] He discussed how a very attractive extraterrestrial female, Elyense (dubbed 'Lya' by the Professor), from the constellation Andromeda had befriended him and revealed her origin. Zitha Rodriquez revealed how Prof. Hernandez approached her while she was researching another story about earthquakes at the Instituto Nacional de Energia Nuclear.

> In 1978-1979, I directed the magazine *OVNI* [UFO].... Well, ... I was writing a book on earthquakes. A friend suggested I talk to a certain person in the Instituto Nacional de Energia Nuclear, one Professor Carlos Graef, who was an experienced seismologist... One day, desperate to make contact ... I went in to look for someone, and when I came out I passed Professor Hernandez. The professor immediately showed interest in what I was doing and how was my work. He had important responsibility at the institute and was a high executive at the university ... I went into his office the first time without knowing exactly what was going to happen.... He invited me to sit down and began to question me... He asked me if I knew any people who had seen UFOs and I told him yes... He got up, walked around his desk, struck the desk with his fist and made an unusual confession. I have traveled in a ship and have a friendship with a woman who said she came from ... Andromeda. I at first did not believe it, said the professor, not all of it.[254]

Hernandez described in detail the free energy principles, advanced technology, and galactic history he learned about from his Andromedan contact. 'Lya' told him that humanity was descended from extraterrestrial civilizations that had established themselves on Earth. After destructive conflicts involved advanced technology, the DNA of the survivors began to degenerate. She told him that the Andromedans and other extraterrestrial civilizations were giving assistance to restore humanity's inherent abilities and former stature. 'Lya', however, said that some extraterrestrial groups were trying to sabotage these efforts and were dedicated to exploiting humanity:

> You had asked me if there were beings more aggressive than the Earth humans inhabiting this universe. I mentioned that there were and spoke about those who have been coming on various occasions to your world... they scorn mercy to your empiricism and the rickety form of science that you posses. They have been coming to your world with complete freedom and have captured living beings, children, ancients, men, women, animals, fish and they rob you of oxygen, hydrogen and even absorb electric fluid of the supplies flowing to your great cities. Human who unfortunately disappear and do not return anymore have been kidnapped by them.[255]

Prof Hernandez described how the Andromedans had made an effort to prepare humanity to deal with the threats confronting it by giving needed information to scientists. Lya told him that they had contacted senior officials in the political and scientific establishments, but had been spurned: "we have had contacts with ambassadors, with tenured professors and with other people of your civilization. They simply do not believe us."[256] The Andromedans claimed that they could not directly intervene to prevent future threats. The Andromedans were primarily scientists and ambassadors, and did not have a military history.

Prof Hernandez then explained how his mental and psychic abilities increased dramatically as a result of his interactions:

My mind had expanded and my power of concentration had become sharpened. I could perceive any sound in great detail and surprisingly, could repeat such any time I desired and analyze it completely, including its musical derivations, if it had any... [W]hen I see a man, whatever his ancestry might be, I perceive various characteristics, his extraordinary ones – levels of vibrational frequency, his origins, his blood chemistry compositions ...[257]

Unfortunately, Prof Hernandez invoked the wrath of his wife who was convinced that he was having an affair and succeeded in having him committed to a mental asylum for one month in 1989. Upon his release, Prof Hernandez disappeared and has not been found since. Subsequent investigations by Zitha Rodriquez were unable to extract his papers and records from Mexican security officials or his distraught family. The Hernandez case has also been investigated by Wendelle Stevens who was able to corroborate Zitha Rodriquez research and the identity of Prof Hernandez.

Another contactee, Alex Collier, also claims to have encountered extraterrestrials from the Andromeda constellation. Collier says the Andromedans are direct descendents of the Lyrans who experienced some difficulty when first leaving the Lyran system due to predatory extraterrestrial races. The Lyrans eventually settled in the Andromeda constellation in the star system 'Zenetae'. Collier describes the nature of the Andromedans as follows:

Everything that they create technologically is used for the advancement of their race. It is for educational purposes only. But, it can be used in defense. No, they do not have a military, per se, they are scientists. What they do is send their children to school anywhere from 150 to 200 years, in our linear time. They teach their students all of the arts and sciences. They are literally masters at everything. Then, at that point, they have the choice in what it is they want to do, and they can change their minds anytime and do something else. So, they are given all the tools. Everything is for education. Nothing is for distraction. They would never conceive of creating television as a distraction. Never. Everything is to help them evolve, and their science and their technology can be used for defensive purposes -- mostly the holographic stuff.[258]

The most significant feature of the Andromedans is that they were instrumental in founding the "Andromeda Council" which is a grouping of approximately 140 star systems that deliberate upon Earth in addition to other stellar affairs. In a 1997 Interview, Collier described the Council's deliberations as follows:

Now, in our galaxy there are many councils. I don't know everything about all those councils, but I do know about the Andromedan council, which is a group of beings from 139 different star systems that come together and discuss what is going on in the galaxy. It is not a political body. What they have been recently discussing is the tyranny in our future, 357 years from now, because that affects everybody. Apparently what they have done, through time travel, is that they have been able to figure out where the significant shift in energy occurred that causes the tyranny 357 years in our future. They have traced it back to our solar system, and they have been able to further track it down to Earth, Earth's moon and Mars. Those three places. The very first meeting the Andromedan Council had was to decide whether or not to directly intervene with what was going on here. According to Moraney, there were only 78 systems that met this first time. Of those 78, just short of half decided that they wanted nothing to do with us at all, regardless of the problems. I think it is really important that you know why they wanted nothing to do with us. We are talking about star systems that are hundreds of millions of light years away from us. Even some who have never met us. They just knew the vibration of the planet reflected those on it. The reasons why they wanted nothing to do with us is that from their perspective, Earth humans don't respect themselves, each other or the planet. What possibly can be the value of Earth humans? Fortunately, the majority of the council gave the opinion that because Earth has been manipulated for over 5,700 years, that we deserved an opportunity to prove ourselves - to at least have a shot at proving the other part of the council wrong.[259]

Another alleged contactee with the Andromedans is an individual who uses the pseudonym 'Tolec'. Tolec emerged into the public arena in early 2011 claiming to have been taken onto an Andromedan mothership and recruited to be a representative to Earth for the Andromedan Council. He claims:

> The Andromeda Council is an intergalactic and interstellar governance & development body of aligned benevolent star systems & planets of sentient intelligent life... for worlds in both the Milky Way and Andromeda galaxies. The Andromeda galaxy is also known as M31 to the people of Earth. The chaired members of the Andromeda Council comprise a total of twelve (12) different, distinct member worlds & races.[260]

Tolec says he is in regular communication with the Andromedan Council, and coordinating with them on how to best transform the Earth into a Galactic society. His website has much material about recent Andromedan activities and echoes the testimony of Alex Collier who he supports as a genuine contactee.[261] Tolec offers no physical evidence to support his claims and believes that his material stands by itself.

Important corroboration for Collier's claims of the Andromedans forming 'galactic' advisory councils and for Tolec's Andromedan Council is Billy Meier. Meier claims he was told by the Pleiadians that the Andromedans belong to a Council that advise the Pleiadians in their interactions with Earth.

Another contactee who mentions the Andromedans playing a Galactic advisory role is 'Adrain' – (real name Manuel D'Escandon). Adrain experienced contacts while living in Miami. He claimed to be soul fragment of a very tall Pleiadian of Lyran descent. He was extensively interviewed by researchers Randolph Winters and Sean David Morton, and found to be credible. Adrain's testimony was supported by extensive photos, film and witness testimonies.[262] Much of this evidence was shown in a video documentary produced by Winters that demonstrates how Adrain's testimony was well supported.[263] Controversy was later to engulf Adrain over some witnesses withdrawing their earlier support of him, thereby calling into question some aspects of his testimony.

According to 'Adrain', the Andromedans play an important role in forming councils that deliberate on Earth's future, thereby helping confirm Collier's, Meier's and Tolec's testimony. The Andromedans are one of the main extraterrestrial races most responsible for crop circles. Adrain argues that the crop circles are intended both to inspire humans with the possibility of extraterrestrial communications, and to warn negative extraterrestrials of the consequences of their actions to control and manipulate humanity.

The Andromedans' chief activity appears to be facilitating decisions of the Galactic community in dealing with difficult problems such as the current Earth situation, innovative strategies for resolving conflict, the education of youth and inspiring humanity with the possibilities of extraterrestrial contact. The manner of the Andromedans interaction with humans suggests they are Intervention Type B 'extraterrestrials'; they establish physical contacts with individuals to assist human evolution. The global solutions they promote include assisting the growth of psychic/crystal/rainbow children, peace education, exposing elite manipulation, promoting improved global governance, and diplomacy and conflict resolution.

Sirians from Sirius A

The next group comprises two extraterrestrial races coming from Sirius. Sirius is a binary star system allegedly harboring advanced life around its two main stars, Sirius A and B. Sirius A is a blue white star approximately 8.6 light years from Earth, a relatively young 250 million years old, and twenty times brighter than our sun.[264] In contrast, Sirius B is a white dwarf sun that ranges between 8 to 32 astronomical units from Sirius A in a highly elliptical orbit. In chapter three I examined claims that extraterrestrials from planets orbiting Sirius B are part of a network of extraterrestrials that have technology exchange agreements with U.S. government entities.

According to Stewart Swerdlow, the main planet in the Sirius A star system is called Khoom, and it comprises humans.[265] Collier, describes the human looking extraterrestrials from a planet circling Sirius A as follows:

> There is a race of beings on [a planet] Sirius A, the humans there are called the Katayy. They are considered benevolent. … Many of the human races there are red-skinned. Their ancestry is some of the first Lyrans that escaped with the women and children during the war. In their oceans they have whales, octopus and sharks. They are a race that is artistic. They have music and are connected to nature. They are builders and not very political. Their governments are based on "spiritual technology," which uses sound and color.[266]

'Adrian' describes the human looking Sirians as a tall dark race. He says the "original Sirians, that came over are mainly tall dark people. But their noses are very big, not flat like a black person."[267] The racial characteristics of the Sirians suggest that they were originally colonists from the Vega star system. If the Sirians were originally Vegans escaping some interplanetary war in the constellation of Lyra, then it is understandable why they developed an interest in building as Collier claims. Building a new civilization on a new world in the relatively young star system of Sirius A, would have been an urgent requirement.

The second extraterrestrial race described to originate from Sirius A are described as a cat-like or 'Lion people'. UFO Researcher Mary Rodwell describes a contactee's account of the cat-like beings from Sirius who built the pyramids: "[T]he cat-like beings from Sirius were the prominent builders of the pyramids…. The Sirius cat-like beings are physical beings, capable of building complex, physical structures."[268] Swerdlow describes the Sirian cat-like beings as follows:

Another planet in orbit around Sirius A is a world called Kilroti. Here, the Sirians created high-intelligence cat-like beings. Those cat-like beings are called the Lion People.... In the high astral levels, there is an etheric race of Lion Beings who are gold, have wings, and violent eyes.... The Ari created the Ohalu Council that governs the Sirius A star system. The Kilroti were created by mixing the genetics of the Sirians with the energy of the Ari. This is what was bought to ancient Egypt... The Sirians also built the Sphinx as a symbolic reminder of the blending of human genetics with lion frequency. This was a way to energetically bind future civilizations to the Sirians.... The face on the Sphinx is identical to the face on the Mars monument that looks down to the Earth at the Sphinx.[269]

Significantly, Richard Hoagland who is best known for his initial analysis of a human "Face on Mars" seen in the original Viking I photos from 1976, updated his analysis with the subsequent Mars Global Surveyor photos of 1998. With updated analysis what he could now see was not a human face, but two faces, one of which was of a lion, just as on the sphinx![270]

We have maintained for over nine years, since Enterprise Mission principal investigator Richard C. Hoagland's appearance at the United Nations, in February, 1992, that the Eastern half of the Face, the portion that until now had only been seen in shadow, was *feline* in appearance. The Western half, we have always maintained, was humanoid. We do not believe that this object was ever intended to be a fully human visage.[271]

Collier refers to the Sirians using sound and color as a kind of 'spiritual technology' which suggests that they specialize in terraforming planets and making them suitable for the evolution of life by altering the 'bio-magnetic energy' grid. This would be a planetary model of the bio-magnetic system of the human body. [272] Such a role is alluded to by Robert Temple and Graham Hancock in their respective examinations of the intervention of Sirians in early human cultures, and the relationship between the star Sirius and the Giza Pyramid complex.[273] Stewart Swerdlow elaborates on the role the Sirians played in assisting the establishment of ancient Egypt: "[T]he Egyptians, who were Atlantean/Lyran refugees, were in the process of building a new civilization from the remnants of their two major ancestral ones that were destroyed. The beings from Sirius A helped them, as they were a major factor in the interactions of Atlantis."[274]

Figure 10. Drawing of Feline humanoid. Credit. ECETI

Alex Collier claims that the intervention of extraterrestrials from Sirius A is due to mistakes made by those from Sirius B in terms of technology transfers and other forms of assistance given to governments: "My understanding is that those from the Sirius A system are trying to be beneficial and assist, because they feel responsibility in that those who colonized Sirius B system were originally from Sirius A."[275]

In conclusion, the main activity that can be attributed to those extraterrestrials from Sirius A is to assist in building a sustainable civilization using sacred geometrical designs. They help create a suitable ecological system for (human) evolution on Earth by altering the 'bio-magnetic energy grid' of the planet. The manner of the Sirians interaction with humans suggests they are Intervention Type C 'extraterrestrials'; they have a largely hands off approach, they work with the biosphere, and use esoteric communications to collaborate with humans. Those from Sirius A can assist in global solutions such as understanding the purpose of building according to sacred geometrical designs, environmental protection, promoting biodiversity, assist in consciousness raising; and evolution of the biosphere.

Ummites

The Ummites are described as extraterrestrials from the planet Ummo which is claimed to be 14.6 light years away, and possibly located in the star system Wolf 424.[276] They played a significant role in disseminating scientific technical literature and objects through Spain and then relayed to the rest of Europe in the 1960s and 1970s from a hidden base near a small town in the French province of 'Basses Alps' (Lower Alps). The Ummites contacted a select number of individuals and distributed to them detailed technical information on different technologies and revolutionary theories that would expand scientific knowledge beyond the prevailing orthodoxies.

A number of prominent Spanish UFO researchers investigated the Ummo affair. Among the most thorough was Antonio Ribera who claims he was first contacted by the Ummites in 1969. After a six year investigation, he wrote *The Ummo Mystery* in 1975 and concluded that the scientific letters genuinely displayed an understanding beyond conventional scientific principles. Significantly, an eminent French scientist agreed with Ribera. Dr J.P. Petit worked for the elite French scientific institution, CNRS (Centre National de la recherche Scientifique). He was a "Directeur de Recherche," and specialized in Magnetohydrodynamic propulsion (MHD), and has written numerous books and scientific papers.[277] He claims that in 1992 he also received scientific papers from the Ummites and learned principles about MHD, and the elimination of shockwaves at supersonic speeds. He wrote: "the scientific information given in the documents are not easy to use. One must have a large mathematical knowledge. General relativity is, as you may think, not understandable by every man. But working several years on the subject, I could transform this information into science, and gave to the UMMO case scientific existence."[278] Petit more recently has discussed the Ummite material in a book discussing UFOs in relation to advanced propulsion systems developed by the U.S. military.[279] He also conducted an investigation of the Ummites alleged base in the French countryside and believes he found it at Digne, thereby giving greater credibility to their existence. [280]

The only physical contact the Ummites had with anybody, aside from phone calls and sending technical information by regular mail, was with a hired typist who described how he worked for and eventually discovered the identities of the Ummites:

> Between 1967 and 1975 the members of the Madrid group [Spanish UFO researchers aware of the Ummites] received a letter from a man who claimed to be the Ummites' typist. Apparently, he had advertised for work in a newspaper and had subsequently been visited by two tall, fair-haired respectable dressed men. They told him that they were Danish doctors and asked if he could type out scientific material for them on a regular basis. Initially all went well, until the day he read the following sentence: 'We come from a celestial body named Ummo which is 14.6 light years from the Earth. - He took this at its face value and questioned the doctors - eventually they admitted that they were not Danish doctors at all, but extra-

terrestrial visitors. To prove their identity they produced a tiny sphere just an inch or so in diameter, which one of them placed in mid-air before the typist. He looked into it and to his amazement saw a scene that had taken place in that same office on the preceding day.[281]

There was a well recorded public event in the form of an Ummo spacecraft that landed near Madrid on June 10, 1967 that was announced by the Ummites several days before to a select group of UFO researchers.[282] The Ummite's approach appears to be one of helping scientists develop innovative technologies and theories that assist in addressing global problems requiring technical solutions.

In 1973, due to the uncertainty over a nuclear war on Earth, the Ummites allegedly terminated their residence on Earth and departed. They apparently sent the following message in 1980 to Dr Antonio Ribera:

For 30 years we have studied your science, your culture, history and civilizations All this information we have carried from your Earth to Ummo in our titanium crystals codified with data. We HAVE DEMONSTRATED to you our culture and our technology in purely descriptive form - so you cannot convert them or realize them practically. We have done this because we note with sadness that you employ your sciences primarily for war and the destruction of your own selves, which cont[inue] as your principal objective. You are like children playing with terrible and dangerous toys which will destroy you. WE CAN DO NOTHING! A cosmic law says that each world must take its own path, to survive or to perish. You have chosen the second. You are destroying your planet - annihilating your species, and contaminating your atmosphere and your seas until now this is irreversible. With sadness we contemplate your insanity, and understand that the remedy is only in yourselves. We can not look forward a great distance into your future because your psyche are completely unpredictable and capricious bordering on paranoia. As your elder brothers in this cosmos, we urgently desire with all our hearts your salvation. Do not destroy your beautiful blue planet, a rare atmospheric world that floats so majestically in space, so full of life. IT IS YOUR CHOICE.[283]

The Ummo case continues to remain controversial due to an early supporter, Jose Luis Jordan Pena, recanting his earlier support and later claiming he faked the Ummo letters. Pena's claims are widely rejected by objective researchers of the Ummite case due to the extensive scope and scientific depth of the letters. Dr Petit, for example, claims that the letters contain scientific principles at the cutting edge of contemporary MHD research. Something well beyond Pena's training as a psychologist. Given the extensive interest in the Ummite case, and scientific competence of its main supporters, it can be concluded that the Ummite case involves extraterrestrials visiting and integrating with the human population.

While it cannot be known exactly how influential the Ummites assistance has been since it was largely covert, it certainly appears to have been significant in sparking innovative scientific initiatives by range of technically competent professionals, scientists and private citizens. It can be concluded that the Ummite's main activity lies in sharing technical information, transforming scientific culture, and in providing global education. The manner of the Ummites interaction with humans suggests they perform exclusively Intervention Type A activities; i.e., they have 'ground teams' on Earth's surface to monitor and share information with chosen individuals. The Ummites can assist in global solutions surrounding the transformation of scientific paradigms, development of environmentally friendly technologies, and educational reform.

Arcturians

The final extraterrestrial race to be examined due to their significance claim to originate from the star system of Arcturus. Arcturus is the brightest star in the constellation Bootes, and is 37 light years away. It is a red giant, over 110 times more luminous than our sun, and is approximately 4.6 billion years old. Its age is comparable to

149

our sun, and therefore capable of having a number of planets that harbor life that has naturally evolved.

The Arcturians are described as once having seeded the Earth with colonies and presumably peacefully coexisted with other races. According to George Andrews: "In antiquity this planet was divided into sectors among four different groups: Blonds, Grays, large lizard-like beings from the Capella system, and beings from the Arcturus system."[284] Andrews goes on to describe the Arcturians as currently playing an observer role in the current battle between extraterrestrial groups over Earth and her population. Alex Collier describes the Arcturians as also being one of the races interacting with the Earth and "trying to help."[285] According to the contactee 'Adrain', the Arcturians are the extraterrestrial race most responsible for crop circles.[286] He argues that the crop circles are intended both to inspire humans with the possibility of extraterrestrial communications, and to warn negative extraterrestrials of the consequences of their actions to control and manipulate humanity. Another source mentioning the Arcturians is Stewart Swerdlow who argues that their "pure society lives without violence, war, disease, poverty, or pollution on their planet."[287]

Most information on the Arcturians comes from those claiming to have telepathically communicated with them. For example, Dr Norma Milanovich in her book, *We, The Arcturians*, describes her communication with the Arcturians through a form of computer aided automatic writing.[288] She claims the Arcturians are here to:

> ... assist Earth as it enters a New Age of spirituality. They cannot interfere with the free will or decision-making process of any Earthling, but are here to educate and help raise the vibrations of all who choose to journey to the new dimension the Earth is entering. [289]

The Arcturians are described as having a highly developed spiritual culture and technological sophistication that gives them great influence in the galaxy. Patricia Pereira has written four books based on telepathic communication and also claims they are peaceful spiritually evolved extraterrestrial here to inspire and uplift humanity.[290]

H.M., another individual who telepathically communicates with the Arcturians, claims they have the following mission on Earth:

> The Arcturians are the overall guides or administrators of the contact experience. They have a desire generally to see this go well. To see you learn as much as possible by this process and to assist you in any way they can. However, their affinity is to the future of the planet as a whole and they tend to have a hands-off approach as much as possible. They will tend to do the least amount of work for the greatest effect. You'll find them to be efficient and quite creative in this. They may be useful to you in learning how to play, how to wait for the right timing, and how to do the very few important things that you must do to succeed.[291]

The Arcturians' main activity therefore appears to be one of integrating spiritual values with advanced technologies, in providing strategic advice in transforming planetary systems, and inspiring humanity with the possibilities of extraterrestrial contact. They are an Intervention Type C extraterrestrial civilization. The global solutions the Arcturians contribute to include transparent and accountable global governance; integrating global financial, political and societal systems; helping humanity coordinate effectively with all extraterrestrial races, and diplomacy and conflict resolution.

The main activities of the Arcturians and other extraterrestrial races that lie outside of the Military-Industrial-Extraterrestrial Complex has been summarized in Table 2. These can be distinguished on the basis of the Extraterrestrial Intervention Types identified earlier. Intervention Type A extraterrestrials establish 'ground teams' and Earth bases with members integrating into human society for monitoring and influencing humanity's evolution. Intervention Type B extraterrestrials physically contact individuals, share information, take individuals into their ships to witness advanced technologies, and/or take individuals to extraterrestrial bases or societies. Intervention Type C extraterrestrials intervene to protect the planet's biosphere, and/or esoterically communicate with individuals collaborating in projects related to human evolution. These can all be distinguished from Intervention Type D extraterrestrials to be discussed in chapter five who enter into agreements with governmental authorities and political elites.

Conclusion

Testimonial evidence reveals that extraterrestrials described in this chapter are very respectful of the vital interests of humanity at the individual, societal and global levels. They have interacted with individuals in a largely voluntary basis, and appear to be very interested in assisting human evolution, and helping resolve a number of systemic global problems. As far as galactic diplomacy is concerned, they appear to be highly suitable partners for conducting "principled negotiations" as described in the *Getting to Yes* model discussed earlier. [292] Together with the "intraterrestrials" and "Solarians" described in chapter three, "Getting to Yes with ET" appears to be a very viable option for humanity. Unfortunately, as will be discussed in the next chapter, governments and their military/corporate allies have sought out another kind of extraterrestrial partner with whom to negotiate.

Table 4. Extraterrestrial Races Outside the Military-Industrial-Extraterrestrial Complex

ET Races	Main Activities	Assist in Global Solutions
Intra-terrestrials (Earth)	Helping surface humanity learn of its ancient Earth history, restore human longevity, developing psychic abilities, ending militarism & protecting the environment. Intervention Type B.	• environmental protection • promoting bio-diversity • human health & longevity • recovery of humanity's history • developing psychic abilities
Solarians (Venus, Mars, Saturn, etc.)	Assisting the evolution of human consciousness, discouraging the use of destructive military technologies, advising political leaders, helping introduce new technologies, and greater respect for all forms of sentient life. Intervention Types A, B & C.	• discouraging militarism • environmental protection • promoting bio-diversity • introducing new energy technologies • promoting spiritual awareness • dealing with 'rogue' extraterrestrials
Alpha Centaurians (Alpha Centauri)	Promoting world peace, social justice, human rights, freedom, and responsible use of advanced technology. Intervention Type B.	• social justice at a global level • human rights and freedom • zones of peace • human rights • sustainable development
Lyrans (Lyra)	Disseminating the unique history of Nordic human race in the galaxy, and assisting in understanding human	• recovery of humanity's history and Lyran heritage • understanding galactic history • discovery of the human essence • diplomacy & conflict resolution • global education

	motivations and potentials. Intervention Type C.	
Vegans (Lyra)	Disseminating the unique history of the darker/blue skinned human race in the galaxy, and assisting in understanding human motivations and potentials. Intervention Type C.	• recovery of humanity's history and Vegan heritage • understanding galactic history • discovery of the human essence • diplomacy & conflict resolution • global education
Pleiadians (Pleiades)	Helping humanity find freedom from oppressive structures through consciousness raising. Intervention Type B.	• universal human rights • participatory democratic systems, • evolution of human consciousness • global education
Procyons (Procyon)	Promoting effective resistance to extraterrestrial subversion, developing 'multidimensional consciousness', using mental imagery to prevent ET mind control, monitoring unfriendly ET activity. Intervention Type B.	• Exposing ET subversion • ending global secrecy of ETs • multidimensional consciousness • deprogramming mind control • universal human rights • internet & global communication
Tau Cetians (Tau Ceti)	Exposing ET subversion & control, identifying corrupt elites & institutions, uplifting human consciousness, negating ET mind control and dealing	• exposing government/ financial corruption & elite manipulation • monitoring ET infiltration, • multidimensional consciousness • deprogramming mind control • conflict resolution • uncovering humanity's origins

	with militarism. Intervention Type B.	
Andromed-ans (Andromeda)	Facilitating decisions of the Galactic community in dealing with the current Earth situation, innovative strategies for resolving conflict, the education of youth, and crop circles. Intervention Type B.	• education of psychic/crystal kids • peace education • exposing elite manipulation • improved global governance • diplomacy & conflict resolution • extraterrestrial communications
Sirians (Sirius A) Human & Feline Humanoid	Assisting in building a suitable ecological system for (human) evolution on Earth by altering the 'bio-magnetic energy grid' of the planet. Intervention Type C.	• Environmental Protection • Promoting bio-diversity • raising human consciousness • helping building new civilizations • evolution of the biosphere
Ummites (Ummo)	Sharing technical information, transforming scientific culture, and global education. Intervention Type A.	• Transforming scientific paradigms • Developing alternative technologies • Educational reform
Arcturians (Arcturus)	Integrating spiritual values with advanced technologies, in providing strategic advice in transforming planetary systems, and crop circles. Intervention Type C.	• global governance • integrating global financial, political and societal systems • coordinating relationships with ETs • diplomacy and conflict resolution • extraterrestrial communications

ENDNOTES - CHAPTER 4

[185] Elizabeth Klarer, *Beyond the Light Barrier* (H. Timmins, 1980) 32. Online information on Klarer is available at: http://tinyurl.com/a9ufba2

[186] Elizabeth Klarer, *Beyond the Light Barrier,* 32.

[187] Elizabeth Klarer, *Beyond the Light Barrier,* 32.

[188] Elizabeth Klarer, *Beyond the Light Barrier,* 36.

[189] Elizabeth Klarer, *Beyond the Light Barrier,* 36.

[190] Elizabeth Klarer, *Beyond the Light Barrier,* 68.

[191] Elizabeth Klarer, *Beyond the Light Barrier,* 80.

[192] Elizabeth Klarer, *Beyond the Light Barrier,* 16.

[193] Elizabeth Klarer, *Beyond the Light Barrier.*

[194] See Project Camelot, "An Interview with Henry Deacon, A Livermore Physicist," (2006) available online at: http://projectcamelot.org/livermore_physicist.html

[195] Project Camelot, "An Interview with Henry Deacon, A Livermore Physicist," (2006) available online at: http://projectcamelot.org/livermore_physicist.html .

[196] John Quinn, *Phoenix Undead: The Montauk Project and Camp Hero Today* available online at: http://www.konformist.com/1998/jquinn/phoenix.htm

[197] Al Bielek Interview, 1991. Available online at: http://educate-yourself.org/ab/ab91interviewsoverignscribe.shtml

[198] See Sixto Paz Wells, *The Invitation* (1st World Library, 1997) 116; Alex Collier, "Leading Edge Interviews 1996," *Defending Sacred Ground,* ch. 4. Available online at: http://www.exopolitics.org/collier-dsg1.pdf ; and Stewart Swerdlow, *True Blood, Blue Blood,* 17.

[199] One of these sources claim that "Those from [Alpha] Centaurus have an open society, a trusting and loving one, so they would be useful to you as you begin to design the social rules for an alternative to a combative or competitive social structure. See Arcturian Channel, " (January 10, 2004) available online at: http://tinyurl.com/brcnpsp

[200] See "NASA finds three habitable super-earths increasing chances of alien life," http://www.examiner.com/article/nasa-finds-three-habitable-super-earths-increasing-chances-of-alien-life

[201] Stewart Swerdlow, *Blue Blood, True Blood,* 10-11.

[202] See Kinder, *Light Years: An Investigation into the Extraterrestrial Experiences of Eduard Meier* (Publisher Group West, 1987); Wendelle Stevens, *UFO Contact from the Pleiades: A Preliminary Investigation Report* (UFO Photo Archives, 1978); and Wendelle Stevens & Lee Elders, UFO... Contact from the Pleiades, Volume 1 (Genesis III, 1998).

[203] Wendell Stevens, *UFO Contact from the Pleiades,* ch. 4.

[204] See Joshua David Stone, *Hidden Mysteries: ETs, Ancient Mystery Schools and Ascension* (Light Technology Publishing, 1995) 38.

[205] For an interview with Alex Collier, see Paola Harris, *Connecting the Dots,* 140-45. Also available online at:

http://web.archive.org/web/20120320093351/http://utenti.multimania.it/paolaharris/aco llier_eng.htm . Another UFO researcher that found Collier to be consistent with her own independent research and extensive database of whistleblower testimonies is Kerry Cassidy co-founder of Project Camelot: http://projectcamelot.org/lang/en/alex_collier_awake_and_aware_en.html

[206] For independent witness testimony, go to: http://www.truthcontrol.com/forum/jon-robinson-alex-collier-witness-testimonie-supporting-alex-colliers-legitimacy-contactee

[207] See Alex Collier, *Defending Sacred Ground* available online at: http://www.alexcollier.org/alex-collier-defending-sacred-ground-1996.pdf. See also, "Our Ancient Heritage," available online at: http://www.bibliotecapleyades.net/sumer_anunnaki/reptiles/reptiles33.htm#Our%20Ancient%20Heritage .

[208] See Dan Sherman, *Above Black.*

[209] See interviews with Clifford Stone available at: http://www.exopoliticsinstitute.org/Journal-vol-1-1-Stone-pt-1.pdf and http://www.exopoliticsinstitute.org/Journal-vol-1-2-Stone-pt-2.pdf

[210] For a discussion of different evidentiary sources for exopolitical analysis, see Michael Salla, *Exopolitics: Political Implications of the Extraterrestrial Presence* (Dandelion Books, 2004), ch. 1. Also available online at: http://exopolitics.org/Study-Paper1.htm

[211] Lyssa Royal and Keith Priest, *The Prism of Lyra: An Exploration of Human Galactic Heritage* (Royal Priest Research Press, 2000) 23-23.

[212] "Arcturian Channel" (January 10, 2004) available online at: http://web.archive.org/web/20101226001710/http://galacticdiplomacy.com/Arcturians-2004-01-10.htm

[213] For an online list of the different extraterrestrials that physically contacted or communicated with Meier, see http://web.archive.org/web/20011006063452/http://www.figu.org/us/ufology/statistics.htm

[214] For online reference to Vedas, go to: http://www.haryana-online.com/History/vedas.htm

[215] Jefferson Souza is cited in Branton, *The Dulce Wars: Underground Alien Bases and the Battle for Planet Earth* (Inner Light, 1999), ch. 27. For online reference to Souza, see http://www.thewatcherfiles.com/dulce/chapter27.htm

[216] Alex Collier on 'The Next Dimension' (October 10 1998) in *Defending Sacred Ground,* available online at: http://www.alexcollier.org/alex-collier-defending-sacred-ground-1996.pdf

[217] Billy Meier Interview – November 20, 1988, available online at: http://web.archive.org/web/20060217060905/http://www.figu.org/us/figu/billy_meier/interview.htm

[218] R.H. Charles, ed. *The Book of Enoch* (Book Tree, 1998). For an online version of the *Book of Enoch*, go to: http://reluctant-messenger.com/enoch.htm

[219] Billy Meier Interview – November 20, 1988, available online at: http://web.archive.org/web/20060217060905/http://www.figu.org/us/figu/billy_meier/interview.htm

[220] Billy Meier Interview – November 20, 1988, available online at:
http://web.archive.org/web/20060217060905/http://www.figu.org/us/figu/billy_meier/interview.htm

[221] Lyssa Royal and Keith Priest, *The Prism of Lyra,* 24.

[222] Lyssa Royal and Keith Priest, *The Prism of Lyra,* 24-25.

[223] For description of starseeds, see Brad and Francine Steiger, *The Star People* (Berkley Books, 1982).

[224] Wendell Stevens, *UFO Contact from the Pleiades,* ch. 4. Available online at:
http://www.etcontact.net/Other/ContactMeier/MeierChap4.htm

[225] For online description of Erra, see
http://web.archive.org/web/20061222094357/http://www.billymeier.com/Plejarans/PlanetErra.html

[226] For description of the Pleiadians first meeting with Meier and the special role they ascribed to him, see Meier, "First conversation with the UFO person," Tuesday, January 28, 1975, available online at:
http://www.ivantic.net/Billy%20Meier/Billy%20Mejers%20Contact.pdf

[227] Wendell Stevens, *UFO Contact from the Pleiades,* ch. 4.

[228] Meier, "First conversation with the UFO person," Tuesday, January 28, 1975, first published online at:
http://www.ivantic.net/Billy%20Meier/Billy%20Mejers%20Contact.pdf

[229] Collier, "The ET Global Connection: A Lecture by Alex Collier," *Defending Sacred Ground,* ch. 1.

[230] Meier, "First conversation with the UFO person," Tuesday, January 28, 1975, available online at:
http://www.ivantic.net/Billy%20Meier/Billy%20Mejers%20Contact.pdf

[231] For description of the Pleiadians dismissive comments of many other contactees, see Meier, "Second Contact," Monday, February 3, 1975, available online at:
http://ca.figu.org/uploads/2nd_Contact.pdf

[232] "Alex Collier - on Reptilians: Leading Edge Follow-up Interview," Leading Edge Interview by Val Valerian, May 5, 1996. Reprinted in *Defending Sacred Ground,* available online at: http://www.alexcollier.org/alex-collier-defending-sacred-ground-1996.pdf

[233] Swerdlow, *Blue Blood, True Blood,* 160.

[234] See Graham Bethune, *Pleiadians from Alcyone* (Cosmic Intelligence Awareness, 1998).

[235] George Andrews, *Extra-Terrestrial Friends and Foes,* 141.

[236] Andrews, *Extra-Terrestrial Friends and Foes,* 149.

[237] Andrews, *Extra-Terrestrial Friends and Foes,* 147.

[238] Swerdlow, *True Blood, Blue Blood,* 31.

[239] See Andrews, *Extra-Terrestrial Friends and Foes,* 143.

[240] Andrews, *Extra-Terrestrial Friends and Foes,* 153.

[241] Andrews, *Extra-Terrestrial Friends and Foes,* 164.

[242] Alex Collier, "More on The Sirians," *Defending Sacred Ground:* ch 5. For online quote see Alex Collier, Leading Edge Followup Interview by Val Valerian, May 5, 1996, http://www.reptilianagenda.com/cont/co121099h.html

243 See Forest Crawford, In the issue of "UFO JOURNAL OF FACTS" (Box 17206., Tucson, AZ 85710), Spring, 1991. For online references, see Branton, "Secrets of the Mojave," http://www.v-j-enterprises.com/mojave.html

244 Forest Crawford, quote from Branton, "Secrets of the Mojave," http://www.v-j-enterprises.com/mojave.html Original source is, Crawford, "UFO JOURNAL OF FACTS" (Box 17206., Tucson, AZ 85710), Spring, 1991.

245 Swerdlow, *Blue Blood, True Blood,* 31

246 This torture allegedly occurred under the orders of the astronomer Frank Drake who was claimed to have headed the covert mission, see Alex Collier, "Galactic Interplay Behind the Scenes," *Defending Sacred Ground*," ch, 4.

247 Lear also claims that Frank Drake was involved in torturing a captured Tau Cetian, http://www.coasttocoastam.com/shows/2003/11/02.html

248 "Arcturian Channel" (January 10, 2004) available online at: http://galacticdiplomacy.com/Arcturians.htm. I have personally interviewed, questioned and listened to the individual receiving these telepathic communications from Arcturians and found the information to be consistent, coherent and credible.

249 Forest Crawford, *UFO Journal of Facts* (Spring, 1991). For online references, see Branton, *Secrets of the Mojave*, http://www.v-j-enterprises.com/mojave.html

250 Forest Crawford, *UFO Journal of Facts* (Spring, 1991). For online references, see Branton, *Secrets of the Mojave*, http://www.v-j-enterprises.com/mojave.html

251 Jerry Wills testimony is revealed in an interview on Exopolitics TV with Alfred Webre and is available on Youtube: http://www.youtube.com/watch?v=rI8a4oSJ6do

252 A 2006 Fox News story on Jerry Wills is available here: http://www.youtube.com/watch?v=J0e7uUPtALs

253 Published as Zitha Rodriquez Montiel & R. N. Hernandez, *UFO Contact from Andromeda: Extraterrestrial Prophesy,* tr. Wendelle Stevens (UFO Archives, 1989). Re-published in Robert Shapiro, *Ultimate UFO Series: Andromeda* (Light Technology, 2004). A chapter of his book is available online at: http://groups.yahoo.com/group/exopolitics/message/213

254 Rodriquez and Hernandez, *UFO Contact From Andromeda*, in Shapiro, *Ultimate UFO Series,* 169-70.

255 Rodriquez and Hernandez, *UFO Contact From Andromeda*, in Shapiro, *Ultimate UFO Series,* 239-40.

256 Rodriquez and Hernandez, *UFO Contact From Andromeda*, in Shapiro, *Ultimate UFO Series,* 245.

257 Rodriquez and Hernandez, *UFO Contact From Andromeda*, in Shapiro, *Ultimate UFO Series,* 294-95.

258 Alex Collier, "Let's Do Some Questions," http://www.reptilianagenda.com/cont/co121099f.shtml

259 Alex Collier, "The Andromeda Council," *Defending Sacred Ground*," ch 1. For online quote, go to http://www.reptilianagenda.com/cont/co121099b.shtml

260 Source: http://www.andromedacouncil.com/about.html

261 Tolec's website is http://www.andromedacouncil.com/

262 See interview by Sean David Morton, "The Man Who Fell to Earth," *Delphi Associates*, Vol. III: 30 (1996), available online at:

http://www.bibliotecapleyades.net/vida_alien/alien_adrian.htm

[263] Randolph Winters, *The Miami Contacts* (The Pleiades Project, 1995).

[264] For online information on the Sirius star system, see "Sirius 2", http://www.solstation.com/stars/sirius2.htm , and http://www.exoplaneten.de/sirius/english.html

[265] Swerdlow, *Blue Blood, True Blood*, 45.

[266] Alex Collier, "More on Civilizations in Various Star Systems," *Defending Sacred Ground*, ch 6. Available online at: http://www.bibliotecapleyades.net/andromeda/esp_andromedacom_6a.htm .

[267] Sean David Morton, "The Man Who Fell to Earth," http://www.bibliotecapleyades.net/vida_alien/alien_adrian.htm , 12.

[268] Mary Rodwell, *Awakening: How Extraterrestrial Contact can Transform Your Life* (Beyond Publications, 2002) 120.

[269] Swerdlow, *Blue Blood, True Blood*, 45-46.

[270] Richard Hoagland, *The Monuments of Mars: A City on the Edge of Forever*, 5th Edition (North Atlantic Books, 2001).

[271] Enterprise Mission statement, "Face it -- It is a Face!" , May 24, 2001, http://www.enterprisemission.com/about.htm

[272] See Robert O. Becker, *The Body Electric: Electromagnetism And The Foundation Of Life* (HarperCollins Publishers, 1987). See also Bruce L. Cathie, *The Energy Grid* (Adventures Unlimited Press, 1997). The following telepathic communication provides more information on the Sirians playing such a role: "They are the original builders of your grid, the architecture on which your planet was based. So therefore they are useful in discerning the sacred geometry and discerning the physical laws of your home world. They can help you also in constructing the new grid, in constructing a new system that is appropriate for your next challenges. So we would say that the Sirians are excellent allies in the strategic design work that lies ahead. Hugh Matlock, "Arcturian Channel" (January 10, 2004) available online at: http://web.archive.org/web/20101226001710/http://galacticdiplomacy.com/Arcturians-2004-01-10.htm

[273] Robert Temple, *The Sirius Mystery: New Scientific Evidence of Alien Contact 5,000 Years Ago* (Destiny Books, 1998) & Graham Hancock, *Fingerprints of the Gods* (Three Rivers Press, 1996).

[274] Swerdlow, *Blue Blood, True Blood*, 45.

[275] Alex Collier, "More on The Sirians," *Defending Sacred Ground: The Story of Alex Collier and his Lifetime Personal Contact with the Zenetaen Culture of Andromeda* (Brotherton Press, 1997) ch 5. For online quote see Alex Collier, Leading Edge Followup Interview by Val Valerian, May 5, 1996, http://www.reptilianagenda.com/cont/co121099h.html

[276] See Antonio Ribera and Wendelle Stevens, *UFO Contact from Planet Ummo* (UFO Photo Archives, 1986).

[277] Information on Petit's books and articles is available online at: http://www.jp-petit.org

[278] JP Petit, "More on the Ummo Case", available online at: http://www.galactic.no/rune/ummo2.html

[279] His book is titled, From Jean-Pierre Petit's book *Ovnis et armes secrètes américaines : L'extraordinaire témoignage d'un scientifique, [UFOs and secret American weapons : An extraordinary testimony from a scientist]* (Albin Michel, 2002).

[280] See J.P. Petit, "More on the Ummo Case," available online at: http://www.galactic.no/rune/ummo2.html

[281] Quoted in "A case with a high level on the technical information given from UMMO - a civilization in the first steps of interplanetary crossing through space," available online at: http://www.bibliotecapleyades.net/vida_alien/alien_ummites.htm

[282] See Ribera and Stevens, *UFO Contact from Planet Ummo.* For online details of the landing see "A case with a high level on the technical information given from UMMO - a civilization in the first steps of interplanetary crossing through space," available at: http://www.bibliotecapleyades.net/vida_alien/alien_ummites.htm

[283] Quoted in Antonio Ribera, "UMMO EXPEDITION TO EARTH" available online at: http://tinyurl.com/a78asuu

[284] Andrews, *Extra-terrestrial Friends and Foes*, 158.

[285] Alex Collier, "More on The Sirians," *Defending Sacred Ground,* ch 5. For online quote see Alex Collier, Leading Edge Followup Interview by Val Valerian, May 5, 1996, http://www.alexcollier.org/alex-collier-defending-sacred-ground-1996.pdf

[286] See interview by Sean David Morton, "The Man Who Fell to Earth," http://www.bibliotecapleyades.net/vida_alien/alien_adrian.htm

[287] Swerdlow, *True Blood, Blue Blood,* 154.

[288] Norma J. Milanovich, *We, The Arcturians (A True Experience)* (Athena Publishing, 1990).

[289] Milanovich, *We, The Arcturians,* back cover.

[290] Patricia Pereira, *The Arcturian Star Chronicles Series,* Vols 1-4 (Beyond Words Publishing, 1999).

[291] Hugh Matlock, "Arcturian Channel" (January 10, 2004) available online at: http://web.archive.org/web/20110104031403/http://galacticdiplomacy.com/Arcturians-2004-01-10.htm I have personally interviewed, questioned and listened to the individual receiving these telepathic communications from Arcturians and found the information to be consistent, coherent and credible.

[292] Based on the book by Ury and Fisher, *Getting to Yes.*

CHAPTER 5

Extraterrestrial Visitors and Secret Government Agreements – The Military Industrial-Extraterrestrial Complex

1. Introduction [293]

We have seen how the Eisenhower administration spurned extraterrestrials that were not willing to assist the U.S. in technological developments that could have weapons applications. All the extraterrestrial groups and civilizations identified in the previous two chapters adopted this policy of non-assistance due to their perception that governments were not acting in the best interests of their citizens. This policy was not adopted by all the alien visitors or residents of our planet. In this chapter we will see that some extraterrestrial groups were more than willing to assist the U.S. in technological developments, and became part of a vast Military-Industrial-Extraterrestrial-Complex (MIEC). What the aliens got in return, more than compensated for any misgivings they may have had over their policy of ignoring the vital interests of different sectors of humanity. The result has been less than beneficial for humanity as a whole, and caused systemic problems around the planet. I will examine each of the extraterrestrial groups that have reached agreements with U.S. government and military authorities, and how these secret agreements have contributed to global problems.

It's important to first point out that not all of the extraterrestrials identified in each of the following groups have the same mindsets or behaviors when it comes to interacting with humanity. Extraterrestrials, like humans, appear to have a diversity of behaviors that deviate from the group norm. While I will show how the following extraterrestrial groups generally behave in ways that violate humanity's vital interests, at least at an individual level, this does not apply to all the members of each extraterrestrial group. Some of whom may be deeply opposed to the way other members of their species deal with humanity, or the policies adopted by their group's leadership. This is analogous to how many U.S. citizens were actively opposed to their government's policy of preemptive war against Iraq in 2003, but nevertheless were sympathetic towards U.S. troops ordered to participate in an "unjust war."

Extraterrestrial Races Cooperating with the Military-Industrial-Extraterrestrial Complex

Grays

The extraterrestrial races in this group include the ubiquitous (short) Grays from the star system Zeta Reticulum and the Orion Constellation who are described in most of the abduction research and who figure prominently in reports of UFO crashes. The earliest documented description of a Gray is in the leaked 1954 Special Operations Manual (SOM1-01):

> They are bi-pedal, 3 feet 5 inches – 4 feet 2 inches in height and weigh 25-50 pounds. Proportionally, the head is much larger than humans ... the cranium being much larger and elongated. The eyes are very large, slanted, and nearly wrap around the side of the skull. They are black with no whites showing. There is no noticeable brow ridge, and the skull has a slight peak that runs over the crown. The nose consists of two small slits which sit high about the slit-like mouth. There are no external ears. The skin is a pale bluish-gray color, being somewhat darker on the back of the creature, and is very smooth and fine-celled. There is no hair on either the face or the body, and these creatures do not appear to be mammalian. The arms being long in proportion to the legs, and the hands have three long tapering fingers and a thumb which is nearly as along as the fingers.... The feet are small and narrow, and four toes are joined together with a membrane.[294]

Lt Col Phillip Corso who served in the Eisenhower administration and later headed the Foreign Technology Desk at the U.S. Army's Research and Development Department, claims to have witnessed the body of a dead 'Gray' retrieved from Roswell in 1947. What he saw fit the SOM1-01 description of a four foot tall extraterrestrial with a large head, large black almond shaped eyes, thin torso and spindly arms and legs.[295] Another description similar to SOM1-01 is by Travis Walton who had an abduction experience with the Grays:

> They were very short, shorter than five feet, and they had very large bald heads, no hair. Their heads were domed, very large. They looked like fetuses. They had no eyebrows, no eyelashes. They had very large eyes – enormous eyes – almost all brown, without much white in them. The creepiest thing about them were those eyes. Oh, man, those eyes, they just stared through me.[296]

Walton's description is similar to the extraterrestrial biological entity mentioned in the 1954 Special Operations Manual.[297]

First mention of the Grays in UFO abduction literature occurred with the famous Betty and Barney Hill case in 1961. The Grays performed an abduction on the couple which resulted in a missing time experience and psychological trauma. The couple had been subjected to mind control by their extraterrestrial captors both as an instrument of control during the abduction and later with the removal of their memories. This led to the couple receiving psychiatric assistance from Dr Benjamin Simon, and investigations by UFO researchers. The records of Dr Simon's treatment was eventually published in a book by John Fuller in 1966 that sparked widespread public interest.[298]

Robert Dean included the Grays as one extraterrestrial described in NATO's 1964 Assessment.[299] Prominent UFO 'abduction' researchers such as Dr David Jacobs, and the late Budd Hopkins and Dr Karla Turner have provided detailed case studies of the intrusive aspects of UFO 'abductions'.[300] These researchers found disturbing evidence of invasive treatment of individuals taken into UFO craft, of women being involuntarily subjected to a genetic program aimed at producing human-extraterrestrial hybrids.

**Figure 11. Alleged photo of Gray
Alien. Credit: Robert Dean**

In a 1998 book, Jacobs described the Gray agenda as follows:

We now know that the abduction phenomenon as a whole is
not for the purpose of research. The evidence suggests that all
the alien procedures serve a reproductive agenda. And at the
heart of the reproductive agenda is the Breeding Program, in
which the aliens collect human sperm and eggs, incubate
fetuses in human hosts to produce alien-human hybrids, and
cause humans to mentally and physically interact with these
hybrids for the purposes of their development.[301]

166

The most egregious cases involved adult hybrids performing humiliating sexual activities on female abductees. Many researchers agree that the Grays are deeply involved in developing a hybrid human-Gray race that would be a suitable vehicle for the next step in human evolution. Researchers such as Jacobs believe this is a cause for alarm and poses a direct threat to human sovereignty. [302]

According to Col. Corso, the Grays were involved in agreements with the Eisenhower administration that military officials saw as a form of 'negotiated surrender.' This was because the Grays gained permission for abducting civilians and 'expanding' their biological program.[303] Clifford Stone is a retired Staff Sergeant U.S. Army who secretly worked for 22 years in classified projects aimed at the retrieval of crashed extraterrestrial vehicles. In the following he describes a meeting with a Gray extraterrestrial at the Pentagon in 1969 after he first began his military service:

> When I got to Fort Meade where he was supposed to be [a friend at the National Security Agency], they said, well, he is going to be tied up ... This person says, by the way, have you ever been to the Pentagon? Well at this time I had never been at the Pentagon.... Why don't we go ahead and give you the twenty-five cent tour. So we went on over.... When we get out there, there are two monorails there. I mean, there are monorails under the Pentagon.... When we got out, he says, we'll let me show you some interesting sites down this corridor here. So we are going down the corridor and it looked like there was a door at the far end of that corridor.... Well, when you go through the door there is like a field table there. And behind the field table you had this little entity [an extraterrestrial]. The entity was a little bigger than the 3, 3 1/2 foot tall entities that are a lot of times reported. But there were two men on either side of the table slightly behind the creature. When I turned around, I looked right into the eyes of this little creature. And you know, it's like you are seeing it but everything is being pulled from your mind - he was reading my whole life.... I remember going down and grabbing a hold of my head like this

and falling to the floor. The next thing I remember I wake up and I am back in my friend's office [back at Fort Mead].... I will go this far to state that there is an interaction between entities and certain Government agencies within the U.S. Government.[304]

Stone went on to distinguish between 'good' and 'bad' extraterrestrials, and refers to the Grays as part of the 'bad guys' committing egregious abductions and that the U.S. government is unsure how to disclose this to the general public:

The good guys [ETs] are, well, I like to refer to them as being nomadic. What you're talking about, about the non-intervention with other intelligent life forms is a universal law. The nomadics go along with that. The grays violated the universal law.... I think there is the effort for the good guys to make contact with the people within our government, but I think now what is happening is that the U.S. government learned in 1983 or thereabout that they are NOT dealing with the good guys, but really don't know what to do about it.[305]

Another whistleblower confirming the intrusive aspect of Gray abductions is Sergeant Dan Sherman who worked for 12 year in the U.S. Air Force. He was secretly trained to be an intuitive communicator with extraterrestrials he later learned were Grays. He learned that abductions were occurring throughout the U.S. and involved more than one country. He resigned his position after learning about the intrusive aspect of the abductions occurring.[306] Evidence that the number of abductions has greatly exceeded what may have been naively agreed to in a covert agreement comes from a range of public surveys. In 1994, David Jacobs estimated from survey data that the number of abductees in the U.S. alone was as high as 15 million.[307]

Finally, we have the case of Niara Isley who worked for the U.S. Air Force in the late 1970s as a radar specialist. During a three month period from January to March 1980, she was involuntarily recruited into a black project after being asked to get a radar lock on a UFO at the Tonopah Test range. After successfully performing her assigned mission, she describes what happened as a consequence of her viewing a UFO:

> I was dragged down what seemed like an abnormally long staircase through another door in the room. I was placed on the floor of a room with a one-way mirrored observation glass, mirrored of course on my side. Locked in there, I went through the effects of the injection, which was terrifying also. I can only describe feeling like I was coming apart at the molecular level. I don't remember pain, only the fear of dissolving away into nothing. After the effects of the injection were beginning to fade, I was dragged out of the room and raped by two security guards while eight other people watched, one of them a Grey extraterrestrial. I remember quite a bit of detail of this and can draw elements from these memories in detail.[308]

Isley's testimony is further evidence that the (short) Grays actively collaborate with members of the U.S. military in secret projects that routinely violate human rights.

The conclusions emerging from the literature about (short) Grays is that they are very active in human abductions, genetic experiments, monitoring humans through implants, mind control, cloning and creation of hybrid humans. These contribute to systemic global problems such as humans traumatized by abduction experiences, genetically modified humans, implants for monitoring humans, and a pacified population due to hypnotic mind control.

Tall Grays/Whites

The second prominent race in this group of extraterrestrials are the 'Tall Grays' described by Robert Dean as "a very large group, I say large, they were 6-8 maybe sometimes 9 feet tall and they were humanoid, but they were very pale, very white, didn't have any hair on their bodies at all."[309] Tall Grays are described to originate from the Orion constellation, and according to Dr Arthur Horn play an overseeing role vis-à-vis short Grays:

The short greys are overseen within their own ranks by the taller seven to eight foot tall greys. These greys are the ones that actually carry out "diplomatic" missions, such as secretly negotiating treaties with heads of human governments. As mentioned the greys in general, and the small three to five foot greys in particular, have been likened to mercenaries.[310]

Support for the diplomatic role played by the 'Tall Grays' comes from William Cooper, former Navy Intelligence Advisor, who claims he saw classified documents where the 'Tall Grays' did negotiate agreements with the Eisenhower administration in meetings beginning in 1954.

Later in 1954 the race of large nosed Gray Aliens which had been orbiting the Earth landed at Holloman Air Force Base. A basic agreement was reached. This race identified themselves as originating from a Planet around a red star in the Constellation of Orion which we called Betelgeuse. They stated that their planet was dying and that at some unknown future time they would no longer be able to survive there.[311]

In the second chapter, I discussed the evidence that Holloman Air Force Base in New Mexico was where President Eisenhower secretly met with extraterrestrial visitors on February 11, 1955, most likely the Tall Grays as mentioned by Cooper. Bill Kirklin, a former USAF medic who served at Holloman Air Force base, described a clandestine visit by President Eisenhower in 1955 to meet with extraterrestrials that landed at the base. In 1972-73, the producers Robert Emenegger and Allan Sandler, were offered and had witnessed actual Air Force film footage of a meeting involving Tall Grays having occurred at Holloman Air Force base in 1971.[312] It can be inferred that this 'tall Gray' race is a hybrid race representing a fusion of human looking extraterrestrials and 'short Gray' biological material.

Dr David Jacobs concludes from an exhaustive analysis of sixty case studies in *Alien Encounters* that the tall Grays play an overseeing role in abduction cases.[313] The Tall Grays were found to be present in many abductions that Jacobs examined through hypnotic regression of abductees, and were in command of the short grays who performed most of the abductions. According to Jacobs, the Tall Grays would assist in regaining control in abduction situations where humans fought against the (short) Grays performing invasive procedures:

> If the abductee gets out of control, the Small Beings usually back off and let the Taller Being deal with the situation, and the proper procedures for regaining control are instituted. Yet some abductees have learned the areas where defiance and self-assertion are possible.[314]

In 2005, a former U.S. Air Force serviceman came to public attention when he disclosed extensive interactions with a variety of extraterrestrials he called 'Tall Whites' due to their very white chalky skin and white hair.[315] Charles Hall was stationed at Nellis Air Force base from 1965-67 where his duty was to use weather balloons for the Air Force at the Indian Springs location on the base. He describes his interactions with 'Tall Whites' beginning in 1965 and how he and other servicemen coped with their disturbing presence.

Hall described a catalogue of incidents where the 'Tall Whites' terrorized other military servicemen who didn't understand them, surprised them or threatened them in some way. Hall, for example, describes one 'Tall White' who wanted to kill a military serviceman who accidentally hit her child with a stone and broke her arm.[316] The incident led to the 'tall White' threatening the servicemen with death if he didn't leave immediately and promise to never return.

Significantly, the 'Tall Whites' began to be seen in the Mojave Desert area in 1954. This indicates that they were associated with the agreement(s) reached between the 'Tall Grays' and the Eisenhower administration in the mid-1950s.[317] Hall further describes regularly seeing them in the presence of Air Force generals and other senior officials who recognized the ambassadorial status of the Tall White's leader.[318]

Figure 12. Artists impression of the "Tall Whites". Credit: Teresa Barbatelli

The 'Tall Grays' and/or 'Tall Whites' represent a working model of how 'human' and 'Gray' biological material can be combined, and therefore play a lead role in assisting the (short) Grays in 'interacting' with humanity to develop a suitable hybrid species. The 'Tall Grays/Whites' intimidate humans in a variety of reported interactions, and behave in an almost clinical manner reminiscent of a medical doctor conducting an experiment. The Tall Grays/Whites are most involved in genetic experiments, creating a hybrid human-Gray race, mind control and diplomatic agreements with the 'shadow government'. Global problems that are influenced by the Tall Grays/Whites include genetically modified humans, implants for monitoring humans, an overly passive population due to hypnotic mind control, influence over elite decision makers, the infiltration of national security agencies, and human rights abuses.

Praying Mantis

An extraterrestrial race often witnessed accompanying Grays and playing a role in human abductions resemble a giant Praying Mantis. Dr Joe Lewels, a researcher of extraterrestrial encounters with humans, described an experiencer's testimony of such beings accompanying Grays during an abduction experience:

> There were three small gray beings about four feet tall, large heads, big eyes, think bodies – looked like bugs or ants…. At one point I was becoming combative, and a taller being came into the room to clam me down. This being was what I recognized as an insect that I had seen before. It was a seven-foot-tall praying mantis…. He talked with me and asked me not to hit or hurt the Grays any more because they were just doing their job. He said it was important that the procedures be performed – all of this was very important for the future…. All this communication was telepathic.[319]

Another researcher, Mary Rodwell, also describes an experiencer's encounters with Praying Mantis beings that accompanied Gray extraterrestrials:

> I feel a very close affinity with the beings some call the 'Preying Mantis Beings'. They are often extremely tall, two to five metres (six to fifteen feet) and they have huge insect eyes protruding from either side of their head…. They are extremely ancient and possess incredible wisdom. People often witness these beings during experiences with the Gray Zetas, enabling them to understand and work more closely with us.[320]

Dr David Jacobs has found evidence of Praying Mantis beings in many abduction reports. He writes:

> Abductees have reported an alien who seems to have a higher "rank" and supervisory status than even the taller beings [Tall Grays]. He is very tall and is usually wearing a cape or long robe with a high collar. He often is described as an insect like being who looks somewhat like a praying mantis or a giant ant. He examines abductees only infrequently and most often engages in staring procedures.... Generally he stands back, observes the abduction proceedings, and may issue directions to the taller beings.[321]

Finally, according to Dr Richard Boylan, the Praying Mantis, along with the Grays, both short and tall, and a fourth race, the Reptilians (to be discussed in the next section) entered into an agreement with the U.S. in 1964. He writes:

> On April 14, 1964 one of the most extraordinary meetings in the history of the Earth took place.... Present on one side of the meeting room were 24 representatives, personally selected by the Four Governments present. These Governments were: the United States, the Soviet Union, the People's Republic of China, and the Council of Europe.... Present on the other side of the meeting room were three representatives from the High Council of the Star Nations, (the governing body of the galactic federation of star civilizations in contact with Earth): the Councilor For the Tall Zetas, the Councilor For the "Praying Mantis" People, and the Councilor For the Reptoid (Reptilian-Humanoid) People (1). Also present were four Short Zetas, who served as security for the Councilors, and who were prepared to provide a quick exit, utilizing energy field "tunnels", if required.... The purpose of this historic Meeting was to ratify an Agreement about issues that had been under discussion and worked on via Star Nations individual contacts with the Leaders of the Four Governments over the period 1957-1961.[322]

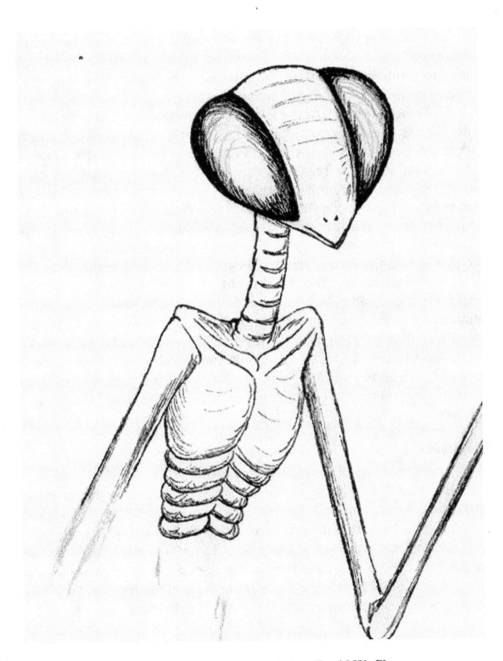

Figure 13. Drawing of Praying Mantis. Permission: David W. Chace

According to Boylan, the extraterrestrials ratified an agreement where abductions would be permitted in an effort to genetically upgrade humanity so that psychic abilities could develop while removing aggression from the human genome.

The observation of the Praying Mantis in many abduction cases and their supervisory role suggests they are assisting in a "genetic upgrade" being performed on humanity by the Grays. The Praying Mantis play a role in regaining control of humans in reported cases where abductees attempt to break free of Grays performing invasive procedures. The Praying Mantis role in coordinating and assisting Grays makes them complicit in the invasive procedures used on humans. The Praying Mantis behave in a clinical manner reminiscent of a medical doctor assisting in an experiment designed to achieve a higher goal.

In conclusion, the Praying Mantis are involved in genetic experiments, creating a hybrid human-Gray race, mind control and diplomatic agreements with the 'shadow government'. Global problems that are influenced by the Praying Mantis include genetically modified humans, implants for monitoring humans, an overly passive population due to hypnotic mind control, influence over elite decision makers, the infiltration of national security agencies, and human rights abuses.

Reptilians

Another prominent extraterrestrial race in this group is described by Robert Dean as humanoids with Reptilian characteristics that are 6-8ft tall.[323] Reptilian extraterrestrial races have been described to be both native to Earth, and also from other star systems. R.A. Boulay, has extensively analyzed a variety of historic sources and argued that there is sufficient evidence to support the conclusion that an ancient extraterrestrial race of Reptilians inhabited the Earth and played a role in the creation of humanity. [324] He writes:

By combining the characteristics of the native ape man … with their own saurian nature, they produced the "Adam" of the Old Testament. This Adam was half human and half reptile…. The homosaurus was modified and given more mammalian traits. The was the Biblical "Fall of Man" where Adam achieved "knowing" or the ability to reproduce sexually.[325]

UFO researcher John Carpenter has analyzed cases of abductions involving Reptilians where the abductees find them to be "hideous, rude and aggressive".[326] Using these abductee accounts he has come up with the following description:

> 6 to 8 feet tall, upright posture, lizard-like scales, greenish to brownish in color, four-fingered hands with claws and webbing between the fingers, a face that looks like a cross between a human and a snake, a central ridge coming down from the top of the head to the snout, cat-like eyes with vertically slit pupils and gold irises. Their manner is usually intrusive, forceful and uncommunicative. Often, they leave claw-like bruises and scratches on the abductees.[327]

In addition to performing their own abductions, Reptilians are also seen supervising (short) Grays in their abductions. According to one case examined by Dr Joe Lewels, the abductee found that the three Grays were accompanied by:

> A taller being [who] had a very different appearance. He looked like a monster. His head was big and seemed to come to a point toward the top. His eyes were huge and seemed to protrude from his face. There was no hair, no eyebrows, no nose, but a chin and mouth area that looked reptilian.... He had claws for hands. He moved slowly and observed and directed the activities of the Greys.[328]

Dr Dale Russell, the former chief of Paleontology of the National Museums of Canada has created a life-size figure of a Reptilian based on his speculation of what a homosaurus would look like. Lewels claims that the "resulting figure resembles so closely what abductees have seen that many of them cannot bear to look at photos of "Homosaurus."[329]

Figure 14. Reptilian – Homosaurus.
Credit. Dr Dale Russell

There are reports confirming that Reptilians have reached agreement with shadow government authorities and work in joint projects. Among the more credible witnesses are claims by Niara Isley who I mentioned earlier worked for the U.S. Air Force in the late 1970s as a radar specialist.[330] Isley claims that she witnessed Reptilians on several occasions during her involuntary recruitment into covert military operations which she details in her forthcoming book. In one incident, she describes being taken on a secret government spacecraft with two extraterrestrials on board. One of whom was a Reptilian:

Well, one of them [Grays] was piloting the craft, and then the Reptilian was in one of the other seats, and then there were two other human beings in the other two seats. There were four seats.[331]

Her experiences suggest that joint operations with Reptilians were commonplace in the MIEC world of covert operations.

More controversial are the claims of Thomas Castello who said he worked as a former security official at a highly classified underground facility in the Archuleta Mesa, near the town of Dulce, New Mexico during the 1970s. He says he witnessed a number of extraterrestrial races cooperating with a number of U.S. national security agencies and corporations. He claims Reptilians indigenous to Earth work side by side with humans and other extraterrestrial races:

> ... some 'reptoids' [Reptilians] are native to this planet. The ruling caste of 'aliens' ARE reptilian.... They were an ancient race on Earth, living underground.... Reptoids rightly consider themselves "native Terrans." Perhaps they are the ones we call the Fallen Angels - maybe not. Either way, we are [considered] the 'squatters' on Earth....Since I was the Senior Security Technician at that base [Dulce], I had to communicate with them on a daily basis. If there were any problems that involved security or video cameras, I was the one they called. It was the reptilian "working caste" that usually did the physical labor in the lower levels at Dulce.[332]

According to Castello, the lower levels of Dulce involved extensive human rights abuses on captive civilians by joint extraterrestrial-human project leaders. Critics have dismissed Costello as a fraud, while others that have claimed to have met him or traveled to Dulce, support his claims.[333] Castello's controversial testimony received a boost with clear evidence emerging at the very first UFO base conference at the town of Dulce in March 2009, which I attended, that there was indeed an underground base hidden in the Archuletta Mesa near Dulce, New Mexico.[334]

Linda Moulton Howe, an investigative journalist and UFO researcher, interviewed a 'contactee/abductee' by the name of Jim

Sparx who claims to have met with a number of Reptilians indigenous to Earth.[335] According to Sparx, indigenous Earth based Reptilians have their own unique culture and have interacted with humanity for millennia, and both assisted humanity and used it as a resource. Sparx was told by the Reptilians that they have reached a number of secret agreements with national governments.[336] Importantly, Sparx did not describe the Reptilians as openly hostile to humanity, only concerned over how humanity was behaving in a way that threatened its, and other species, existence.

Sparx's claims are very consistent with the experience of another 'contactee' Ole K., who claims to have met with a female Reptilian, Lacerta, and interviewed her on a number of occasions and distributed the interviews as the 'Lacerta Files'. According to Lacerta, Reptilians who have evolved on Earth are distinct to 'off-world' Reptilians who periodically visit the Earth.[337] While there is some debate over the credibility of Ole K, the testimony is coherent and consistent with Sparx and other research on the Reptilian species, and worth considering to better understand Reptilian activities.[338] According to Lacerta, the Reptilians disposition towards humanity is cautious since they view humans as a primitive species that is the 'property' of other extraterrestrial races that seeded the planet. The Earth based Reptilians, according to Sparx, 'harvest' humans in a way that does not challenge the human presence on the planet. This suggests that the Reptilians are following agreements 'imposed' upon them by more powerful off-world extraterrestrial races mentioned by Lacerta.

In sum, according to the whistleblower and contactee testimonies discussed thus far, it can be concluded that some, but not all, indigenous Earth based Reptilians are involved in secret government agreements that have led to human rights violations. While Reptilians generally have a tendency of isolationism towards humanity, they have nevertheless historically influenced religious belief systems, and regard humanity as a barbaric species that needs to be manipulated for its own good. The systemic global problems that a significant number, but not all, (indigenous) Reptilians contribute to include human rights abuses, genetic engineering, elite corruption and domination, and religious dogma.

Draconians

The most controversial 'whistleblower'/'contactee' cases concern an off-world 'master Reptilian race' described as the Draconians who are claimed to originate from the Alpha Draconis star system which is 215 light years distant and was formerly the pole star.[339] UFO researcher, John Rhodes has described a number of different reptilian races raised in abduction reports and in archeological records.[340] He describes the Draconian Reptilians or "Draco Reptoids" as follows:

> The Draco reptoids, usually standing seven to twelve feet tall, have been reported to be the royal elitists of the reptoid hierarchy. They are seen far less often than other reptoids types. The Draco are similar in appearance to the Reptoid, but they have distinct physical differences. Draco have wings. These wings are made of long, thin bony spines or ribs that protrude out of their backs. The ribs are adjoined by flaps of leathery, blackish-brown skin. The wings are usually in a retracted position. In some instances, such as reported by author John Keel ('MothMan Prophecies), the beings matching descriptions of the Draco have been seen to actually fly by use of their wings.... In several contacts, people have seen reptilian looking beings wearing capes draped over their shoulders and down their backs.... What strikes eyewitnesses the most about the Draco beings is that they have horns... These may be long, bony ridges that run back along their slightly conical heads or they may also be actual, horny protuberances that developed midway between the brow and the top of the Dracos skull.[341]

Stewart Swerdlow claims to have been forcibly indoctrinated into a series of classified projects due to his advanced psychic abilities. One of these programs was called "Project Talent" and involved mind control procedures used against gifted young children.[342] Swerdlow was involved as a youth in programs conducted at the Montauk facility on Long Island New York. He says he came across a number of extraterrestrial civilizations during his classified work at Montauk, one of which were the Draconians or 'Draco'. He says:

> The leader group is a seven to eight foot tall winged reptilian-type creature…. Harsh, warlike beings who feel little emotions, the Draco have no regard for culture or other beings. Most Draco are androgynous and reproduce by parthenogenesis, or cloning.[343]

Adrain also describes Draconians as a very large powerful warrior cast:

> There are beings from Alpha Draconis and Ursa Major that are most amazing. They are half man and half lizard. Big people, you know. Very strong … very big up to 1,5000 to 1,800 pounds. They are totally unemotional warriors, and that's a problem.[344]

Another who has given information on the Draconians is Alex Collier. According to Collier, the Draconians or Dracos have two main castes, the first of which is a warrior caste that are in the 7-8 foot range, and who are apparently feared throughout the galaxy for their fighting abilities. [345] The second caste are a 'royal line' of Draco Reptilians that he describes as 'Ciakars' which, because of their alleged size, psychic ability and wings, might be confused as the proverbial Dragon, if Collier is correct:

> The Draconians are a very large reptilian race, otherwise known as "the Dracs". There is royal line of the reptilian race called the Ciakar. They range from 14 to 22 feet tall and can weigh up to 1,800 pounds. They do have winged appendages and they are awesome beings. They're extremely clairvoyant and extremely clever, and they can also be extremely sinister.[346]

Collier claims that according to the Draconian world view, they were the first intelligent species in the galaxy and seeded many worlds with their biological off-spring. [347] The Draco Reptilians therefore, see themselves as the natural rulers of inhabited worlds such as Earth, and view humans as an inferior species. Swerdlow similarly believed Reptilians have a mindset of conquerors with Draconians at the top of the pyramid:

> The Reptilians are programmed to believe that they are the superior physical form. Scientifically speaking, Reptilian DNA does not change very much over eons of time.... For them, this is the proof that they are already perfect, without any need to adapt.... Due to their ethnocentric values, they also consider it their right to control and conquer all of space and time.[348]

The Draconians are interested in harvesting the Earth's resources while ensuring that these resources are efficiently exploited.

There appears to be a strict hierarchy involving the Draco-Reptilians and other extraterrestrial races so far described in this group. According to Thomas Castello, Reptilians from Alpha Draconis, the 'Dracos', are in command of the Earth based Reptilians.[349] Earth based Reptilians are in turn in command of the 'Tall Grays', who are in command of the smaller 'Grays'. Interestingly, Castello also describes the Draconian ruling caste as Ciakars who are winged and therefore could be easily confused as dragons. Jefferson Souza, a Brazilian UFO researcher confirms the existence of a hierarchy involving the Grays and a Master Reptilian race.[350] The relationship between the Draconians and Praying Mantis is still not clear. One abductee reported seeing a Praying Mantis come to take over from a Reptilian supervisor when she was becoming combative. This suggests that Praying Mantis may have specialized skills that makes them subordinate only to the Draconians in the extraterrestrial hierarchy involved in secret technology agreements.

All of the extraterrestrial races described so far, Grays, Praying Mantis, Reptilians and Draconians appear to have a number of interlocking agreements between them that have a common interface in the agreements with U.S. national security agencies. The Draconians form the (hidden) apex of the military-industrial-extraterrestrial complex (MIEC) that controls information and technology related to the extraterrestrial presence. The Draconians appear to be very active in controlling human elites, institutions and financial systems; promoting militarism; creating a climate of scarcity, struggle and insecurity; harvesting humans and manipulating Grays and other Reptilian races. Draconian activities directly contribute to global problems such as concentrated wealth, corrupt elites and institutions, ethnic/religious violence, human rights abuses, a culture of violence and terrorism, and the drug trade and organized crime.

Sirians from Sirius B

In addition to the above extraterrestrials, there are a number of human looking extraterrestrials from Sirius B which is part of a binary star system. Alex Collier describes extraterrestrials from Sirius B as follows:

> The cultures around Sirius B have a very controlling vibration. Some of the humans are red, beige and black-skinned. The planets around Sirius B are very arid and generally occupied by reptilian and aquatic-type beings... The society is more obsessed with political thought patterns instead of spiritual attributes. [351]

An African tribe called the Dogon, had an intricate understanding of this elliptical orbit of Sirius B around the main star, Sirius A. This knowledge was apparently given to their ancestors by advanced extraterrestrials from the Sirius star system.[352] The Dogon described the Sirians as amphibians from a planet around Sirius B, which is consistent with Collier's claim that one of the planets around Sirius B is "generally occupied by reptilian and aquatic-type beings."[353] The dark racial characteristics of the humans from Sirius B suggests that these are descendents from the star system Vega which will be described later.

Preston Nichols claims to be a 'whistleblower' who participated in a clandestine project at Montauk that involved a number of extraterrestrial groups. An independent investigator found Nichols "to be a very reliable and solid witness and that for myself, his information checked out across the board--right down the line; to the extent that it was at all possible to verify particular information."[354] The humans from Sirius B, according to Nichols, played a role in providing exotic technology such as time/inter-dimensional travel to clandestine government agencies involved in both the Philadelphia Experiment and Montauk Project.[355] Stewart Swerdlow also claims that Sirians based at Montauk specialized in technology transfers.[356]

Alex Collier elaborates on the role of this group of extraterrestrials in technology exchanges with national security agencies: "those from Sirius B have come here and really messed with our heads, and they are the ones who originally gave our government the Montauk technology."[357] This exotic technology was provided for the purpose of encouraging national security agencies to develop offensive military capabilities vis-à-vis possible extraterrestrial threats. This technological assistance even involved biological weapons research according to Collier who claims: "the biological material that has been added to the Ebola [virus] was given to the government by the humanoids from Sirius B. I don't know if was one of their viruses that they picked up somewhere or whether it is actually from them."[358]

According to Daniel Salter another whistleblower with long military service which included a period in the National Reconnaissance Office, extraterrestrial related issues drive human-extraterrestrial cooperation in a clandestine organization in the National Security Agency called the Advanced Contact Intelligence Organization (ACIO).[359] According to leaked information from an alleged whistleblower on a popular website called the Wingmakers, information which Salter affirms to be accurate, ACIO is cooperating with a consortium of extraterrestrials to develop sophisticated time travel technologies for future extraterrestrial threats.[360] According to the Wingmakers website:

> Blank Slate Technology or BST ... is a form of time travel that enables the re-write of history at what are called intervention points. Intervention points are the causal energy centers that create a major event like the break-up of the Soviet Union or the NASA space program. BST is the most advanced technology and clearly anyone who is in possession of BST, can defend

themselves against any aggressor. It is, as Fifteen [leader of the Labyrinth] was fond of saying, the freedom key. Remember that the ACIO was the primary interface with extraterrestrial technologies and how to adapt them into mainstream society as well as military applications. We were exposed to extraterrestrials and knew of their agenda. Some of these extraterrestrials scared the hell out of the ACIO.[361]

It is likely that this consortium of extraterrestrials includes those from Sirius B who allegedly provided some time travel/inter-dimensional travel technology for the Montauk Project, and assistance in researching biological weapons.

The Sirians do not appear to be closely connected to the Gray or Reptilian groups that have been the main extraterrestrial groups involved in technology transfers. The Sirian interaction with the shadow government appears to have been an independent initiative designed to provide an alternative source of extraterrestrial technology. Nevertheless, Collier's description of humans from Sirius B co-habiting their worlds with Reptilians suggests a deep historical experience with Reptilians. This suggests that concern with the Reptilian/Gray technology exchange agreements may have been a major factor in the Sirians' efforts.

In conclusion, this human extraterrestrial group from Sirius B is mainly active in technology exchange programs that have assisted the government in the acquisition of various technologies that have had military applications. This appears to be aimed at promoting military cooperation to potential extraterrestrial threats against Earth, both through subversion and external intervention. The global problems that the humanoids from Sirius B have contributed to include: covert weapons research, use of exotic technologies, and abuse of civilians used in time travel experiments.

Anunnaki

Finally, there is reported to be a race of tall human looking extraterrestrials that have played a role in seeding the Earth. They periodically return to determine how effectively Earth's resources have been utilized by humanity and extraterrestrials 'managing' humanity. These are described by the Sumerians as the Anunnaki from the world 'Nibiru' in the extensive cuneiform texts translated by Zecharia Sitchin.[362] These tall humanoids form the chief 'founding' extraterrestrial race that were the gods described in many ancient mythologies and religions.[363] According to the accounts of the Sumerians, the Anunnaki's chief god is Anu. The pantheon of Anunnaki, as described by Sitchin, form key figures in the hierarchy that secretly oversee management of humanity and the planet Nibiru which periodically returns to the vicinity of Earth. According to Sitchin, the Anunnaki created humanity as a slave race to work deep underground gold mines. The early humans were then genetically upgraded in order for them to be better utilized by the Anunnaki.

Sitchin claims that the Anunnaki were deeply divided over the wisdom of creating a race from their own genetic material that could be used first as slave labor and later as mercenaries. The two Anunnaki factions were led by Enlil and Enki, both sons of the Anunnaki supreme leader, Anu. The two Anunnaki factions regularly had conflicts and used human mercenaries for proxy wars against one another. The result was an escalating series of battles that culminated in the use of nuclear weapons that destroyed the Anunnaki's main space ports. According to Sitchin, the biblical accounts of Sodom and Gomorrah describe the use of nuclear weapons whose radioactive fallout made life too dangerous for the resident Anunnaki. [364] Most Anunnaki chose to leave the Earth but a few likely remained to secretly observe and manage their hidden facilities.

Sitchin says little about the origin of the Anunnaki other than them originating from the 'tenth planet' of our solar system, Nibiru, that orbits the sun in a 3600 year cycle. For an account of their origins we can turn to Alex Collier who claims, according to the Andromedans, that the Anunnakis' history is as follows:

> A very long time ago, colonies on Sirius B and the Orion Group were having trouble with each other. In order to bring peace, there was a marriage between members of each group. The woman came from the Orion Group, where the hierarchy

includes a queen – the matriarchal paradigm. The male was from Sirius B. Both members were considered royalty of their respective line. When these two came together in marriage, their offspring had the genetics from both lines. Because of these genetics, the new race that was created was given the name "Nibiru", which I am told by Moraney [Andromedan Counselor] in the Orion tongue means "divided amongst two". This is who they literally are – a cross between those from Sirius B and a race from the Orion system. They formed a new "tribe" which has continued to flourish for at least hundreds of thousands of years. So, they are a tribe that has become a race.[365]

It appears that the Anunnaki's mode of operation is to exploit planetary resources by using 'primitive' species such as humanity to extract resources and for mercenary purposes. Due to their propensity for factional fighting, it appears that these experiments result in failure as factions maneuver for advantage over one another. A crisis situation results where the primitive species is left to its own devices while most Anunnaki leave the planet as a result of widespread destruction. The Anunnaki presumably leave behind a small team to secretly manage what remains of their hidden infrastructure and to manage humanity by carefully chosen proxies. The remaining Anunnaki form a kind of regulatory mechanism to ensure that the Earth's resources, and humanity in general, are responsibly 'managed' until the return of Nibiru and the main body of Anunnaki.

The Anunnaki have a relationship with the Earth based Reptilians based on whatever historical agreements they reached concerning management of humanity. It is also likely that the Anunnaki have some form of agreement with the Draconians over how the latter intervene in worlds where the Anunnaki have established 'human experiments'. Finally, those members of the Anunnaki who have remained secretly on Earth, have played a role in the creation of elite human organizations to manage human affairs.[366] These elite organizations are run by privileged families whose loyalty is to the Anunnaki. Currently, these organizations are based in Europe and led by secret societies such as the Illuminati. Due to emphasis on bloodlines and ancestral loyalties, Anunnaki controlled secret societies compete with U.S. based organizations that specialize in technology transfers with the extraterrestrial groups discussed so far: Grays, Reptilians and Praying Mantis. These historic 'agreements' and/or secret control of human elite groups make the Anunnaki a part of the military-industrial-extraterrestrial complex.

Figure 15. Ancient Sumerian depiction of Anunnaki

According to Robert Dean, the Anunnaki are major players in human affairs and this is likely to become more significant as their home planet, Nibiru, returns to the vicinity of Earth.[367] According to

Neil Freer, humanity has to prepare for the return of the Anunnaki to "break the Godspell" created in early human history where they were worshipped as gods.[368] It is the apparent return of the Anunnaki that appears to be a wild card that concerns national security agencies. They are unaware of how the Anunnaki will impact on global humanity and the military-industrial-extraterrestrial complex that has been created to manage extraterrestrial affairs.[369] The main activities of the Anunnaki are to influence the long term human evolution through elite groups, systems and institutions, and by influencing human consciousness. They appear to be in competition with the Draconians for control of Earth. The main global problems they contribute to include elite domination, religious fundamentalism, a patriarchal global culture, and a culture of violence.

The main activities of the various races that cooperate with the Military-Industrial-Extraterrestrial Complex can now be summarized as in the following table.

Table 5. Extraterrestrial Races Cooperating with the Military-Industrial-Extraterrestrial Complex

ET Races	Main Activities	Resulting Global Problems
'Short Grays' (Zeta Reticulum & Orion)	Abducting civilians, genetic experiments, mind programming, monitoring humans through implants, cloning and creation of human-Gray hybrids.	• Traumatized 'abductees', • genetically modified humans • humans monitored with implants • mind programmed 'abductees' • human rights abuses
'Tall Grays-Tall Whites' (Orion)	Genetic experiments, creating a hybrid human-Gray race, mind control and diplomatic agreements with the 'shadow government'.	• genetically modified humans • humans monitored with implants • mind programmed 'abductees' • political elites compromised • national security agencies infiltrated • human rights abuses
Praying Mantis	Oversee genetic experiments, help control human resisting Grays, mind control and diplomatic agreements with the 'shadow government'	• genetically modified humans • humans monitored with implants • mind programmed 'abductees' • political elites compromised • national security agencies infiltrated • human rights abuses
Indigenous Reptilians (Earth)	Participate in agreements with national security agencies that involve human rights abuses,	• human rights abuses • genetic engineering • elite corruption & domination

	manipulating human elites, and influencing religious belief systems.	• religious dogma
Draconian Reptilians (Alpha Draconis)	Controlling human elites, institutions & financial systems, militarism, creating a climate of scarcity, struggle and insecurity, harvesting humans, manipulating Grays and Earth Reptilians.	• Concentrated global wealth & poverty • Corrupt elites & institutions • ethnic/religious violence, • human rights abuses • culture of violence & terrorism • drug trade & organized crime
Sirians (Sirius B)	Participate in technology exchange programs that promote military cooperation to potential extraterrestrial threats.	• Covert weapons research • use of exotic weapons • abuse of civilians in time travel experiments.
Anunnaki (Nibiru)	Control long term human evolution through elite groups, systems and institutions, and manipulating human consciousness. Compete with Draconians for control of Earth.	• Elite manipulation • religious fundamentalism • patriarchal global culture • culture of violence

Conclusion

While there are a number of other extraterrestrial civilizations that have been reported by whistleblowers and/or contactees, evidence points to the 19 examined in this and the previous two chapters as having most significance for humanity.[370] The primary means of distinguishing the extraterrestrial civilizations is the degree to which they participate in technology exchanges and joint projects with the shadow governments in the U.S. and elsewhere. Agreements have been reached where the evidence suggests the vital interests of individuals, communities and even the biosphere have been ignored.

According to the negotiating model I have used so far based on the book, *Getting to Yes*, these agreements can be described as resulting from "unprincipled negotiations." Those extraterrestrials civilizations that are part of these unprincipled negotiations (discussed in this chapter) are to varying degrees part of a military-industrial-extraterrestrial complex (MIEC). The MIEC secretly consumes vast resources through black budgets in the U.S. and elsewhere, and initiates covert projects that harm private citizens, developing nations, and the global environment.[371]

In contrast, those extraterrestrial civilizations outside of the MIEC due to their respect of the vital interests of individuals, societies and the biosphere (described in chapters three and four), have only minimal impact on human society. This is because they are prevented from any large scale interaction due to the agreements that bind together the MIEC. These agreements are exclusive as to which extraterrestrials civilizations can cooperate with shadow governments. As a response, civilizations outside the MIEC have adopted three types of intervention strategies described earlier as Intervention Types A, B & C. These contrast with agreements entered into by some extraterrestrials that I describe as Intervention Type D.

The systemic global problems caused by the MIEC are an increasing burden and immediate threat to human freedom and sovereignty. [372] Continuing with the current strategic response to the extraterrestrial presence by shadow governments, plays into the hands of human elites and extraterrestrials that wish to deprive humanity of its sovereignty and freedom. The alternative is to work with those extraterrestrials outside the MIEC that appear to have the best interests of humanity at heart. Cooperating with extraterrestrial races outside of MIEC provides an important opportunity for those private citizens who are concerned about the secret agreements between government agencies and those extraterrestrial races who are part of the MIEC.

Working with extraterrestrial civilizations whose activities lie in the realm of human emancipation, consciousness raising and conflict resolution, provides important global solutions to the harmful effect of a vast MIEC that continues to remain clandestine, non-accountable, and unrepresentative. The opportunity to address the systemic global problems caused by almost 60 years of secret agreements with extraterrestrial civilizations lies before each individual concerned with the future of humanity and the Earth. Private citizens and small groups have the ability to identify, find and cooperate with those extraterrestrial civilizations that can assist in providing global solutions that lead to the liberation, consciousness raising and sovereignty of humanity. This can be achieved by implementing negotiating principles through citizen initiatives based on a model outlined in Ury's and Fisher's book, *Getting to Yes* – as discussed in the first chapter.

ENDNOTES – CHAPTER 5

293 I sincerely thank Hugh Matlock for his generous support of this research, editorial assistance, and the many hours spent discussing and clarifying the roles of the various races discussed in this chapter.

294 Robert Wood and Ryan Wood, *The Majestic Documents*, 6. Available online at: http://www.bibliotecapleyades.net/sociopolitica/sociopol_som1-01.htm

295 See Philip Corso, *The Day After Roswell* (Pocket Books, 1997) 34-35.

296 Quoted in George C. Andrews, *Extraterrestrials Among Us* (Llewellyn Publications, 1993) 246-47.

297 Robert Wood and Ryan Wood, *The Majestic Documents*, 6. Available online at: http://www.bibliotecapleyades.net/sociopolitica/sociopol_som1-01.htm

298 John G. Fuller, *The Interrupted Journey: Two Lost Hours "Aboard a Flying Saucer* (The Dial Press, 1966).

299 Bob Hieronimus, "Transcript of Interview with Bob Dean, March 24, 1996," published online at: http://www.ufoevidence.org/documents/doc1156.htm

300 See David Jacobs, *The Threat* (Simon and Schuster, 1998); Budd Hopkins, *Intruders* (Ballantine Books, 1987); & Karla Turner, *Taken: Inside the Alien-Human Abduction Agenda* (Kelt Works, 1994).

301 David Jacobs, *The Threat: Revealing the Secret Alien Agenda* (Fireside Books, 1998) 61.

302 See David Jacobs, *The Threat: Revealing the Secret Alien Agenda* (Simon & Schuster, 1999).

303 Corso, *The Day After Roswell*, 292.

304 "Testimony of Clifford Stone," *Disclosure*, ed., Stephen Greer (Crossing Point, 2001) 332.

305 Robert W. Boyajian, "Exclusive Interview with Sergeant Clifford Stone, on assignment at Roswell, New Mexico," UFO UNIVERSE (Spring of 1989) available online at: http://www.eboards4all.com/866799/messages/23.html

306 Sherman, *Above Black*, 134.

307 David Jacobs, *Alien Encounters: First-hand accounts of UFO abductions* (Virgin Books, 1994) 306.

308 Niara Isley, "Nellis AFB Radar Specialist Witnesses UFO," http://www.ufodigest.com/news/1208/dreamland.html

309 Bob Hieronimus, "Transcript of Interview with Bob Dean, March 24, 1996," published online at: http://www.ufoevidence.org/documents/doc1156.htm

310 Arthur Horn, *Humanity's Extraterrestrial Origins: extraterrestrial Influences on Humankind's Biological and Cultural Evolution* (A & L Horn, 1994) 259. See also Dr Arthur Horn, "The Orion Empire," available online at: http://tinyurl.com/c85kv4n

311 Milton William Cooper, "Origin, Identity, and Purpose of MJ-12," in *Behold a Pale Horse* (Light Technology Publishing 1991) Also available at: http://www.bibliotecapleyades.net/sociopolitica/esp_sociopol_mj12_1.htm

[312] See Grant Cameron, "1972 Film Disclosure Offer,"
http://www.presidentialufo.com/ufo-disclosure/197-disclosure-pattern-1972-75
[313] David Jacobs, *Alien Encounters: First-hand accounts of UFO abductions* (Virgin Books, 1994).
[314] Jacobs, *Alien Encounters,* 279
[315] Charles Hall, *Millennial Hospitality* (Authorhouse, 2002) vols 1-3. Hall has a website where sample chapters and summaries are available:
http://www.millennialhospitality.com
[316] Hall *Millennial Hospitality,* vol. 1, 245-48. For further description of the Tall Whites and their disturbing behavior, see Michael Salla, "Charles Hall, Tall Whites and Richard Boylan," *Exopolitics.Org* (Nov 27, 2004) http://www.exopolitics.org/Exo-Comment-22.htm
[317] See chapter two for Eisenhower-Extraterrestrial agreement. For information on when the Tall Whites were first seen, see Hall, *Millennial Hospitality,* vol. 1., 236.
[318] Hall, *Millennial Hospitality,* vol. 1., 440-54.
[319] Joe Lewels, *The God Hypothesis: Extraterrestrial Life and its Implications for Science and Religion,* 2nd ed. (Wildflower Press, 2000) 171.
[320] Mary Rodwell, *Awakening: How Extraterrestrial Contact Can Transform Your Life* (Beyond Publications, 2002) 119.
[321] David Jacobs, *The Threat: Revealing the Secret Alien Agenda* (Fireside, 1998) 94.
[322] Richard Boylan, "The Day the Earth Stood Still," available online at:
http://drboylan.com/1964agreement.html
[323] Bob Hieronimus, "Transcript of Interview with Bob Dean, March 24, 1996," published online at: http://www.ufoevidence.org/documents/doc1156.htm
[324] R. A. Boulay, *Flying Serpents and Dragons: The Story of Mankind's Reptilian Past* (Book Tree, 1999).
[325] R. A. Boulay, *Flying Serpents and Dragons*, 9. Also cited in Joe Lewels, The God Hypothesis, 201.
[326] Cited in Joe Lewels, *The God Hypothesis,* 167.
[327] Paraphrased by Joe Lewels in *The God Hypothesis,* 167,
[328] Lewels, *The God Hypothesis,* 170-71,
[329] Lewels, *The God Hypothesis,* 203,
[330] Niara Isley, "Nellis AFB Radar Specialist Witnesses UFO,"
http://www.ufodigest.com/news/1208/dreamland2.html
[331] Cited in Niara Isley, *Facing the Shadow, Embracing the Light* (forthcoming 2013). Purchase details available here: http://facingtheshadowembracingthelight.com/
[332] See Branton "A Dulce Base Security Officer Speaks Out," in *The Dulce Wars: Underground Alien Bases and the Battle for Planet Earth* (Inner Light, 199) ch. 11. For online version go to:
http://www.bibliotecapleyades.net/branton/esp_dulcebook11.htm
[333] See Michael Salla, *Exposing U.S. Government Policies on Extraterrestrial Life* (Exopolitics Institute, 2009) 46-86. An earlier version of the chapter is available online at: http://exopolitics.org/Dulce-Report.htm
[334] See Michael Salla, http://www.examiner.com/article/dulce-underground-ufo-base-conference-ends

335 Linda Moulton Howe, "Meetings With Remarkable Aliens," *Nexus Magazine,* Vol. 7, no.2 (February-March 2000). http://www.bibliotecapleyades.net/sumer_anunnaki/reptiles/reptiles32.htm
336 Linda Moulton Howe, "Meetings With Remarkable Aliens," *Nexus Magazine,* Vol. 7, no.2 (February-March 2000). http://www.bibliotecapleyades.net/sumer_anunnaki/reptiles/reptiles32.htm
337 Lacerta File, "Interview with a Reptiloid," http://www.whale.to/b/lacerta.html
338 For a discussion of the credibility of Ole K. see "A Swedish Tale Of An Alien Reptile Woman," http://tinyurl.com/bucwxpp
339 For online information on the Draco Constellation and Alpha Draconis, go to: http://starryskies.com/The_sky/constellations/draco.html
340 John Rhodes has a website where he places his research, http://www.reptoids.com
341 John Rhodes description is available online at: http://www.reptoids.com/Vault/phydes_ver1.htm
342 For discussion of mind control techniques developed by the CIA see John Marks, In Search of the Manchurian Candidate: The CIA and Mind Control (Norton and Co., 1991). For discussion of Project Talent, see testimony of Duncan O'Finioan, available online at: http://projectcamelot.org/duncan_o_finioan.html
343 Stewart Swerdlow, *Blue Blood, True Blood: Conflict and Creation* (Expansion Publishing Co., 2002) 158.
344 Sean David Morton, "The Man Who Fell to Earth," p. 13.
345 Alex Collier, "Let's Do Some Questions," http://www.reptilianagenda.com/cont/co121099f.shtml
346 Alex Collier, "Let's Do Some Questions," http://www.reptilianagenda.com/cont/co121099f.shtml
347 See Alex Collier, "The Draconians," Defending Sacred Ground, ch. 1, available online at: http://www.alexcollier.org/alex-collier-defending-sacred-ground-1996.pdf
348 Swerdlow, *Blue Blood, True Blood,* 15.
349 See Branton "A Dulce Base Security Officer Speaks Out," in *The Dulce Wars: Underground Alien Bases and the Battle for Planet Earth* (Inner Light - Global Communications, 1999) ch. 11.
350 See Branton, *Secrets of the Mojave* (Creative Arts & Science Enterprises, 1999), available online at: http://www.v-j-enterprises.com/mojave.html
351 Alex Collier, "More on Civilizations in Various Star Systems," *Defending Sacred Ground*, ch 6, available online at: http://www.alexcollier.org/alex-collier-defending-sacred-ground-1996.pdf
352 See Robert Temple, *The Sirius Mystery* (Destiny Books, 1987) 204-27.
353 Alex Collier, "More on Civilizations in Various Star Systems," *Defending Sacred Ground*, ch 6, available online at: http://www.alexcollier.org/alex-collier-defending-sacred-ground-1996.pdf
354 John Quinn, *Phoenix Undead: The Montauk Project and Camp Hero Today* (NewsHawk Inc, 1998) available online at: http://www.konformist.com/1998/jquinn/phoenix.htm
355 Preston Nichols, *Montauk Experiments in Time* (Skybooks, 1999) 65,70
356 Swerdlow, *Blue Blood, True Blood,* 18.

[357] Alex Collier, "More on The Sirians," *Defending Sacred Ground,* ch 5. For online quote see Alex Collier, Leading Edge Followup Interview by Val Valerian, May 5, 1996, http://www.reptilianagenda.com/cont/co121099h.shtml

[358] See Collier, "Leading Edge Follow Up Interview, 1996" *Defending Sacred Ground,* ch 5. Available online at: http://reptile.users2.50megs.com/cont/co121099h.shtml

[359] Daniel M. Salter, *Life With a Cosmos Clearance* (Light Technology, 2003) 186-88.

[360] See Salter, *Life With a Cosmos Clearance* 181-85.

[361] See Neruda Interview #1, http://www.wingmakers.com/neruda1.html

[362] See Zecharia Sitchin, *The Twelfth Planet* (Harper Collins Publishers, 1978).

[363] Zecharia Sitchin, *Genesis Revisited* (Hearst Books, 1990).

[364] Zecharia Sitchin, *The Wars of Gods and Men* (Harper Books, 1999).

[365] Alex Collier, "The Nature of Nibiru," *Defending Sacred Ground,* ch. 6.

[366] See Jim Marrs, *Rule By Secrecy: The Hidden History that connects the Trilateral Commission, the Freemasons, and the Great Pyramids* (Perennial, 2001).

[367] See Rick Martin, "Interview with Robert Dean," The Spectrum (December 11, 2001) 22; available online at: http://www.bibliotecapleyades.net/vida_alien/esp_vida_alien_22f.htm

[368] Neil Freer, *Breaking the Godspell: The Politics of Our Evolution* (Book Tree, 2003).

[369] For description of the power politics system created to deal with extraterrestrials, see Michael Salla, *Exposing U.S. Government Policies on Extraterrestrial Life*, 152-79. Earlier version published as "The Failure of Power Politics as a Strategic Response to the Extraterrestrial Presence – Developing Human Capacity as a Viable Global Defense Strategy ," Research Study #7 (January 1, 2004). Available online at: http://exopolitics.org/Study-Paper-7.htm

[370] A list of other extraterrestrial races can be found online at: http://www.exopaedia.org/Extraterrestrial+Civilizations

[371] See Michael Salla, Exposing *U.S. Government Policies on Extraterrestrial Life* (Exopolitics Institute, 2009) 87-127. Earlier version published as: "The Black Budget Report, An Investigation into the CIA's 'Black Budget' and the Second Manhattan Project," *Scoop* (30 January, 2004) http://www.scoop.co.nz/mason/stories/HL0401/S00151.htm

[372] For an online description of systemic global problems, see Richard H. Robbins, *Global Problems and the Culture of Capitalism*, 2nd edition (Alyn and Bacon Publishing, 2001). For online information, go to: http://faculty.plattsburgh.edu/richard.robbins/legacy/default.htm

CHAPTER 6

Extraterrestrials Among Us

Introduction

On December 7, 2012 the current Russian Prime Minister and former President, Dmitry Medvedev, made some startling off-air comments to reporters while his microphone was still switched on. He was asked whether the President is given any secret files on extraterrestrials while in office. In his responses, Medvedev not only confided that extraterrestrials are visiting the Earth, but that some are actually living among us.[373] There is startling evidence from a number of independent sources supporting Medvedev's claim that 'human looking' extraterrestrial visitors have integrated with and lived in major population centers up until recently. This is known by a select number of government agencies and military departments. A range of highly classified government documents and military programs give credence to this phenomenon, as revealed by a number of whistleblowers.

Command Sergeant Major Robert Dean, I mentioned in chapter two, claims that a top secret NATO document he witnessed in 1964 described how senior political and military leaders had been visited by and interacted with 'human looking' extraterrestrials who could easily blend into human society. What really concerned NATO leaders, according to Dean, was that extraterrestrials could be walking in the corridors of key political and military institutions. Aside from whistleblower testimonies supporting Medvedev's claim, a number of private individuals claim to have encountered extraterrestrials posing as ordinary citizens in major cities around the planet.

George Adamski was the first to write about extraterrestrials secretly living among the human population. In his second non-fiction book describing his extraterrestrial contact experiences, *Inside the Flying Saucers*, Adamski discussed how human looking extraterrestrials had established a presence among the human population. They apparently looked so much like us that they could get jobs, lived in neighborhoods, drove cars, and could blend in easily with the human population. Adamski wrote about how they contacted him to set up meetings that led to his famous flights aboard extraterrestrial vehicles. While controversy over Adamski's contact experiences and his credibility continues, Adamski's UFO sightings and contacts with extraterrestrials were supported by an impressive collection of witnesses, photographs and films that a number of independent investigators concluded were not hoaxes.[374]

Adamski's testimony offers important insights into how extraterrestrials may be living incognito among the human population. After discussing the Adamski case and the strongest evidence supporting it, I will then discuss other contactees similarly claiming to have encountered extraterrestrials acting like ordinary citizens. Finally, I return to Medvedev's candid off-air remarks, and will examine a number of whistleblowers who claim to have witnessed documents or events confirming official government knowledge that extraterrestrials live among ordinary citizens. We will see that Medvedev was not joking.[375]

Contact Testimonies of Extraterrestrials Among Us

Adamski's famous Desert Center meeting with an extraterrestrial emerging from a 'scout ship' on November 20, 1952 was seen by six witnesses who signed affidavits confirming Adamski's version of events in his subsequent book, *Flying Saucers have Landed* (1954). In fact, four of the witnesses immediately reported what had happened to a nearby newspaper, the *Phoenix Gazette*, that published a story on November 24 featuring photos and sketches. The Desert Center encounter was among those of Adamski's claims regarding extraterrestrial contact that, according to UFO researcher Timothy Good, were "accurately reported," and "sensible and verifiable".[376] Given the clear supporting evidence supporting Adamski's first meeting with an extraterrestrial traveling in a scout craft, it is worth examining closely his alleged subsequent meetings with extraterrestrials living on Earth.

In the first chapter of *Inside the Flying Saucers*, Adamski recounts his meeting with two extraterrestrials while he was sitting in the lobby of a Los Angeles Hotel on February 18, 1953.

> I looked at my wrist watch and saw that it said ten-thirty. The lateness of the hour, with still nothing of extraordinary significance having taken place, sent a wave of disappointment through me. And just at this moment of depression, two men approached, one of whom addressed me by name. Both were complete strangers, but there was no hesitancy in their manner as they came forward, and nothing in their appearance to indicate that they were other than average young businessmen.... I noted that both men were well proportioned. One was slightly over six feet and looked to be in his early thirties. His complexion was ruddy, his eyes dark brown, with the kind of sparkle that suggests great enjoyment of life. His gaze was extraordinarily penetrating. His black hair waved and was cut according to our style. He wore a dark brown business suit but no hat. The shorter man looked younger and I judged his height to be about five feet, nine inches. He had a round boyish face, a fair complexion and eyes of grayish blue. His hair, also wavy and worn in our style, was sandy in color. He was dressed in a gray suit and was also hatless. He smiled as he addressed me by name. As I acknowledged the greeting, the speaker extended his hand and when it touched mine a great joy filled me. The signal was the same as had been given by the man I had met on the desert on that memorable November 20, 1952. (Described in the book, *Flying Saucers Have Landed.*)[377]

Significant in Adamski's description is how the two extraterrestrials could pass off as businessmen. Aside from a penetrating stare, nothing struck him as unusual in their appearance. Adamski goes on to explain how he went with them in their car to travel to a remote desert location:

Together we left the lobby, I walking between them. About a block north of the hotel, they turned into a parking lot where they had a car waiting. They had not spoken during this short time, yet inwardly I knew that these men were true friends. I felt no urge to ask where they proposed to take me, nor did it seem odd that they had volunteered no information. An attendant brought the car around, and the younger man slid into the driver's seat, motioning me to get in beside him. Our other companion also sat with us on the front seat. The car was a four-door black Pontiac sedan. The man who had taken the wheel seemed to know exactly where he was going and drove skillfully. I am not familiar with all the new highways leading out of Los Angeles, so I had no idea in which direction we were headed. We rode in silence and I remained entirely content to wait for my companions to identify themselves and explain the reason for our meeting. [378]

What's significant here is that the two extraterrestrials possessed a car and knew how to navigate on the newly completed Los Angeles highway system. This is no mean feat and suggests that the extraterrestrials had taken the time to learn the road traffic rules and how to navigate through Los Angeles. The next passage is quite remarkable for the information Adamski reveals:

Lights and dwellings thinned as we left the outskirts of the city. The taller man spoke for the first time as he said, "You have been very patient. We know how much you are wondering who we are and where we are taking you. I acknowledged that of course I had been wondering, but added that I was entirely content to wait for this information until they chose to give it to me. The speaker smiled and indicated the driver. "He is from the planet you call Mars. I am from the one you call Saturn." His voice was soft and pleasant and his English perfect. I had noticed that the younger man also spoke softly, although his voice was pitched higher. I found myself wondering how and where they had learned to speak our language so well. [379]

What's interesting here is Adamski's observation that the two extraterrestrials could speak the English language so well without any hint of an accent. What follows in the next passage is truly remarkable insofar as it reveals the true extent to which extraterrestrials have merged with the ordinary human population.

> As the thought passed through my mind, it was immediately recognized. The Martian now spoke for the first time since our meeting in the hotel. "We are what you on Earth might call 'Contact men.' We live and work here, because, as you know, it is necessary on Earth to earn money with which to buy clothing, food, and the many things that people must have. We have lived on your planet now for several years. At first we did have a slight accent. But that has been overcome and, as you can see, we are unrecognized as other than Earth men. "At our work and in our leisure time we mingle with people here on Earth, never betraying the secret that we are inhabitants of other worlds. That would be dangerous, as you well know. We understand you people better than most of you know yourselves and can plainly see the reasons for many of the unhappy conditions that surround you. [380]

This passage is most significant since it describes how the extraterrestrials have spent years living on Earth, learning the language, getting jobs and mixing with the human population. Furthermore, it appears as though extraterrestrials living among the human population may work in pairs, a kind of buddy system that would make sense in terms of ensuring safety and communications with the home world if an emergency ever occurred. If Adamski is accurate in his recollections and the extraterrestrials are telling the truth, then it would appear that there could be a significant number of extraterrestrials who are living incognito among the normal population in many if not most major cities on the planet. Upon examining other contactee cases and the testimonies of whistleblowers, it does appear as though this is indeed the case.

Galactic Diplomacy: Getting to Yes with ET

On July 4, 1949, Daniel Fry had an encounter with an extraterrestrial at White Sands Proving Grounds. Fry was employed as a Technician with Aerojet General Corporation where he was working on rocket propulsion systems. According to Fry, the extraterrestrial, 'Alan' showed Fry his ship, explained its propulsion system and took him for a ride to New York and back in 30 minutes. Alan explained to Fry the efforts he was undertaking to integrate with the human population:

> I am not, as you call it, a 'Yank'; although my present assignment requires me to become one. The fact that you believed me to be one of your countrymen, is a testimonial to the success of the effort I have expended during the last two of your years to learn and practice the use of your language and idiom. As a matter of fact, I have never yet set foot upon your planet. It will require at least four more of your years for me to become adapted to your atmosphere and gravity and to become immunized to your biotics."381

The extraterrestrial furthermore told Fry:

> We have made a careful analysis of the steps to be taken so that I may move easily, and unnoticed, among your people... I must have a profession, or at least a gainful occupation... The ideal occupation would be that of a purchasing agent in an international trading concern. Such a position would furnish a means of livelihood, a good background cover, and an excellent excuse to visit other countries whenever it might become necessary.382

The extraterrestrials asked Fry to assist him in integrating with the Earth population. Fry supplied textbooks on English and Math. Alan asked Fry to get a forged birth certificate & passport:

> Since my origin was actually extraterrestrial, there is no legal way in which I can obtain either a birth certificate or a passport, yet I must have both … It was therefore necessary to find a

County Registrar who could the need for my being here, and be willing to assist, even at some risk to himself…. We will arrange for you to meet him, and you must become well acquainted since it will be up to you to conduct the negotiations.[383]

Fry supplied evidence in the form of photographs, film and was available for interviews. Good investigated Fry's case and found his "story to be essentially true."[384] Furthermore, Good asserts that "Fry did take at least one genuine photograph of a UFO."[385]

Adamski and Fry were not the only contactees claiming that extraterrestrials were blending in with the human population. Howard Menger also claimed to have been contacted by extraterrestrials posing as ordinary human citizens while he was training to be a spokesperson for the space brothers. In one case, the extraterrestrial was posing as a real estate salesperson and asked Menger to accompany him in one of the extraterrestrial's car where he was taken to a new contact location to meet at appointed times with the space brothers' ships. Menger describes the incident as follows:

In the fall of 1947, a young man, neatly dressed in fall clothing, entered the shop. Though he said he was a real estate man, there was something odd about him. And he didn't act like other extroverted, back slapping real estate men I knew…. He told me he was thinking of putting up some "For Sale" signs near a place called Pleasant Grove, about eight miles from the shop, and would like some advice…. I agreed to go with him. He did not introduce me to a young lady waiting in the car… Halfway there the conversation fell off and there was silence. Very abruptly the man changed the subject. "Howard, we know you are keeping your contacts with our brothers a secret as you have been instructed." I didn't know if I should feign surprise or not since I had detected something unusual from the beginning… Oh, you ARE …" and I chuckled. He simply came out with a wide grin, and drove a few hundred yards without speaking further. You see, Howard, I have been taught much of real estate, but little of acting.[386]

Menger's extraterrestrial friends went on to describe a secret location where he would later rendezvous with the extraterrestrial vehicles at appointed times. Menger's contact experiences and UFO sightings are supported by independent witnesses, photographs, film and even scientific analysis of a potato allegedly grown on the moon. Timothy Good conducted a thorough investigation of Menger and concluded that at least some of his extraterrestrial contact experiences and photographs/films were genuine.[387] It is the manner by which Menger was contacted in 1947 that alerts us to the presence of extraterrestrials blending in with the human population. The extraterrestrial had learned about the real estate trade, was driving an ordinary car, and was accompanied by a female. Both extraterrestrials had assumed the identities of real estate agents and could in that way evade detection while learning much about human society. Again, as in the case of Adamski's two extraterrestrials, they worked as a pair suggesting a buddy system.

In chapter three I explained that at one of Howard Menger's 'conventions' at his home in April 1957, three visitors from Venus were allegedly photographed by veteran UFO researcher August Roberts. As I discussed earlier, several of the photos were given to Frank Stranges who showed the photos at his UFO lectures. At one of these lectures in December 1959, Stranges claims that he was approached by a Pentagon official who offered him the chance to meet with one of the Venusians. Stranges then describes elaborate security procedures he had to undergo, and his subsequent meeting with Valiant Thor at the Pentagon for thirty minutes. Thor was apparently a guest of the US government for three years, and regularly met with senior officials including President Eisenhower and Vice President Nixon. Stranges claims he was told never to reveal what had happened. Nevertheless, he eventually wrote a book about his encounter, *Stranger at the Pentagon* (1967). In his book and subsequent interviews, he describes the messages of world peace and spirituality delivered to him and senior US officials by Thor.

Predictability, Stranges' claims were greeted with widespread ridicule from UFO researchers given the lack of evidence that such a meeting had occurred. Yet Stranges' prominence as an evangelical theologian suggested that his account was much more than an outright hoax. I explained in chapter five how Phil Schneider's testimony gave Stranges' account some support. According to Schneider, Valiant Thor worked for or was 'a guest' of the Pentagon as Stranges claims. At a September 1995 lecture, Schneider showed a photo of Valiant Thor with Schneider's father standing in the background, and claimed Thor had been working for the Pentagon for 58 years (since 1937).[388] While there is discrepancy in the amount of time Valiant Thor has been located at the Pentagon according to Stranges and Schneider, Schneider's testimony helps substantiate the core of Stranges' testimony.

If Stranges' testimony is accurate, then the Pentagon housed a visitor from Venus for at least three years who was able to meet with senior national security officials. He was also able to travel to UFO gatherings such as the Menger's to meet with private citizens. If Valiant Thor (and his associates) was able to interact with a range of private citizens during his three year stay, these interactions would have been closely monitored by intelligence agencies, and individuals sworn to secrecy.

Another contactee who claimed to have met with extraterrestrials, posing as an ordinary civilian, involves the case of a tenured professor in the medical school at the University of Mexico, who was also a senior member of the Mexican Atomic Energy Commission. The Professor used the pseudonym of 'Prof Hernandez' and worked with a Mexican journalist, Zitha Rodriguez to release his amazing story.[389] I introduced the Hernandez case in chapter four when discussing examples of extraterrestrials from the Andromeda constellation. To repeat, Hernandez discussed how a very attractive extraterrestrial female, Elyense (dubbed 'Lya' by the Professor), from the constellation Andromeda posed as a student and visited him in his lecture classroom on several occasions from 1972-1974. After realizing that she wasn't one of his students, he eventually confronted her, and asked why she was coming to his lectures. After having several conversations where she displayed remarkable knowledge of physics as well as paranormal abilities, Hernandez was eventually told by Lya that she was from another world. After further meetings in 1975, she eventually persuaded him to join her as a co-pilot in her space vehicle. This how Hernandez described the incident on 22 April 1975 in his diary:

> I had gone to participate in a conference on the theme of effective neutralizers for anesthesia. That afternoon I felt particularly exhausted... As I headed for the parking lot, I scarcely imagined that Lya was waiting for me in the car... "Hello," she said in greeting... Are you in much of a hurry?" No, it is only that I want to rest," I said. Would you like to go on a mission as a copilot?" ... "Today has been an especially tiring day.... Couldn't this be another day?" I asked, almost pleading. "It is important, I cannot assure you that you will have another opportunity like this...." "Very well... " I said as I locked the door, "if it is not too far, I accept...."[390]

At this point, Hernandez drove his car to a remote location directed by Lya. He then goes on to describe how they proceeded to enter Lya's space vehicle and left the Earth's atmosphere.

> A round object of more or less three meters diameter was some meters in front of us. Lya took out an apparatus of metal that was like a small box of cigarettes and pressed a button. At that moment the door of that ship opened itself from below, and we went through into the interior by means of a small ladder... She touched a small lever with various buttons and pressed one.. The ship silently rose into the air.... The Earth withdrew more and more, and thus I could contemplate the night, the stars and alter dozens of satellites of all types orbiting the Earth.[391]

Hernandez story was investigated by Lt Col Wendelle Stevens who corresponded with Zitha Rodriquez. Stevens found many similarities with other contactee cases even though Hernandez could not have known of these. He decided to translate Rodriquez book of Hernandez experiences and eventually concluded that Hernandez was credible. As in the Adamski and Menger cases, Hernandez reveals that his extraterrestrial contact could easily blend into the Mexican population. In contrast to the Adamski and Menger cases, Lya was alone and did not appear to have a buddy. While she did not own a car, she knew how to navigate Mexico City's road system to ensure that Hernandez could reach the destination of her flying vehicle. Her ability to meet with Hernandez in city locations and knowledge of how to travel to rural areas, again suggests familiarity with the location and customs of the native population.

ETs Among Us in Italy

The most widespread reports of extraterrestrials walking among us come from Italy. Indeed, the most extensive case of mass contact occurred over the years from 1956 to 1978 in the Pescara region of Italy. This involved a group of extraterrestrials calling themselves 'Amicizia' or Friendship. The Friendship case was first revealed in *Mass Contact*, a book detailing the history of a mysterious group of human looking extraterrestrials that established underground bases in Italy and regularly met with local residents.[392] The author, Stefano Breccia (now deceased) was a well regarded Italian UFOlogist with an electrical engineering background who taught at several Italian and foreign universities. He investigated the Amicizia (Friendship) case over a period of several decades during which he got to meet and question many of the primary witnesses. In his book, Breccia includes the testimony of Bruno Sammaciccia, a highly qualified Italian scholar with degrees in psychology and psychiatry, and author of 160 books. Sammaciccia's testimony contains his claims of direct physical contact with extraterrestrials over several decades. Leading Italian UFOlogist, Dr Roberto Pinotti wrote the Preface to the book and acknowledged his own decades long knowledge of the Friendship case, and the extensive evidence supporting it. Some of the many photos taken of UFOs and extraterrestrials in the Friendship case rank among the best quality ever taken. In terms of its overall impact, number of participants involved, and documentary evidence compiled, *Mass Contact* is the most astonishing case of human extraterrestrial contact in modern history.

In the Preface, Dr Pinotti describes his amazement at overhearing his university professor talking about extraterrestrials while taking his final doctoral exam at the University of Florence in 1969. Upon approaching the professor and telling him of his interest in UFOs, the Professor asked Pinotti: "Are you aware of the underground alien base near Pescara and of its logistics." Pinotti said it quickly became apparent that his professor belonged to the secret fellowship "which had been created in order to help the aliens in their enterprises on our planet." Pinotti was able to confirm that "a group of human looking aliens from far away stars had built a huge underground structure along the shore of the Adriatic sea." It was only with the passing away of Sammaciccio in 2003 that Pinotti decided to come forward to reveal his own knowledge of the case: "because in his will there was the request that his story be made known, without causing problems to anyone, I acknowledged that [it] was my duty to contribute to the truth, as much as possible."

The story of *Mass Contact* began in 1956 when Bruno Sammaciccia and two friends met with two mysterious individuals who said they were extraterrestrials. One was over 8 foot tall while the other was just over 3 foot. Sammaciccia and his friends, initially skeptical, were eventually taken into a large underground base where they saw more of the alleged extraterrestrials. They also saw their children being educated, some of the advanced technologies they used, and their space ships. Finally convinced that they were really having physical contact with extraterrestrials, Sammaciccia and his friends decided to help the extraterrestrials. They began with material support by arranging for truckloads of fruit, food and other material to be transported and unloaded at an extraterrestrial base. Eventually, two truckloads of supplies were being delivered every month to bases in different regions of Italy where Sammaciccia and his assistants lived.

Sammaciccia describes the various people involved in the case and who had direct meetings with the extraterrestrials. The individuals involved grew over time as Sammaciccia assisted the extraterrestrials in helping prepare humanity for the reality of human looking extraterrestrials from other planets. Breccia said that he personally met and interviewed almost 80 people who worked with or met the extraterrestrials. Most involved were in Italy, but others were from other countries that also had been exposed to the same group of extraterrestrials.

Sammaciccia finally described a violent conflict between two factions of extraterrestrials trying to influence humanity's development and future. While his 'Friendship' faction promoted cosmic unity and ethical development, the other faction promoted technological development at all cost. This led to periodic violent clashes between the factions. Eventually, the underground bases of Sammaciccia's extraterrestrial friends was destroyed in 1978. Survivors had to leave the Earth but promised to return at a future time when humanity was ready for a more ethical future of humanity interacting with extraterrestrials.

Sammaciccia's astounding story sounds like an episode from Star Trek, but it is well supported by documentary evidence, some of Italy's finest UFO researchers, and first hand witnesses of the events described. Some of the witnesses were leading statesmen, scholars and high society figures from Italy and Europe. According to Breccia, a general in the Italian Carabineers, Gaetano Tamborrini Orsini, an additional three Italian military generals, as well as diplomats, Nobel Laureates and politicians were all involved. This reveals that Italian and foreign authorities were closely monitoring the situation. Significantly, the Italian authorities did nothing to close down the bases and apparently did not interfere in private efforts to keep the extraterrestrials supplied. The only condition appeared to be that the witnesses keep their contacts secret. A condition that the main witness, Bruno Sammaciccia, insisted upon until his death in 2003. The Friendship case helps confirm the accounts of Adamski, Fry, Menger and 'Hernandez' that human looking extraterrestrials have blended into human society and have walked among us.

A possibly related and more recent case involves Italian contactee Maurizio Cavallo who had been contacted by extraterrestrials first in 1959 when he was seven, and later in September 1981. He says he was telepathically summoned to travel to a remote location where he met with and boarded an extraterrestrial vehicle. He then began to have a series of meetings with the

211

extraterrestrials who said they came from the planet Clarion in a nearby galaxy 150 thousand light years away. On one occasion when he was aboard an extraterrestrial vehicle, he met with an extraterrestrial called Suell.

Figure 16. Photo of Suell. Credit: Paola Harris

Unlike the 'Clarions' he had met with so far, Suell could communicate verbally in flawless Italian. In addition, Suell was dress in normal civilian attire unlike his companions who wore distinctive uniforms. Cavallo was told that this was to enable Suell to integrate into the population. In the Spring of 1986, Cavallo says that he was telepathically summoned to travel to a large northern Italian city where he knew he would meet with an extraterrestrial living among us. He writes: "That big town I will not mention, for many obvious and less obvious reasons, linked with the extraterrestrial visitors who live and work among us, enwrapped me and intimidated me."[393] Upon entering a crowded bar, Cavallo waited a long time and began to doubt whether he had correctly interpreted the telepathic directions he had received. Then it happened:

> Somebody knocked from outside on the shop window, made a quick gesture and ran into the crowded bar. "Am I late?" said Suell, looking amused. All my fighting emotions broke down in that moment and I had to force myself not to cry. He came closer and said he had been delayed by a trite bureaucratic problem. So I learned he was employed in a public administration office ... He added he had his car parked outside and with that we had to go to his friends who were waiting for us.[394]

Cavallo was then driven by Suell to a remote location approximately 75 miles away where they disembarked and walked some distance in the woods to a 'safe house'. There they met with another two extraterrestrial companions of Suell who claim to have been on Earth for almost eighty years. The extraterrestrials occupied what appeared to be a typical rural dwelling, but had a secret underground greenhouse where they grew vegetables with extraordinary nutritional value:

> I could not say how deep we went, I remember we walked for several minutes before arriving to a strongly illuminated dome-shaped space. It was an immense place in which its structure, totally built in a wonderful transparent material, permitted me to see the external rock enwrapping it. Innumerable sections intersected that place and each one contained infinite quantities and qualities of plants and vegetable forms.[395]

Cavallo has supplied photographs of Suell and other extraterrestrials he has met. Cavallo's case has been investigated by Italian-American journalist Paola Harris who finds him to be credible. As in the cases of Menger, Adamski and Hernandez, extraterrestrials can easily blend into modern society to take ordinary jobs and drive cars. Furthermore, Cavallo's account is very similar to the Friendship case and suggests he was dealing with the same group of human looking extraterrestrials based in northern Italy. It is not only contactees that have discussed extraterrestrials living among us. A Russian Prime Minister made candid off-air remarks confirming that such a phenomenon is real. His comments, and those of the contactees, are supported by the testimonies of highly credible whistleblowers.

Russian Prime Minister admits that extraterrestrials live among us

After completing an on-air interview with five television reporters on December 7, 2012, Prime Minister Medvedev continued to respond to reporters and made some off-air comments without realizing that the microphone was still on, and that he was being filmed. He was then asked by one reporter if "the president is handed secret files on aliens when he receives the briefcase needed to activate Russia's nuclear arsenal," Medvedev's response was captured on video and widely circulated:

> I will tell you for the first and last time. Together with the hand-over of a suitcase with nuclear codes the President of the country is brought a special folder. On it is written, [Medvedev draws his hand horizontally in the air] "Top Secret". And it is entirely devoted to the aliens who have visited our planet. At the same time, a report is provided by the absolutely closed special forces who are engaged in the control of aliens on the territory of our country. These two folders are given over together with the nuclear suitcase. After the termination of authority, respectively, these folders are transferred to the new president. You can get more information on this subject by watching the well known newsreel-documentary film "Men in Black".[396]

The reporter then asked him: "How many are among us?" Medvedev responded: "How many of them are among us I will not say, because it might cause a panic."[397]

After giving his detailed comments to the reporter on extraterrestrials, Medvedev was translated as follows in a Reuter's report: "More detailed information on this topic you can get from a well-known movie called 'Men In Black.'"[398] The Reuters translation was used by a number of media sources in concluding that Medvedev was joking, and his comments needed to be taken with a grain of salt. For example, one reporter said:

> ... before Russian alien conspiracy theorists can say "told you so," the Russian PM quickly indicated that his comment was a joke. "More detailed information on this topic you can get from a well-known movie called 'Men In Black,'" he said.[399]

However, a more accurate translation of what Medvedev actually said about the Men in Black phenomenon was, as quoted above: "You can get more information on this subject by watching the well known newsreel-documentary film "Men in Black.'" So Medvedev was referring to a Russian "documentary film" titled "Men in Black", not the Hollywood blockbuster by the same name. Since the Russian documentary was recent and not well known outside of Russia, most Western media accepted the Reuter's translation. The documentary was translated into English and released on Youtube on December 18, 2012.[400]

It's true that while Medvedev was giving his detailed response to a female reporter's question on extraterrestrial life, the reporter was broadly smiling, and other reporters could be heard laughing in the background. Yet Medvedev appeared very serious throughout his elaborate response, and did not appear to be joking. So was Medvedev referring to the Men in Black Hollywood comedy to, at best, reveal valid information to the reporter using dry humor? Or was Medvedev instead giving a candid admission about Russian Presidents being given a secret briefing paper on a secret agency created to monitor extraterrestrials living among us, and referring to a recent Russian documentary for the reporter to follow up?

In the Russian Men In Black (MIB) documentary, a number of prominent UFO cases in Russia and the USA are discussed. The Roswell

UFO crash is covered, along with a number of extraterrestrial abduction cases, and UFOs disabling nuclear weapons facilities. The documentary examines testimony that extraterrestrial bases have been established on Earth, and that some are in restricted US military areas with the full knowledge of the Pentagon. The documentary even goes on to seriously discuss President Eisenhower's alleged meeting with extraterrestrials, where agreements were reached with some of the visitors giving them permission to take some of the Earth's resources in exchange for advanced technology. As we learned in chapter two, this is actually what occurred according to witness testimony. If Medvedev wanted the female Russian reporter to explore some of the information he was revealing, then it makes sense that he was in fact referring to the Russian MIB documentary.

Figure 17. Alleged photo of military officer meeting Gray alien. First emerged nearly 20 years ago & may have been leaked by Soviet KGB. Were photos like this in the folder received by Russian Presidents?

This leads to an incredible conclusion. If Medvedev was in fact referring to the Russian MIB documentary, then he was implicitly endorsing information that extraterrestrials have established bases on remote US military facilities with Pentagon approval. Even more startling is that Medvedev was endorsing the claim that President Eisenhower had in fact met with extraterrestrials, and reached agreements for advanced technologies to be traded for planetary resources. Initial media reports of Prime Minister Medvedev's off-air comments were simply unaware of a Russian documentary titled Men In Black, and wrongly concluded that he was referring to the MIB comedy. As the translated text of his comments now makes clear, Medvedev was referring to a Russian documentary exposing the Men in Black phenomenon, and was candidly advising the Russian reporter to investigate some of the claims found in it to learn about a worldwide cover up of extraterrestrials among us. So aside from the contactee testimonies we have already seen, is there more reliable evidence supporting Medvedev's claims?

Whistleblower Testimonies of Extraterrestrials Living Among Us

Early contactee claims and Medvedev's more recent claim that extraterrestrials are living among us received a significant boost by the whistleblower testimony of Command Sergeant Major Robert Dean which I described in chapter two. To briefly repeat, Dean worked at NATO's Supreme Headquarters from 1963-1967, and during this time was stationed in the Operations Center with a Cosmic Top Secret clearance. He claims to have viewed a secret NATO study that was commissioned to analyze the threat posed by UFOs to NATO operations in Eastern Europe. Nato's report, "An Evaluation of a Possible Military threat to Allied Forces in Europe," focused on the dangers of UFOs being mistakenly identified as an incoming ballistic missile attack from the Soviet Union. Dean claimed that the NATO study identified four different extraterrestrial civilizations visiting the Earth. He said that what really worried the NATO top brass was that some of the visitors looked so much like us that they were virtually indistinguishable. Dean says that NATO generals were paranoid over the possibility that some of the extraterrestrial visitors could be walking in the corridors of NATO or the Pentagon, or even the White House itself. In an interview he said:

There was a human group that looked so much like us that that really drove the admirals and the generals crazy because they determined that these people, and they had seen them repeatedly, they had had contact with them…. These people looked so much like us they could sit next to you on a plane or in a restaurant and you'd never know the difference. And being military and being primarily paranoid, that bothered the generals and the admirals a little bit. That the fact that these intelligent entities could be involved with us, walking up and down the corridors of SHAPE, walking down the corridors of the Pentagon. My God, it even dawned on a couple of them that these guys could even be in the White House! Of course, as I said, being paranoid in those years it really shook things up a little bit.[401]

Dean's testimony is a vital key in unlocking the truth of extraterrestrials living among the human population. His testimony conclusively demonstrates that official military and government agencies are aware of this possibility, and in fact would undoubtedly have been developing strategies for such a contingency. While NATO viewed extraterrestrials living among us in the context of a classified Study assessing UFOs as a potential security threat, based on contactee testimonies, it appears that the extraterrestrial visitors are blending in to learn about the human population. In addition to learning about human values and civilization, it appears that the visitors were conducting a low key education effort to promote awareness of their presence to a limited number of individual 'contactees'.

Another important case confirming the existence of extraterrestrials living among us is that of Ingo Swann. Swann was the first psychic employed in the CIA's remote viewing program that began in 1975: Project Star Gate. Swann's successive rate was so impressive that by 1975 he was recruited by a covert government operative, "Mr Axelrod" to spy on extraterrestrials as a private consultant. Swann remote viewed extraterrestrials on the moon that had bases on the dark side. In later interviews and in his book, *Penetration*, Swann claimed that he viewed various structures on the surface and observed extraterrestrials near them who were able to breath unaided, thereby suggesting an atmosphere on the moon.[402] Swann's remote viewing was confirmed by Axelrod who sent Swan a book by George Leonard describing similar structures he viewed on the moon using photographic analysis of NASA images.[403] The success of Swann and Project Star Gate in delivering accurate remote viewing data to intelligence agencies quickly led to military agencies asking Swann to develop the necessary protocol for training military remote viewers.[404] Swann's involvement with the covert activities of "Mr Axelrod" provides valuable evidence on extraterrestrials living among us.

In one incident, Swan describes how he was taken by Axelrod to a remote location, thought to be Alaska, where they traveled to a lake to view UFO activity. The goal was for Swann to psychically gain information on what the extraterrestrials were doing at what appeared to be a secret UFO base. Swann described in detail an incident involving a UFO coming out of a lake, drawing in some of the lake's water, and expanding in size from a tiny spot into a large triangular vehicle.[405] He passed on the psychic information to Axelrod before they quickly left the area in order to escape detection by the UFO. What is most remarkable in Swann's testimony about his covert work for Axelrod is a supermarket incident where he encountered a strikingly attractive female who he psychically intuited was extraterrestrial.

Swann claims that he was shopping in a Los Angeles supermarket when he noticed a very attractive, scantily clad woman. He claims that his body physically began tingling and he intuitively received information about her non-earthly origins:

> For absolutely no reason at all I experienced an electrifying wave of goosebumps throughout my whole body. The hair on my arms practically stood at attention, and the hair on my neck definitely did. Without rhyme or reason or forethinking or anything at all I suddenly "knew" she was an alien, an extraterrestrial.[406]

At first dismissing the idea, he got independent confirmation of her extraterrestrial identity by observing her being followed by two of Mr

Axelrod's operatives, whom he called the 'twins', also in the supermarket:

> Way down the line-up of vegetable cases I recognized, of ALL astounding and possible things, ONE OF THE TWINS. HE was watching the woman. HE saw that I saw him and there immediately arose in my mind an image of a white card. Please do not speak, and please act normal.... Well, if one of the twins is HERE, of all places, then the other must be, too. And sure enough, the other twin was at the opposite end of the vegetable line-up- and he was watching the woman too.[407]

Swan reasoned that the "twins' presence, coupled with my psychic alert, confirmed that the woman WAS an ET."[408] Frightened by the presence of Axelrod's operatives Swann quickly exited the venue due to his fear of what might happen. He then watched her from outside loading her groceries into a "broken-down yellow Volkswagon." [409]

Further confirmation that the woman was extraterrestrial followed not long afterward when Axelrod spoke with Swann by phone. Axelrod had undoubtedly been told by his two operatives (the 'twins') that Swann had been in the presence of the extraterrestrial and had possibly communicated with her. Axelrod wanted to know if the woman had telepathically communicated with or was attempting to communicate with Swann. He was very worried about this possibility and Swann assured him that no telepathic communication had occurred. Axelrod began their conversation by asking: "What WAS she like", Swann replied, "I nearly choked on the word. Extraterrestrial!"[410] "Have you felt you have seen people like her before?" Axelrod asked. Swann responded, "If you mean have I seen extraterrestrials before, the answer is no." When satisfied that no telepathic contact between Swann and the woman had occurred, Axelrod warned: "I feel obliged to tell you that she is very dangerous. If you ever see her again, especially if she approaches you, make every effort to put distance between you and her. But act natural, always do it naturally." [411] Axelrod's efforts to monitor the extraterrestrial female, his concern about Swann being in telepathic communication with her, and his warning that she was dangerous suggested that Axelrod's efforts were part of an official policy to prevent any ordinary civilians from fraternizing with extraterrestrials.

The above supermarket episode helps confirm the testimonies of Dean, Adamski, Fry, Menger, Hernandez and Cavallo that extraterrestrials are living and working among the human population. While they generally appear to be very attractive, they can blend in without standing out too much. Nevertheless, it does appear that they can be identified by shadow government agencies who apparently attempt to monitor the activities of extraterrestrials living among us.

The Swan episode demonstrates that not only are extraterrestrials blending in with the general population, but covert government agencies go to great effort to monitor extraterrestrials, and to deter private citizens from interacting with extraterrestrials.

Another noteworthy aspect to Swann's encounter with an extraterrestrial is that she was followed by two of Axelrod's covert operatives. This helps confirm that extraterrestrials blending in with the general population are monitored by covert personnel who are drawn from various special forces units in the military and intelligence services. Another whistleblower case that helps illustrate the use of special forces for such monitoring work is testimony from an alleged former member of Britain's elite Special Boat Service who claims that during his employment he had to arrest two females that he believed were extraterrestrials. This is what he said according to a third party recalling his testimony at a confidential gathering of UFO researchers:

> He claimed that he was once in the S.B.S., or the 'Special Boat Service', which is a lesser known special intelligence service like the S.A.S. within the United Kingdom. He was told to travel to the London Underground, to South Kensington tube station if memory serves me correctly. When he boarded a train, the supervisor with him pointed out two women on the train that he was ordered to take away. These females were tall, blonde and blue eyed, and had the appearance of twins. He described them as having quite high foreheads, and that they were the most beautiful women he had seen, with perfect physiques. He

described how everyone else on the train seemed to be in a trance, and reacted to the abduction of two people from a public train, with complete indifference. He had not been told why they were being abducted, and was concerned for their safety. As he took them away he said that they conveyed a feeling of peace towards him. The man had been concerned that he may have been indirectly responsible for bringing these two women into harm's way. It was after about a week or two that he was sitting in a restaurant in Canary Wharf London, when one the two women that he had abducted, came over to his table and smiled at him, and generally conveyed that they were safe to him and that there was no need to worry.[412]

The above incident provides a valuable example of how extraterrestrials living among us are monitored by various branches of the intelligence community, including special forces personnel. This is precisely what Prime Minister Medvedev admitted in his off-air comments in December 2012.

It appears that extraterrestrials living among us can be taken into custody to gain intelligence of their activities and subsequently released. Such a policy suggests that responsible government authorities have determined that while extraterrestrials themselves don't pose a national security threat, it is the unauthorized disclosure of their presence which would constitute a national security threat. The behavior and concern of one of the women, who reassured the intelligence operative responsible for arresting her that she was safe, helps illustrate the benign nature of the extraterrestrials living among us and how they don't directly pose a national security threat.

A final case to consider concerns Catherine Austin Fitts, a former Assistant Secretary of the Department of Housing and Urban Development (HUD). She is best known for implementing financial tracking software first at HUD and later her own financial securities company, Hamilton Securities, that exposed financial improprieties at HUD and BCCI; and the Iran-Contra Savings & Loan scandal. She claims that in 1998 the Undersecretary of the U.S. Navy had commissioned a "high level strategic plan" to prepare the American public for an official announcement that extraterrestrials exist and live among us.

> In 1998, I was approached by John Peterson, head of the Arlington Institute, a small high quality military think tank in Washington, DC. I had gotten to know John through Global Business Network and had been impressed by his intelligence, effectiveness and compassion. John asked me to help him with a high level strategic plan Arlington was planning to undertake for the Undersecretary of the Navy. At the time I was the target of an intense smear campaign that would lead the normal person to assume that I would be in jail shortly or worse. John explained that the Navy understood that it was all politics ---- they did not care.
>
> I met with a group of high level people in the military in the process --- including the Undersecretary. According to John, the purpose of the plan --- discussed in front of several military or retired military officers and former government officials--- was to help the Navy adjust their operations for a world in which it was commonly known that aliens exist and live among us.
>
> When John explained this purpose to me, I explained that I did not know that aliens existed and lived among us. John asked me if I would like to meet some aliens. For the only time in my life, I declined an opportunity to learn about something important.[413]

I have been able to confirm that Fitts served on the Board of Directors of the Arlington Institute during the period in question, and that extraterrestrial life was discussed at some of its closed door meetings as a hypothetical "wildcard event." However, Fitts' specific claim of there being a strategic plan sponsored by the U.S. Navy to prepare the public for disclosure of extraterrestrial life, or of a possible meeting an extraterrestrial, was not supported by other Board members.[414] I contacted Fitts to elaborate or clarify her earlier recollection, she had nothing to add to what was released to the public.[415] Essentially, she stood by her version of events as reported. Given her former senior position with HUD, and refusal to amend her earlier public statement, a prima facie case can be made for accepting her claims as credible. What can be concluded from Fitts' claims is that official efforts may be secretly underway to prepare the American public for the reality that extraterrestrials are living and working among us.

Another whistleblower case involves Sir Peter Horsley, a former Air Marshall for the Royal Air Force, who also served as Equerry to Britain's Queen Elizabeth and Prince Philip. At a time he was directly working for Prince Philip, who was known to be interested in UFOs, Sir Peter was invited to meet with someone that he eventually concluded was an extraterrestrial. The meeting was set up by a retired senior RAF officer, General Martin, and involved Horsley meeting with a very unusual individual who called himself Janus. Janus requested Horsley to arrange for him to meet with Prince Philip. In his autobiography, Horsley recounts Janus' narrative about extraterrestrial visitors to Earth that he called 'observers':

> Since time immemorial there have been tales of vessels coming out of the sky bringing strange visitors. Observers do come among you and make contact on a very selective basis where they judge that such contact could not harm either party. These observers have studied earth for a long time. With advanced medical science may have been fitted with the right sort of internal equipment to allow their bodies to operate normally until they leave. It is not very difficult to obtain the right sort of clothes and means to move around quite freely.... The observers are not interested in interfering in your affairs, but once you are ready to escape from your own solar system it is of paramount importance that you have learned your responsibilities for the preservation of life everywhere. While you are still far away from traveling in deep space, such contacts will be infrequent and must be conducted with great secrecy.[416]

Janus went on to explain how extraterrestrials secretly operating on Earth could move relatively freely in the open societies of Western democracies:

The observers have very highly developed mental powers, including extra-sensory, thought reading, hypnosis and the ability to use different dimensions.... They do not use weapons of any kind and rely solely on their special powers to look after themselves. They make contact only with selected people where secrecy can be maintained. In the loosely-knit societies of the Western world, particularly in England and America, it is fairly easy with the help of friends to do this but not in police and dictators states. [417]

Horsley then recounts how he arrived at his conclusion about Janus' extraterrestrial origins:

It was what Janus had left unsaid that was fantastic. He had subtly separated himself during the conversation to leave me with the impression that he was not one of us, gradually insinuating that he was an observer. His personality was so powerful and hypnotic that already I was wondering what to do with him.[418]

Significantly, Janus explained that the secrecy extraterrestrials adopted in living among the human population was done with the clear intention of not disrupting human affairs. Combined with official military and government secrecy, this makes it possible for human looking extraterrestrials to live on Earth with official government/military knowledge, but no public awareness. This explains why, for example, in the Italian "Friendship" case, human extraterrestrial contact could quietly continue over two decades with official knowledge and without any effort to prevent civilians from assisting the extraterrestrials. Bruno Sammaciccia's emphasis on secrecy appeared to be the condition upon which such contacts could continue.

The emphasis on maintaining secrecy concerning extraterrestrial living among is also found in Swann's encounter. It is worth recalling Swann's claims of Axelrod's concern over the extraterrestrial female's possibly having made contact with Swann. This suggests that extraterrestrials are presumably under clear instructions not to disclose their true origins to private citizens. Furthermore, Axelrod's 'extreme concern' that Swann had made telepathic contact, indicates that any individual who uncovers the actual identities of extraterrestrials could be taken into custody for debriefing or further action. It is therefore worth discussing the importance of the government laws and regulations dealing with citizens having unauthorized contact with extraterrestrials in the United States.

Extraterrestrial Exposure Law

In 1969, NASA passed a federal regulation dealing with "Extra-terrestrial Exposure". The Extraterrestrial Exposure law offers a legal precedent for the detention and indefinite imprisonment of any individual who comes into contact with extraterrestrials.[419] The most relevant passages concern the power of NASA administrator or his/her designee to:

> Determine that a particular person, property, animal, or other form of life or matter, whatever is extra-terrestrially exposed and quarantine such person, property, animal, or other form of life or matter whatever. The quarantine may be based only on a determination, with or without the benefit of a hearing, that there is probable cause to believe that such person, property, animal or other form of life or matter whatever is extra-terrestrially exposed.[420]

Most disturbing about this federal regulation was that such detention could not be appealed and due legal process, could be denied to citizens on the basis of "probable cause" that they have been extraterrestrially exposed. Given that the general public and elected representatives are not aware of an extraterrestrial presence, this NASA regulation gives a green light to practices and decisions concerning extraterrestrial exposure that are not subject to congressional oversight or media scrutiny. While the Extraterrestrial Exposure law was "officially removed" and placed on reserve status in

1991, it nevertheless creates a precedent that the legal counsel of any government agency or military department could cite for possible enforcement against individuals who have extraterrestrial contact.

NASA's regulation, and similar laws or regulations in other countries, provide a powerful means of silencing individuals who come into contact with extraterrestrials who have merged into the general population. Essentially, anyone encountering such extraterrestrials could be subjected to indefinite detention without any legal protection. This would not only deter individuals from disclosing such interactions with extraterrestrials, but would also help deter extraterrestrials from disclosing their origins to ordinary citizens.

Laws and regulations passed in the United States and elsewhere can be used as legal means of coercing private citizens who discover the true identity of extraterrestrials living among us. Accepting evidence that extraterrestrials are closely monitored and covert agencies are responsible for ensuring that such information does not get into the public domain, the conclusion is that private citizens are at great risk if they make contact and government agencies wish to suppress this. Private citizens can be denied their constitutional rights despite such laws or regulations prohibiting unauthorized contact with extraterrestrials being withdrawn and placed on reserve status.

Conclusion

The evidence provided above in terms of the testimonies of different contactees and whistleblowers suggest that extraterrestrial visitors who are virtually indistinguishable from humans are living among us. These extraterrestrial visitors appear to have very attractive physical characteristics, extraterrestrial females being described as among the most beautiful women that male observers have witnessed. The extraterrestrials go to great trouble in learning the indigenous language of the culture they are immersed in, learning how to drive and navigate on highways systems, and taking innocuous jobs over several years. The fact that these extraterrestrials visitors are monitored and even taken into custody before being released suggests that a vast covert monitoring system is in place. The testimonial evidence examined in this chapter supports the claims made by Russian Prime

Minister Medvedev that such a covert monitoring system does exist for extraterrestrials embedded among the human population. Elements within the U.S., British, Russian, Italian and other NATO countries are aware of extraterrestrials among us, and assist in a global monitoring system.

Extraterrestrials living among us appear to be operating in a manner similar to a galactic peace corps where they try to blend in. They presumably wish to learn about Earth culture and behavior; and to, perhaps, assist in passing on information to selected individuals. The fact that these extraterrestrials are monitored rather than immediately taken into permanent custody suggests that decisions have been taken by responsible government agencies to tolerate such a presence. The extraterrestrials themselves accept secrecy as a necessary condition for their presence on Earth. The case involving Valiant Thor suggests that the monitoring system created extends even to such visitors being given VIP status and allowed to regularly meet with senior officials. Consequently, it can be concluded that such extraterrestrials do not directly pose a national security threat, though knowledge of their origin is deemed to be a national security threat where individuals are sworn to secrecy. This would account for the great difficulty in gaining information about extraterrestrials that have merged with the general population given the very high security classification attached to this phenomenon.

As far as national laws and regulations concerning "extraterrestrial exposure" are concerned, the only means to ensure that private citizens are protected if they do encounter extraterrestrials, is to have the right to interact with extraterrestrials formally recognized. While there is growing awareness of the need to have such a right recognized based on eventual government disclosure of UFO's as extraterrestrial in origin, it may require concerted public action to ensure this right. Some progress to this end has occurred with the issuing of a "Declaration on Promoting Peaceful Relations with Extraterrestrials" that explicitly refers to such a right, and was adopted at a conference in Hawaii on June 11, 2006.[421] The third article of the Declaration states that signatories and supporters: "Affirm the natural right of all citizens to have open contact with representatives of extraterrestrial civilizations in all cases, and to engage in non-official diplomacy." Another initiative provides a draft bill for an Extraterrestrial Contact Act to be passed in the US Congress that would protect citizens experiencing extraterrestrial exposure.[422] It is likely that similar bills will eventually be presented in most national parliaments.

The fact that a number of extraterrestrials have chosen to blend in with the general population will come as a great surprise to many still unsure about the reality of the UFO phenomenon and the extraterrestrial hypothesis. Even more startling is the possibility that extraterrestrial visitors are given VIP status and have met with senior officials in major Western nations such as the US and Italy. The presence of extraterrestrial visitors quietly learning about human languages, culture, politics and science will give to many, great reassurance that humanity is being quietly assisted in preparing for a future of open contact with extraterrestrials. For many others, the opportunity to discover extraterrestrials living among us will motivate individuals to quietly explore this possibility with friends or acquaintances whose behavior may be a clue to an other worldly origin.

ENDNOTES – CHAPTER 6

373 See Michael Salla, "Russian Prime Minister claims extraterrestrials live among us," http://exopolitics.org/russian-prime-minister-claims-extraterrestrials-live-among-us

374 An impartial assessment of the Adamski case is provided by Lou Zinsstag and Timothy Good in *George Adamski- The Untold Story* (Ceti Publications, 1983).

375 See Michael Salla, "Russian PM not joking – extraterrestrials live among us according to MIB documentary," http://exopolitics.org/russian-pm-not-joking-extraterrestrials-live-among-us-according-to-mib-documentary/

376 Timothy Good, *Alien Base: The Evidence for Extraterrestrial Colonization of Earth* (Avon Books, 1998) 154-55.

377 Cited from an online version of *Inside the Flying Saucers* at: http://www.thenewearth.org/InsideTheSpaceShips.html

378 Cited from an online version of *Inside the Flying Saucers* at: http://www.thenewearth.org/InsideTheSpaceShips.html

379 Cited from an online version of *Inside the Flying Saucers* at: http://www.thenewearth.org/InsideTheSpaceShips.html

380 Cited from an online version of *Inside the Flying Saucers* at: http://www.thenewearth.org/InsideTheSpaceShips.html

381 Daniel Fry, *White Sands Incident* (Horus House, 1992) 24. Available online at: http://danielfry.com/index.php?id=1120

382 Cited in Timothy Good, *Alien Base,* 73.

383 Cited in Timothy Good, *Alien Base,* 72.

384 Cited in Timothy Good, *Alien Base,* 74.

385 Timothy Good, *Alien Base,* 77.

386 Howard Menger, *From Outer Space* (Pyramid Books, [1959] 1974) 49-50. Available online at http://tinyurl.com/d7xfhel

387 Timothy Good, *Alien Base,* 194-95.

388 Schneider's September 1995 lecture is available online at: http://www.alienvideo.net/0702/phil-schneider-shot-2-alien-greys.php

389 For an online summary of his case go to: http://tinyurl.com/bb8vpen and for a chapter from his book go to: http://groups.yahoo.com/group/exopolitics/message/213

390 Zitha Rodriquez Montiel & R.N. Hernandez, *UFO Contact from Andromeda*, ch. 3 republished in *Ultimate UFO Series: Andromeda*, ed., Robert Shapiro, 2004, 193-95

391 Zitha Rodriquez Montiel & R.N. Hernandez, *UFO Contact from Andromeda*, ch. 3 republished in *Ultimate UFO Series: Andromeda*, ed., Robert Shapiro, 2004, 193-95

392 Stefano Breccia, *Mass Contact* (Author House, 2009).

393 Maurizio Cavallo, *Beyond the Heavens: A Story of Contact* (Author House, 2008) 88.

394 Cavallo, *Beyond the Heavens: A Story of Contact,* 89.

395 Cavallo, *Beyond the Heavens: A Story of Contact,* 99.

396 Translated by Hugh Matlock on January 6, 2013. Distributed to a private email list.

397 See also: "Dmitry Medvedev muses on aliens and Vladimir Putin's lateness," *The*

Telegraph, Dec 8, 2012, http://www.telegraph.co.uk/news/worldnews/vladimir-putin/9731278/Dmitry-Medvedev-muses-on-aliens-and-Vladimir-Putins-lateness.html

[398] "Russian PM talks Father Christmas, aliens and "jerks," Reuters, December 7, 20122. http://tinyurl.com/c9hlycf

[399] Zack Tran, "Secret Files on Aliens: Extraterrestrials Living in Russia Jokes PM Medvedev," December 10, 2012: http://tinyurl.com/d8nv9cn

[400] Available online at: http://www.youtube.com/watch?v=CrjXmDlAYzo

[401] Bob Hieronimus, "Transcript of Interview with Bob Dean, March 24, 1996," published online at: http://www.ufoevidence.org/documents/doc1156.htm

[402] Ingo Swann, *Penetration: The Question of Extraterrestrial and Human Telepathy* (Ingo Swann Books, 1999) 56-57; and interview by Bob Hieronimus, 28 Feb, 1999.

[403] Leonard, *Somebody Else is On the Moon* (Pocket Books, 1977).

[404] See Gary Bekkum, "To the Moon and Back, With Love," *American Chronicle,* Aug 3, 2006. Available online at: http://www.americanchronicle.com/articles/viewArticle.asp?articleID=12104

[405] See Swann, *Penetration,* 91-93.

[406] Swann, *Penetration,* 74.

[407] Swann, *Penetration,* 74.

[408] Swann, *Penetration,* 75.

[409] Swann, *Penetration,* 76.

[410] Swann's conversation with Axelrod is described in *Penetration,* 80-81.

[411] Swann *Penetration,* 80-81. For an online description of the LA incident see Garry Bekkum, "To the Moon and Back, With Love," *American Chronicle,* August 3, 2006, http://www.americanchronicle.com/articles/viewArticle.asp?articleID=12104.

[412] Story was described by David Hughes Narborough who posted it on an online public forum, http://groups.yahoo.com/group/prepare4contact/message/4624

[413] Available online at: http://www.scoop.co.nz/stories/HL0209/S00126.htm

[414] In private email communications with John Petersen, Joe Firmage and a third Board member during March 2008, none confirmed Ms Fitts version of events, or that she was present at meetings when extraterrestrial life was discussed. To varying degrees, they suggested there was no substance to her story. It was suggested that she was untrustworthy and had contrived the story.

[415] Private email received on Thursday, March 27, 2008.

[416] Peter Horsley, *Sounds from Another Room: Memories of Planes, Princes and the Paranormal* (Leo Cooper, 1997) 194.

[417] Horsley, *Sounds from Another Room,* 195.

[418] Horsley, *Sounds from Another Room,* 195.

[419] For online information on the Extraterrestrial Exposure Law go to: http://www.abovetopsecret.com/pages/etlaw.html and http://groups.yahoo.com/group/exopolitics/message/187

[420] Title 14 National Aeronautics and Space section 1211.102 A3

[421] See chapter 8.

[422] Go to: http://web.archive.org/web/20070705191850/http://www.contactact.org/eca_bill.htm

CHAPTER 7

Galactic COINTELPRO – Exposing the Covert Counter-Intelligence Program against Extraterrestrial Contactees

Introduction

In chapter six I discussed how in the early 1950's a select group of individuals began to publicly make claims of having had direct physical contact with 'human looking' representatives of different extraterrestrial civilizations. These 'contactees' claimed to have been given knowledge of the extraterrestrials' advanced technologies, philosophical beliefs and their efforts to assist humanity in becoming part of a galactic society where open contact with off world civilizations would occur. The contactees described the extraterrestrials as benign, very respectful of human free will, and ancestrally linked to humanity (thus dubbed the "space brothers"). They further revealed that the extraterrestrials, who were in many cases indistinguishable from humans, had secretly integrated into human society.[423] The apparent goals were to better acquaint themselves with different national cultures, and/or to participate in an educational uplift program to prepare humanity for galactic status. Contactees began to disseminate to the general public the nature of their experiences and knowledge gained through interaction with extraterrestrials.

Information revealed by contactees presented an unrivaled national security crisis for policy makers in the U.S. and other major nations. Two main elements made up this crisis. First, the advanced space vehicles and technologies used by extraterrestrial civilizations were far more sophisticated than the most developed aircraft, weapons and communications systems possessed by national governments. This presented an urgent technological problem that required vast national resources to bridge the technological gap with extraterrestrials. It led to a second Manhattan project whose existence and secret funding would be known only to those with a "need to know."[424] Manhattan II, along with evidence of extraterrestrial visitors and technologies, would be kept secret from the general public, the media and most elected political representatives.

Second, extraterrestrial civilizations were contacting private individuals, and even having some of their representatives integrate into human society.[425] This was encouraging growing numbers of individuals to participate in a covert extraterrestrial effort to prepare humanity for "galactic status" - where the existence of extraterrestrials would be officially acknowledged and open interaction would occur. Also included was the issue of nuclear disarmament. Tens of thousands of individuals supported the contactees who distributed newsletters, spoke at conferences and traveled widely spreading their information for peacefully transforming the planet, and calling for an immediate end to the development of nuclear weapons. Nuclear weapons threatened more than humanity's future according to the extraterrestrials. Every detonation disrupted the fabric of space-time that could also seriously affect their own worlds in destructive ways.

Directly confronted were the policies of major nations that were actively building nuclear weapons. Enormous revolutionary potential for the entire planet was put forward. Thus, contactees presented an urgent national security need for an extensive counter-intelligence program. Preventing the contactee movement from becoming a catalyst for global changes through the teachings and experiences gained from extraterrestrials became the highest priority. Consequently, a highly secret and ruthless counter-intelligence program was finally implemented that directly targeted contactees and their supporters.

A series of covert intelligence programs were implemented that aimed to neutralize the revolutionary potential of the contactee movement. These programs evolved in three stages that resulted in the final counter-intelligence program that was adopted to eliminate any threat posed by contactees.

- Stage one was the initial surveillance of contactees by intelligence agencies that attempted to discern the scope and implications of human and extraterrestrial interaction.

- Stage two was the more active phase of debunking and discrediting contactees and their supporters.
- Finally, stage three was integrated into the FBI's COINTELPRO which provided the necessary cover for comprehensively neutralizing any possible threat by contactees who might join other dissident groups for comprehensive policy changes.

All three stages of the covert programs employed against contactees were secretly run by the CIA, the Air Force Office of Special Investigations (AFOSI), the NSA and other U.S. intelligence agencies supporting these efforts. Field agents were briefed on the reality of extraterrestrial life, and the contact and communications occurring with private citizens. This chapter concentrates on the covert counter intelligence program adopted by U.S. national security agencies that targeted contactees ever since the 1950's. The goal was to nullify, discredit and debunk evidence confirming private citizen contact with extraterrestrial civilizations, and the revolutionary potential this had to transform the planet.

Phase One: Intelligence Agencies Monitor Contactees

There is extensive documentation to establish that the FBI closely monitored contactees, and were keenly interested in determining the scope of their activities resulting from communications and interactions with extraterrestrials.[426] Declassified FBI documents establish that prominent contactees were subjected to close monitoring where their statements and activities were investigated, and field agents directly issued reports to the FBI Director, J. Edgar Hoover. Field agent reports suggest that the FBI Director was seriously trying to understand the revolutionary potential posed by contactees and the threat to U.S. national security. This is not surprising given documentation that suggests the FBI was largely left out of the intelligence loop concerning extraterrestrial technologies. [427] Hoover was probably relying on surveillance of contactees to apprise himself of the true situation concerning extraterrestrials.

George Van Tassel claims that in August 1953, he had a physical meeting with human looking extraterrestrials from Venus. He subsequently established regular 'telepathic' communications with them where he was given information that he shared with his many supporters and public authorities. Popularity grew rapidly for Van Tassel who had many thousands that read his newsletters and attended his public lectures. Thousands also attended Van Tassel's annual Giant Rock Flying Saucer conventions in the Mojave Desert that began in 1954. Over a 23 year period his convention became the key annual event for the contactee movement.

FBI interest in Van Tassel dates from November 1953, just over a year after he sent a letter to the Air Technical Intelligence Center (ATIC) at Wright Patterson Air Force base on behalf of 'Commander Ashtar' to deliver a "friendly warning" concerning the destructive weapons then under development.[428] This led to a meeting between Major S. Avner of the Air Force Office of Special Investigations (AFOSI) who met with a liaison for the FBI, and culminated in Van Tassel being interviewed by the two Special Agents on November 16, 1954. The agents sent an extensive memo to J. Edgar Hoover detailing Van Tassel's claims to having been visited by extraterrestrials.[429] Revealed by the memo is Hoover's special interest in what the extraterrestrials had to say about the atomic weapons, an upcoming Third World War, and their ability to telepathically communicate with Van Tassel. Undisputedly, Van Tassel was closely monitored by the FBI as evidenced in a document dated April 12, 1965 which states: "Van Tassel has been known to the Los Angeles FBI Office since 1954.[430]

Another contactee who received much FBI attention was George Adamski. Adamski first became known in 1947 for his photos of flying saucers and motherships taken with an amateur telescope on Mount Palomar, California, that received wide coverage. He became the most well known of all contactees due to his internationally bestselling books describing his meetings with extraterrestrials. The first book, *Flying Saucers Have Landed* (1953), was based on his November 20, 1952 Desert Center encounter with 'Orthon" the Venusian occupant of an extraterrestrial scout craft. Orthon proceeded to tell Adamski about the dangers posed by nuclear weapons and the possibility that all life could be destroyed in an uncontrolled nuclear reaction. Four months later, in February 1953, Adamski claimed to have had another encounter. In chapter six I described how he was picked up by two extraterrestrials at a Los Angeles hotel lobby, and driven to a secret location where he again met Orthon and was taken inside a Venusian mothercraft.[431] Adamski's UFO sightings and contacts with extraterrestrials were supported by an impressive collection of witnesses, photographs and films that a number of independent investigators concluded were not hoaxes.[432]

Interest in Adamski by the FBI began in September 1950 when a confidential source began relaying information to the FBI's San Diego office. According to the source, Adamski explained that the social system used by the extraterrestrials most closely resembled communism. This "raised eyebrows within the FBI, and led to continued, deep monitoring."[433] Also according to the FBI source, Adamski claimed, "this country is a corrupt form of government and capitalists are enslaving the poor."[434] Predictably, such comments led to Adamski being viewed as a "security matter."[435] The source was never revealed by the FBI and so there was no way to evaluate the source's objectivity in relaying such prejudicial information. Adamski's claims that the extraterrestrials viewed the development of nuclear weapons as a threat of the future of humanity, was a cause of deep concern among officials. It was such views that led to the FBI considering him, along with George Van Tassel, as a subversive that required close monitoring according to an official 1952 document.[436]

A lecture by Adamski at a California Lions Club on March 12, 1953, was covered by a local newspaper that reported that Adamski had official FBI and Air Force clearance to present his material to the public. According to Adamski this newspaper report was 'incorrect', but led to a visit by FBI and Air Force representatives who were apparently concerned by references to official clearance.[437] The representatives demanded that Adamski sign a document that his material did not have official clearance. J. Edgar Hoover's office received the FBI and Air Force representatives' report, together with the signed document. Popularity and Adamski's international travel led to the FBI, and other intelligence agencies, paying close attention to his statements and public reactions. Adamski claimed to have been given private audiences with Pope John XXIII, Queen Juliana of the Netherlands and other VIP's.[438] In February

1959 Adamski traveled to New Zealand, and spoke before packed audiences. A one page Foreign Service Dispatch with Adamski's key talking points was circulated to the FBI, CIA, Air Force and Navy thus confirming continued monitoring of Adamski.

Other contactees who were monitored by the FBI according to declassified documents included Daniel Fry, George Hunt Williamson, and Truman Bethurum.[439] Information relayed by contactees concerning the social and economic systems of the extraterrestrials, together with the extraterrestrials' criticism of the nuclear weapons development occurring around the globe, led to them and their supporters being considered a security threat. Given U.S. national hysteria over communism during the McCarthy Era, this led to counter-intelligence programs being implemented against the contactees. Debunking and discrediting contactee claims were the most significant activities that occurred.

Phase Two: Debunking & Discrediting Contactees

An active role was played by the CIA in creating the necessary legal, political and social environment for the debunking of flying saucer reports and discrediting contactee claims. It did so by depicting flying saucer reports as a national security threat insofar as mass hysteria over them could be exploited by foreign enemies. Solid justification for such a psychological warfare program was built on the famous 1938 radio broadcast by Orson Welles. A renowned book on Wells' broadcast by Dr Hadley Cantril focused on the psychology of panic, and was later widely cited by national security experts in relation to public interest over flying saucer reports.[440] Consequently the CIA led covert psychological operations that would 'educate' the American public about the 'correct facts' concerning flying saucer reports and contactee claims. One of the first actions taken by the CIA was to initiate the creation of an inter-agency government group called the Psychological Strategy Board that would deal with national security threats through covert psychological operations.

A Presidential Directive on April 4, 1951, created the Psychological Strategy Board "to authorize and provide for the more effective planning, coordination, and conduct within the framework of approved national policies, of psychological operations."[441] Initially set up by Gordon Gray, a top advisor to President Truman at the time (and also later with President Eisenhower), the Psychological Strategy Board was an interagency organization that was initially located within the CIA, but reported to the National Security Council. Ostensibly the Psychological Strategy Board would lead covert psychological operations to deal with the Cold War threat.

The Cold War threat was a cover for its true function. In reality, the Psychological Strategy Board was created to deal with the national security threat posed by flying saucer reports and contactee claims that could undermine the authority of the U.S. government. Evidenced in leaked government documents, Gray is described as a founding member of the secret control group, allegedly titled Majestic-12 Special Studies Group (MJ-12), which took charge of the extraterrestrial issue.[442] According to one of the leaked Majestic Documents, President Truman created the Psychological Strategy Board after recommendation by the head of MJ-12.[443] Gray's leadership and the role of MJ-12 in its creation, helps confirm that the Psychological Strategy Board was created to run psychological operations to shape public opinion on the extraterrestrial issue.

Psychological Strategy Board success, together with its successor the Operations Coordinating Board, and all covert psychological operations concerning extraterrestrial life, was to only disclose the truth to those with a "need to know."[444] This required the creation of a suitable national security cover for psychological operations against the American public. Victory would be achieved by the formation of a panel of experts that could shape government policy and intelligence activities against those involved in extraterrestrial affairs. Consequently, the CIA secretly convened a public panel of 'impartial' experts to discuss the available physical evidence.

Named after its chairman, Dr Howard Robertson, the Robertson Panel reviewed cases of flying saucers over a four-day period for a total of 12 hours and found none of them to be credible. Conclusions by the Panel were released in a document called the Durant Report. It recommended ridiculing the 'flying saucer phenomenon' and the possibility of extraterrestrial life, for national security reasons. The

Report is key to understanding the institutionally sanctioned debunking and discrediting of evidence concerning extraterrestrial life. Confirmation of the leading role of the CIA in convening the panel and choosing experts appears in the Durant Report itself, despite efforts to suppress the CIA's role in early releases of sanitized versions. The CIA's Intelligence Advisory Committee had agreed that the "Director of Central Intelligence will ... [e]nlist the services of selected scientists to review and appraise the available evidence in the light of pertinent scientific theories..."[445]

Almost exclusively the Report focused on the national security threat posed by foreign powers exploiting the American public's belief in the flying saucer phenomenon. It declared: "Subjectivity of public to mass hysteria and greater vulnerability to possible enemy psychological warfare ... [and] if reporting channels are saturated with false and poorly documented reports, our capability of detecting hostile activity will be reduced."[446] Consequently, the Robertson panel recommended an 'educational program' to remove the threat posed by enemy nations exploiting the public's belief in flying saucers:

> The Panel's concept of a broad educational program integrating efforts of all concerned agencies was that it should have two major aims: training and "debunking." ...The "debunking" aim would result in reduction in public interest in "flying saucers" which today evokes a strong psychological reaction. This education could be accomplished by mass media such as television, motion pictures, and popular articles.... Such a program should tend to reduce the current gullibility of the public and consequently their susceptibility to clever hostile propaganda.[447]

In conclusion, a Panel convened by the CIA, with experts chosen by the CIA, reviewed a selection of flying saucer cases over a 12 hour period spread over four days, and concluded that the public's psychological reaction to flying saucers was the basis of a possible security threat.

The Cold War provided the necessary security environment for the CIA and interagency entities such as the Psychological Strategy

Board, to claim that flying saucers could be exploited by the Soviet Union using psychological warfare techniques. Consequently, psychological operations would have to be conducted through the mass media and official agencies to debunk flying saucer reports, and remove the possible threat. Irrespective of the truth of contactee's claims of having met with extraterrestrials, this meant the public's possible reaction to the reality of flying saucers and extraterrestrial life justified debunking all contactee reports. Debunking techniques that could be used to discredit contactees as reliable witnesses and make their claims appear ridiculous included: making fun of contactee claims, media exaggeration of reported events, dismissal of all physical evidence by critics, repeatedly citing prominent authority figures who stressed delusion and fraud, and emphasizing the lack of scientific interest in contactee reports.

The Durant Report created the necessary legal justification to debunk evidence provided by contactees regardless of the merits of their claims. This is evidenced by the way in which the FBI and other intelligence agencies privately interacted with contactees, and then made public statements or leaked information to the media in ways that questioned the integrity of contactees. For example, Adamski had communicated with the FBI, AFOSI and the Pentagon over the content of material he would put in his books, or documents he would present to the public. This is not surprising given that many contactees, like Adamski, were former military servicemen that understood the importance of not doing anything to threaten national security. Adamski was led to believe that he was cleared to distribute a particular document, and had made public statements to this effect. This led to the head of the FBI's public relations department, Louis B. Nichols, instructing Special Agent Willis to meet with Adamski concerning the particular document in question. A subsequent FBI report dated 16 December 1953, stated:

> Willis was told to have the San Diego agents, accompanied by representatives of OSI if they care to go along, call on Adamski and read the riot act in no uncertain terms pointing out he has used this document in a fraudulent, improper manner, that this

Bureau has not endorsed, approved, or cleared his speeches or book.[448]

The FBI made public its views about Adamski's alleged behavior in a way that delivered a "huge blow to Adamski's credibility."[449] At the time when the general public believed unquestionably in the accuracy of statements made by public officials, such negative comments would be sufficient to end one's career or credibility. Certainly, many in the general public interested in the flying saucer phenomenon now believed Adamski to be a fraud. This was especially so for those advocating a scientific investigation of flying saucers. What the public did not realize was that intelligence agencies such as the FBI and AFOSI were intent on debunking contactees as a matter of policy due to the threat they posed to national security. Thus contactees could be easily "set up" to believe something informally told to them by insiders, and then be publicly confronted by other officials claiming they had made fraudulent statements when they could not confirm what they had been told.

Another way in which contactee claims were debunked was to have tabloid newspapers such as the National Enquirer publish sensational reports that embellished actual contactee testimonies or were entirely fabricated by staff reporters. Any subsequent investigations by researchers would demonstrate that such claims were exaggerated or unfounded, thereby tainting the contactees and UFO research more generally. What was not generally known was that the National Enquirer was created and controlled by known CIA assets whose covert assignment was to ridicule the entire flying saucer phenomena. Gene Pope bought the New York Enquirer in 1952, and relaunched it as The National Enquirer in 1954. Pope was listed in his Who's Who biography as being a former CIA intelligence officer and being involved in "psychological warfare."[450] Chief instrument of the covert psychological operations used to debunk contactee claims and flying saucer reports was The National Enquirer with its sensationalistic tabloid style. The National Enquirer along with other media sources covering contactee claims were part of the education program that required the debunking of flying saucer reports. Predictably, the result of the sensationalist tabloid approach to contactee claims was that serious reporters and researchers would avoid stories covered by *The National Enquirer*.

As one of the chief instruments of the covert psychological warfare being conducted by the CIA and other intelligence agencies against contactees, the National Enquirer was a great success. It succeeded so well that influential UFO researchers determined to establish the scientific merit in investigating UFO reports, became unwitting allies to the covert psychological program to dismiss contactee claims. This is evidenced in remarks by leading UFO researchers such as Major Donald Keyhoe who emphasized the need to separate genuine UFO reports from "the mass of wild tales and usually ridiculous "contactee" claims."[451] Keyhoe along with other UFO researchers were greatly concerned about contactee claims that were being exaggerated by the press, "the press unfortunately lump all "spacemen" reports together causing many people to reject all of the UFO evidence."[452] Essentially, Keyhoe viewed contactee reports as an embarrassment that needed to be separated from the more scientifically oriented UFO research. Other prominent UFO researchers followed Keyhoe's approach thus creating a major schism among those convinced extraterrestrial life was visiting the earth. Successful debunking of reports of flying saucers and extraterrestrial life made it possible for the CIA, FBI and military intelligence agencies, to move to the third stage of their covert psychological operations. Next, we will learn about full scale counter-intelligence warfare techniques that were used to disrupt and neutralize the contactee movement.

Phase Three: Galactic COINTELPRO

COINTELPRO was a counter intelligence program initiated in 1956 against political dissidents that reportedly ended in 1971. It was primarily run by the FBI; other intelligence agencies such as the CIA and NSA assisted in select covert activities. COINTELPRO assumed that political dissidents in the U.S. were being influenced by foreign powers in ways deemed a threat to U.S. national security. It is worth reviewing the techniques used by COINTELPRO with regard to political dissidents to understand what occurred against contactees. In the case of both contactees and political dissidents, the influence of "foreign powers" was thought to justify military style counter-intelligence programs to disrupt and neutralize these groups. The "off world" nature of one of these 'foreign powers', extraterrestrials, did not appreciably change the nature of the counterintelligence methods used against both 'contactees' and political dissidents. In both cases, the activities of these groups were deemed to be threats to U.S. national security.

There were two significant differences in how COINTELPRO was respectively used against political dissidents and contactees. First, while intelligence agents were fully briefed about the 'foreign powers' influencing political dissidents, it is unlikely they were fully briefed in the case contactees. Second, while COINTELPRO against political dissidents was exposed and apparently ended in 1971, the COINTELPRO used against contactees was never exposed. It almost certainly continues to the present.

In 1975, a U.S. Senate committee chaired by Senator Frank Church investigated COINTELPRO's methods and targets, and published a detailed report in 1976.[453] The Church Committee described COINTELPRO as follows:

> COINTELPRO is the FBI acronym for a series of covert action programs directed against domestic groups. In these programs, the Bureau went beyond the collection of intelligence to secret action defined to "disrupt" and "neutralize" target groups and individuals. The techniques were adopted wholesale from wartime counterintelligence...[454]

Counterintelligence, as defined by the Church Committee, constitutes "those actions by an intelligence agency intended to protect its own security and to undermine hostile intelligence operations." [455] The Committee described how "certain techniques the Bureau had used against hostile foreign agents were adopted for use against perceived domestic threats to the established political and social order."[456] The Committee described COINTELPRO as a series of covert actions taken against American citizens, and was part of a "rough, tough, dirty business" according to William Sullivan, assistant to the FBI Director.[457]

The Committee learned that: "Groups and individuals have been harassed and disrupted because of their political views and their lifestyle..."[458]

The Committee found that COINTELPRO had "been directed against proponents of racial causes and women's rights, outspoken apostles of nonviolence and racial harmony; establishment politicians; religious groups; and advocates of new life styles."[459] Between the years 1960-1974, over 500,000 investigations had been launched of potential subversives of the U.S. government, but no charges were ever laid under statutes concerning overthrow of the U.S. government.[460] The Committee grouped the activities conducted by COINTELPRO under the following headings: (a). General Efforts to Discredit; (b) Media Manipulation; (c) Distorting Data to Influence Government Policy and Public Perceptions; (d) "Chilling" First Amendment Rights; and (e) Preventing the Free Exchange of Ideas.[461] The Committee found that: "Officials of the intelligence agencies occasionally recognized that certain activities were illegal, ... [and] that the law, and the Constitution were simply ignored."[462] More disturbingly, the Church Committee concluded that: "Unsavory and vicious tactics have been employed."[463]

The Church Committee did not discuss COINTELPRO in regard to the UFO issue or contactee claims. Despite that omission, circumstantial evidence clearly points to COINTELPRO being used against contactees, and was the final stage of well orchestrated counter-intelligence program to "disrupt" and "neutralize" the contactee movement. As shown earlier in the cases of Van Tassel and Adamski, contactee claims dealing with a range of socio-economic and military policies from the perspective of extraterrestrial life, were viewed as subversive and a direct threat to U.S. national security.

The full nature of the threat posed by the reality of extraterrestrial life and technologies was vividly evidenced in the 1961 Brookings Institute Report commissioned by NASA on behalf of the U.S. Congress. Titled, "Proposed Studies on the Implications of Peaceful Space Activities for Human Affairs," the Brookings Report discussed the societal impact of extraterrestrial life or 'artifacts' being found on nearby planetary bodies. The Report described the unpredictability of societal reactions to such a discovery:

Evidences of its [extraterrestrial] existence might also be found in artifacts left on the moon or other planets. The consequences for attitudes and values are unpredictable, but would vary profoundly in different cultures and between groups within complex societies; a crucial factor would be the nature of the communication between us and the other beings.[464]

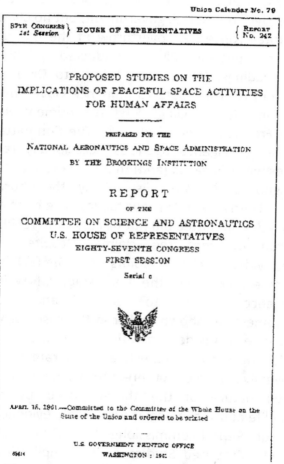

Union Calendar No. 79

| 87TH CONGRESS 1st Session | HOUSE OF REPRESENTATIVES | REPORT No. 242 |

PROPOSED STUDIES ON THE
IMPLICATIONS OF PEACEFUL SPACE ACTIVITIES
FOR HUMAN AFFAIRS

PREPARED FOR THE
NATIONAL AERONAUTICS AND SPACE ADMINISTRATION
BY THE BROOKINGS INSTITUTION

REPORT
OF THE
COMMITTEE ON SCIENCE AND ASTRONAUTICS
U.S. HOUSE OF REPRESENTATIVES
EIGHTY-SEVENTH CONGRESS
FIRST SESSION

Serial c

APRIL 15, 1961.—Committed to the Committee of the Whole House on the State of the Union and ordered to be printed

U.S. GOVERNMENT PRINTING OFFICE
WASHINGTON : 1961

Figure 18. Cover Page. Brookings Report

Devastating societal effects, according to the Report, could result from contact with more technologically advanced off world societies:

Anthropological files contain many examples of societies, sure of their place in the universe, which have disintegrated when they had to associate with previously unfamiliar societies espousing different ideas and different life ways; others that survived such an experience usually did so by paying the price of changes in values and attitudes and behavior.[465]

The Brookings Report went on to raise the possibility of suppressing any announcement of extraterrestrial life or artifacts for national security reasons: "How might such information, under what circumstances, be presented or withheld from the public?"[466] Consequently, it is clear that official fear over societal responses to any official announcement of extraterrestrial life was a paramount national security concern. A powerful justification for the use of COINTELPRO against contactees had been found.

One of the most important tactics used by COINTELPRO was to disrupt dissident groups by creating divisions and suspicion among their supporters. In the 'Galactic' version of COINTELPRO, disruption occurred by dividing those who accepted evidence confirming the reality of UFO's and extraterrestrial life. A division between exponents of a purely scientific approach to UFO data and those supporting the testimonies of contactees was cleverly exploited by COINTELPRO operatives. Victory would be achieved by convincing more technically oriented supporters of a purely scientific approach that the contactee movement would discredit "serious" researchers. To help convince supporters of a scientific approach that their efforts would eventually bear fruit, an official Air Force investigation was launched in 1952. Project Blue Book was little more than a public relations exercise by the U.S. Air Force to convince the general public and UFO researchers that it was taking UFO reports seriously. In reality, Project Blue Book provided minimal resources for a serious UFO investigation and primarily acted as a vehicle for defusing public interest in UFO reports.[467]

One of Project Blue Book's primary functions was to carry out the first plank of the "education program" recommended by the Durant Report. It would "train" the general public how to correctly evaluate the UFO data in ways that would defuse public and media interest in such reports. In short, Project Blue was a key part of the covert psychological operations being conducted to convince the general public and media that UFO reports were not important, and not worth considering. Nevertheless, the status of Project Blue Book as an official Air Force investigation encouraged UFO researchers that rigorous sufficient methods and research would eventually bear fruit. Such hopes were dashed in 1969 by the Condon Committee's final report which publicly put an end to the Air Force investigation and Project Blue Book.

Another primary function of Project Blue Book was to neutralize the contactee movement by depicting personal testimonies of contact with extraterrestrials as unscientific. By providing a highly visible public investigation, Project Blue Book gave the necessary 'training' for scientific research that would systematically exclude contactee reports. UFO researchers would be encouraged to attack contactee reports as unscientific, prone to delusion or fraud, and an insult to 'serious' UFO research. Statements by leading UFO researchers such as Dr Allen Hynek, a former consultant to Project Blue Book, provide evidence that such a process occurred.

In a book purporting to provide the scientific foundations of UFO research, Dr J. Allen Hynek dismissed testimonies of contactees who he regarded as "pseudoreligious fanatics" with "low credibility value:"

> I must emphasize that contact reports are *not* classed as Close Encounters of the Third Kind. It is unfortunate, to say the least, that reports such as these have brought down upon the entire UFO problem the opprobrium and ridicule of scientists and public alike, keeping alive the popular image of "little green men" and the fictional atmosphere surrounding that aspect of the subject.[468]

As Hynek's statement makes clear, UFO researchers attacked contactee reports with great vigor to defuse what they considered to be a major challenge to serious public consideration of UFO reports. By encouraging UFO researchers that a purely scientific method would result in the truth about UFOs and extraterrestrial life eventually coming out, Galactic COINTELPRO succeeded in creating a major schism among those accepting the reality of UFOs and extraterrestrial life. By the end of the 1960's, the contactee movement had been so thoroughly debunked and discredited by UFO researchers, that COINTELPRO no longer needed to have Project Blue Book continue. UFO researchers had become an unwitting accomplice of intelligence agencies secretly conducting the various covert psychological programs that made up Galactic COINTELPRO.

Galactic COINTELPRO also had a more sinister side in terms of "unsavory and vicious tactics" that were employed contactees that reflected methods used against political dissidents.[469] The mysterious Men In Black (MIB) phenomenon has been described by various researchers who discovered that individuals with extraterrestrial related experiences were often threatened and harassed by well dressed men in dark business suits who gave the appearance of being public officials. Evidence that elite intelligence groups were tasked to intimidate, harasses and even "neutralize" contactees or others with direct experience with extraterrestrials or their technology appears in a leaked document that a number of veteran UFO researchers consider to be legitimate.[470] The Special Operations Manual states:

> If at all possible, witnesses will be held incommunicado until the extent of their knowledge and involvement can be determined. Witnesses will be discouraged from talking about what they have seen, and intimidation may be necessary to ensure their cooperation.[471]

Investigations were also conducted by the US Air Force that was concerned by reports that MIB impersonated Air Force officials. A March 1, 1967 memo prepared by the Assistant Vice Chief of Staff described incidents where civilians had been contacted by individuals claiming to be members of NORAD and demanded evidence possessed by witnesses.[472]

The shadowy operations of the MIB and the SOM1-01 document suggests that they were part of an "enforcement" division of the counter-intelligence effort that comprised the FBI, the Air Force's OSI, the Office of Naval Intelligence and even the CIA. It's very possible that MIB were associated with more secretive intelligence agencies such as the National Security Agency (NSA) and National Reconnaissance Office (NRO) where selected agents had higher security clearances for dealing with evidence of extraterrestrial life.[473]

Consequently, a pecking order existed among the intelligence agencies involved in Galactic COINTELPRO where each conducted specific functions. Agents drawn from the FBI, the Air Force OSI (and other military intelligence units including the Navy's ONI) were primarily involved in intelligence gathering, and closely monitoring the activities of contactees as evidenced in FOIA documents. The CIA was involved in coordinating debunking and discrediting efforts against contactees through a public education program outlined in the Durant Report. The NSA and NRO were involved in tracking communications and interactions with extraterrestrial life, and provided enforcement teams to withdraw evidence and intimidate contactees into silence. Galactic COINTELPRO could therefore minimize the amount of extraterrestrial related information held by different sections in each intelligence agency where agents were instructed to perform specific functions. Most out of the loop concerning the reality of extraterrestrial life and the merit of contactee claims was the FBI. On the other hand, the NSA and NRO appeared to be most in the loop due to their monitoring of extraterrestrial activities through electronic communication and satellite imagery. Military intelligence agencies appeared to fill intermediate functions where they supported Galactic COINTELPRO without being given access to all information concerning extraterrestrial life and projects. This is evidenced in Vice Admiral Tom Wilson, the head of Intelligence for the Joint Chiefs of Staff (J-2) in 1998 who reportedly was out of the loop on extraterrestrial related projects.[474]

CONCLUSION

Galactic COINTELPRO against contactees aimed to minimize the threat posed by human looking extraterrestrials to the policies adopted by secretly appointed committees with regard to extraterrestrial life and technologies. Primarily the threat from the extraterrestrials was that they would succeed in having contactees convince large portions of the American and global public for comprehensive policy changes to prepare humanity for status as a galactic society. Such policy changes were considered a direct security threat by policy makers in the U.S. and in other countries who were briefed about the reality of extraterrestrial life. Galactic COINTELPRO involved three interrelated phases that culminated in a comprehensive counter-intelligence program to neutralize and disrupt the threat posed by the contactee movement.

First was a surveillance program orchestrated by the FBI which closely monitored the contactee's public lectures, interactions and communications. Documents released through FOIA have confirmed that the FBI conducted extensive monitoring of prominent contactees, and worked with other intelligence agencies such as the Air Force OSI.

The second phase of Galactic COINTELPRO was a debunking and discrediting program secretly run by the CIA that convened the Robertson Panel which issued the Durant Report in 1953. Its most important finding for the counter-intelligence program was to justify an education program comprising 'training' the public and 'debunking' witness testimonies, including contactees, on the basis of the national security threat posed by the public's belief in UFOs being exploited by foreign enemies. Irrespective of the merit of contactee claims, this meant that evidence and statements would be debunked and discredited on national security grounds. Intelligence professionals in the unenviable position of debunking and discrediting people who they may have privately concluded were genuinely describing actual events that had occurred to them. FBI documents establish that FBI agents and sources played an active role in discrediting prominent contactees as part of the CIA's psychological warfare program against contactees.

Galactic COINTELPRO's final stage was to create a schism between those accepting evidence of extraterrestrial life. A group of

UFO researchers advocating a scientific methodology were encouraged to disassociate themselves from contactee claims that were regarded as unscientific, and unlikely to lead to public support by academics, bureaucrats and congressional representatives. Project Blue Book was created to encourage UFO researchers to hold on to the misguided belief that a strict scientific methodology would be sufficient to overturn government policy on covering up the reality of extraterrestrial life. UFO researchers therefore led the charge against contactee claims being seriously considered. Aided by the Project Blue Book investigation, the public was trained in what categories of UFO evidence ought to be considered legitimate. None of these categories included contactee claims.

Galactic COINTELPRO could not have succeeded without the unwitting assistance of veteran UFO researchers who were all too eager to dismiss contactee claims as unscientific and prone to delusion or fraud. Such researchers failed miserably to anticipate the Galactic COINTELPRO that had been implemented to disrupt and neutralize contactee testimonies, and readily accepted official statements questioning the integrity of contactee claims. Indeed, the eagerness with which UFO researchers established themselves as the gatekeepers of serious scientific research into UFOs, and debunked contactee claims marks the most tragic aspect of nearly seven decades of research into UFOs and extraterrestrial life.

Another key factor in the success of Galactic COINTELPRO to the present has been the compartmentalization of extraterrestrial related information. This made it possible for intelligence agencies to perform specific functions within Galactic COINTELPRO without agents being informed of the truth of contactee claims. The success of debunking and discrediting contactees would have to depend on intelligence agents believing contactees were a genuine security threat. Consequently, extraterrestrial related information was made available on a strict need to know basis ensuring that only a selected group of individuals within different intelligence agencies were briefed at all.

A summary table can be compiled for key intelligence agencies, their respective activities in Galactic COINTELPRO, and their level of access to extraterrestrial related information.

Table 6. U.S. Intelligence Agencies & Galactic COINTELPRO

Agency	Activities	Access to Extraterrestrial Related Information
Federal Bureau of Investigations	Intelligence gathering, withdrawing evidence, and discrediting contactees by local field agents.	*None.* FBI Director Hoover was denied access and did not have capacities for monitoring extraterrestrial activities.
Air Force Office of Special Investigations (with cooperation of other military intelligence units, e.g., Office of Naval Intelligence)	Intelligence gathering, withdrawing evidence, discrediting contactees, through Project Blue Book. Create schisms among UFO/ET researchers	*Partial.* Military Intelligence monitors extraterrestrial activities, possible contacts with civilians, and pass these on to other agencies.
Central Intelligence Agency	Leads a public education program through training the public and debunking contactee reports. Create schisms among UFO/ET researchers	*Partial.* Coordinates an interagency effort to ensure extraterrestrial related information is not made public.
National Security Agency and National Reconnaissance Organization	Provides enforcement teams to withdraw evidence and intimidate contactees into silence.	*Full.* Monitors extraterrestrial life and its interactions with private citizens and governments.
Psychological Strategy Board/ Operations Coordinating Board (successor agency coordinates with control group for ET affairs, MJ-12)	Coordinates interagency efforts in covert psychological programs to deceive public about extraterrestrial life.	*Full.* Has access to full range of information provided by intelligence agencies in order to develop a strategic response to extraterrestrial activities.

In conclusion, many pioneering men and women who may have accurately related their physical contact with extraterrestrials had their reputations and careers systematically undermined by public officials, the mass media and UFO researchers. It appears that such an outcome was intended as part of an official Galactic COINTELPRO that continues to the present day. In contrast to the termination of the FBI's COINTELPRO against political dissidents in 1971; it is very likely that individuals in public office, the mass media and among the UFO research community may be active agents of an ongoing COINTELPRO against contactees. It is hoped that exposure of Galactic COINTELPRO will help dispel the reflexive dismissal of contactee testimonies that has up to the present hindered an objective evaluation of direct physical contact between private citizens and extraterrestrial life.

ENDNOTES – CHAPTER 7

[423] See chapter five. For an earlier version, see Michael Salla, "Extraterrestrials Among Us," *Exopolitics Journal* 1:4 (2006) 284 -300. Available online at: http://exopoliticsjournal.com/Journal-vol-1-4.htm

[424] See Michael Salla, *Exposing U.S. Government Policies on Extraterrestrial Life* (Exopolitics Institute, 2009) 87-127. For an earlier version is available online at: See Michael Salla, "The Black Budget Report: An Investigation into the CIA's 'Black Budget' and the Second Manhattan Project," *Scoop Independent News* (30 January 2004): http://www.scoop.co.nz/stories/HL0401/S00151.htm

[425] See chapter six.

[426] See Nick Redfern, *On the Trail of the Saucer Spies* (Anomalist Books, 2006).

[427] See FBI (FOIA) document released on 06/09/1986 concerning J. Edgar Hoover claim that the FBI was being denied access to recovered Flying Discs, available online at: http://www.cufon.org/cufon/foia_001.htm

[428] See Redfern, *On the Trail of the Saucer Spies*, 24.

[429] Redfern, *On the Trail of the Saucer Spies*, 25.

[430] Available in Redfern, *On the Trail of the Saucer Spies*, 23.

[431] See also George Adamski, *Inside the Spaceships* (Abelard-Schuman, 1955).

[432] An impartial assessment of the Adamski case is provided by Lou Zinsstag and Timothy Good in *George Adamski- The Untold Story* (Ceti Publications, 1983).

[433] Redfern, *On the Trail of the Saucer Spies*, 35.

[434] Cited in Redfern, *On the Trail of the Saucer Spies*, 36.

[435] Cited in Redfern, *On the Trail of the Saucer Spies*, 36.

[436] See Redfern, *On the Trail of the Saucer Spies*, 33.

[437] The incident is described in Timothy Good, Alien Base: The Evidence for Extraterrestrial Colonization of Earth (Avon Books, 1998) 112.

[438] See Timothy Good, *Alien Base*, 135-40.

[439] See Redfern, *On the Trail of the Saucer Spies*, 39.

[440] Hadley Cantril, *The invasion from Mars; a study in the psychology of panic* (Princeton University Press, 1940).

[441] See SourceWatch, "Psychological Strategy Board," http://www.sourcewatch.org/index.php?title=Psychological_Strategy_Board

[442] See: Stanton Friedman, *TOP Secret/MAJIC: Operation Majestic-12 and the United States Government's UFO Cover Up* (Marlowe and Co., 2005) 50,55.

[443] See "Majestic Twelve Project, 1st Annual Report," Robert and Ryan Woods, eds., *Majestic Documents* (Wood and Wood Enterprises, 1998) 114. (p. 10). Also available online at: http://majesticdocuments.com/documents/1948-1959.php

[444] For discussion of how "need to know" was applied to extraterrestrial related information, see Timothy Good, *Need to Know: UFOs, the Military, and Intelligence* (Pegasus Books, 2007).

[445] "Report of the Meetings of Scientific Advisory Panel on Unidentified Flying Objects Convened by Office of Scientific Intelligence, CIA, Jan 14-18, 1953"

(Released November 16, 1978) 1. Available online at:
http://www.cufon.org/cufon/robert.htm

[446] "Report of the Meetings of Scientific Advisory Panel on Unidentified Flying Objects," 15.

[447] "Report of the Meetings of Scientific Advisory Panel on Unidentified Flying Objects," 19-20.

[448] Cited in Redfern, *On the Trail of the Saucer Spies,* 39.

[449] Redfern, *On the Trail of the Saucer Spies,* 38-39.

[450] For discussion of Pope and the CIA connection to the National Enquirer, see Terry Hansen, *The Missing Times* (Xlibris Corporation, 2001) 231-46.

[451] Donald Keyhoe, *Aliens from Space* (Signet, 1973) 198.

[452] Keyhoe, *Aliens from Space*, 198.

[453] United States Senate, *Final Report of the Select Committee to study Governmental Operations with respect to Intelligence Activities together with additional, supplemental, and separate views*, April 26 (Legislative Day, April 14), 1976. Available online at: http://archive.org/details/finalreportofsel06unit

[454] United States Senate, *Final Report of the Select Committee to study Governmental Operations with respect to Intelligence Activities*, Book III., sec. I.

[455] United States Senate, *Final Report of the Select Committee to study Governmental Operations with respect to Intelligence Activities*, Book III., sec. I.

[456] United States Senate, *Final Report of the Select Committee to study Governmental Operations with respect to Intelligence Activities*, Book III., sec. I.

[457] United States Senate, *Final Report of the Select Committee to study Governmental Operations with respect to Intelligence Activities*, Book III., sec. D.1.

[458] United States Senate, *Final Report of the Select Committee to study Governmental Operations with respect to Intelligence Activities*, Book II, Section 1.C.

[459] United States Senate, *Final Report of the Select Committee to study Governmental Operations with respect to Intelligence Activities*, Book II, Section 1.C.2.

[460] United States Senate, *Final Report of the Select Committee to study Governmental Operations with respect to Intelligence Activities*, Book II, Section 1.C.6.

[461] United States Senate, *Final Report of the Select Committee to study Governmental Operations with respect to Intelligence Activities*, Book II, Section 1.C.6.

[462] United States Senate, *Final Report of the Select Committee to study Governmental Operations with respect to Intelligence Activities*, Book II, Section 1.C.4.

[463] United States Senate, *Final Report of the Select Committee to study Governmental Operations with respect to Intelligence Activities*, Book II, Section 1.C.

[464] Brookings Report, 215. For an overview of the Brookings Report, go to: http://www.enterprisemission.com/brooking.html

[465] Brookings Report, 215.

[466] Brookings Report, 215.

[467] For description of the lack of resources and inadequate Air Force support for Project Blue Book, see Edward Ruppelt, *The Report on Unidentified Flying Objects* (Doubleday, 1956).

[468] Allen Hynek, *The UFO Experience: A Scientific Inquiry* (Henry Regnery, 1972) 30.

[469] United States Senate, *Final Report of the Select Committee to study Governmental*

Operations with respect to Intelligence Activities, Book II, Section 1.C.
[470] See Ryan Wood, Majic Eyes Only: Earth's Encounters with Extraterrestrial Technology (Wood Enterprises, 2005) 264-67; & Stanton Friedman, *TOP Secret/MAJIC,* 161-84.
[471] "SOM1-01: Majestic-12 Group Special Operations Manual," *The Majestic Documents,* eds. Robert Wood & Ryan Wood (Wood & Wood Enterprises, 1988) [ch. 3.12b.] 165
[472] Redfern, *On the Trail of the Saucer Spies,* 57.
[473] See Daniel M. Salter, *Life with a Cosmos Clearance* (Light Technology, 2003)15-16, 122-23; & Dan Sherman, Above Black: Project Preserve Destiny – Insider Account of Alien Contact and Government Cover Up (OneTeam Publishing, 1998).
[474] See Steven Greer, *Hidden Truth Forbidden Knowledge* (Crossing Point, Inc., 2006) 158-59.

Introduction to Chapters 8 - 13: Citizen Diplomacy Initiatives

I have so far introduced a significant amount of material revealing extensive First Contact meetings, information and experiences involving extraterrestrials. These have ranged from officially sanctioned meetings resulting in negotiated agreements and experiences by private citizens from around the world. I have also revealed some of the evidence that extraterrestrials have integrated themselves into human society, and how this has been monitored by various government agencies. Finally, I have showed how government agencies have been involved in repressing private citizens with information and experiences involving extraterrestrial life.

As can be easily imagined, many of the policies adopted by the U.S. and other countries on the issue of extraterrestrial life have not had private support or input. Many feel, quite rightly, that the vital interests of individuals, nations and the biosphere have been grossly ignored. Consequently, there have been many attempts by private citizens to address the host of issues raised by government policies on extraterrestrial life. What follows in chapters 8-13, is six citizen diplomacy initiatives that I have been personally involved with to varying capacities. These initiatives have resulted in documents that have been circulated, discussed and endorsed by many other private citizens. These documents are valuable insofar as they reveal some of the sentiments of private citizens concerning extraterrestrial life, their thoughts about government policies and what private citizens need to do in response. Most importantly, the documents identify the vital interests of humanity and the biosphere when it comes to extraterrestrial contact.

I include the documents that were adopted or supported at various conferences or online events where these citizen diplomacy initiatives were first presented. I begin each document with an introduction giving background on the initiative and some of my analysis. The six initiatives discussed in the next six chapters, make up second track galactic diplomacy conducted by private citizens. The documents and processes involved in each initiative are helpful insofar as they reveal the evolution of the thoughts and efforts of private citizens contemplating how best to conduct galactic diplomacy. The documents provide important insights into the vital interests of individuals, communities and the biosphere; that need to be included in *principled negotiations* with extraterrestrial civilizations. It would be wise for any individual contemplating citizen diplomacy initiatives with extraterrestrials to seriously consider these documents in part or whole in reaching any agreements.

CHAPTER 8

Hawaii Declaration on Peaceful Relations with Extraterrestrial Civilizations

Introduction

Speakers and participants at the June 9-11, 2006 conference on Extraterrestrial Civilizations and World Peace (Kona, Hawaii) agreed by consensus on the Hawaii Declaration on Peaceful Relations with Extraterrestrial Civilizations. The Declaration affirmed "the intent of humanity to join in peaceful and cooperative relations with extraterrestrial civilizations." Successive versions of the Declaration had been circulated to all conference speakers and participants for formal discussion. The conference organizers and advisors developed a process for facilitating group consensus over the Declaration.

Figure 19. 2006 ET Conference Banner

A pre-conference draft had been electronically circulated to all speakers for feedback in order to develop a document for physical circulation at the conference. At the opening of the conference on Friday June 9, 2006, a draft was circulated to all participants where they could comment on each principle in written form. Participant feedback was summarized and helped guide speakers at a subsequent luncheon on the second day (Saturday) to discuss the items which had strongest support from conference participants. Speakers present at the luncheon agreed by consensus on the revisions to the Declaration based on participant feedback and speaker comments.

Conference participants were then invited to attend a special session on Saturday afternoon where they could hear the results of the participant feedback process and what was discussed at the Speaker luncheon. Based on further participant comments and suggested revisions, speakers met again on Sunday mid-morning to discuss participant suggests. This led to further revisions of the document and the development of a penultimate draft for the final speaker panel of the conference. During the final panel session, the audience proposed a number of further revisions and after more debate, the proposed revisions were adopted by the speakers. The final version of the Hawaii Declaration on Peaceful Relations with Extraterrestrial Civilizations was formally adopted by consensus.

This was a unique moment in the recent history of human awareness of extraterrestrial life. For the first time consensus had been achieved on how to establish peaceful relations with extraterrestrial civilizations. The consensus process had been chaired by Dr Michael Salla with assistance by Hugh Matlock. Advisors included Angelika Whitecliff, Paola Harris, Dr Tom Hansen and Alfred Webre, J.D. What follows is the Declaration adopted by consensus at the 2006 Conference and subsequently circulated on the internet. To date it has been translated into seven languages.[475]

Hawaii Declaration on Peaceful Relations with Extraterrestrial Civilizations

We, the individuals and institutions participating in and/or supporting the Extraterrestrial Civilizations & World Peace Conference in Kailua-Kona, Hawaii, June 9-11, 2006,

Are a body of concerned private citizens who are promoting world peace and harmonious relations with extraterrestrial civilizations,

Recognizing the overwhelming evidence pointing to the presence of extraterrestrial civilizations, and their generally peaceful interaction with individuals and governmental authorities,

Inspired by the profound significance for humanity of sharing the wisdom, knowledge, culture and technology provided by extraterrestrial civilizations,

Asserting that extraterrestrial civilizations have been observing human evolution for some time with particular interest in humanity's quest for lasting peace among its peoples,

Noting that extraterrestrial civilizations have indicated that the abolishment of nuclear weapons worldwide is a necessary milestone toward peaceful coexistence on earth and as a prerequisite for open contact,

Recalling United Nations resolutions concerning international co-operation in the peaceful exploration and use of outer space, banning atmospheric and underwater nuclear tests, and proscribing hostile acts on the moon and other celestial bodies,

Recognizing a range of initiatives promoted by private citizens and citizen organizations with regard to extraterrestrial civilizations visiting Earth,

Intending for this Declaration to be used as a starting point for a greater public dialogue with those holding similar or diverging perspectives and interests concerning extraterrestrial visitation,

Using a consensual decision making process among speakers, organizers, and participants at the Extraterrestrial Civilizations and World Peace Conference, 2006, we have agreed to, Honor the following principles for establishing peaceful relations with extraterrestrial civilizations:

1. We affirm the intent of humanity to join in peaceful and cooperative relations with extraterrestrial civilizations,

2. Affirm support for United Nations resolutions promoting the peaceful use of Outer Space, and support for UN, International and U.S. Congressional initiatives to prevent an arms race in outer space, including the weaponization of space,

3. Affirm the natural right of all citizens to have open contact with representatives of extraterrestrial civilizations in all cases, and to engage in non-official diplomacy,

4. Declare the need for Civil Society to develop acceptable protocols (standards of behavior) with extraterrestrial civilizations, that the protocols should be representative of the

aspirations of all humanity, and that all nations should work in concert to establish peaceful relations,

5. Cooperate with extraterrestrial civilizations in promoting Earth, Cosmic and Life friendly technologies, and encouraging the right use and open availability of these technologies,

6. Affirm our desire to coordinate the earth's ecological health and biological diversity with extraterrestrial civilizations that can aid us in that endeavor,

7. And express our desire to welcome the open appearance of benevolent extraterrestrial civilizations.

***

Expressions of Support - Conference Organizers and Speakers
Michael E. Salla, PhD (Convenor/Speaker); Angelika Whitecliff (Co-Organizer); Hon Paul Hellyer (Speaker); Thomas Hansen, PhD (Speaker); Joan Ocean, M.Sc. (Speaker); Paola Harris, M.Ed. (Speaker); Alfred Webre, J.D. (Speaker); James Gilliland (Speaker); Robert Salas, (Capt USAF, ret.- speaker); Mary Rodwell, R.N. (Speaker); Neil Freer (Speaker); Scott Jones, PhD (Speaker); Philip Corso, Jr (Speaker); Darryl Anka (Speaker); Wendelle Stevens (Lt Col. USAF ret. - Speaker);
"A New World if you can take it" (Lt Col Philip Corso)
Official Conference website:
http://etworldpeace.earthtransformation.com/
Declaration Online Petition:
http://www.petitiononline.com/ETPeace/petition.html
Conference Sponsor is the Exopolitics Institute:
www.exopoliticsinstitute.org
Kailua-Kona, Hawaii, June 11, 2006
Copyright © 2006 Exopolitics Institute

ENDNOTES – CHAPTER 8

[475] Petition is available for viewing at:
http://www.petitiononline.com/ETPeace/petition.html

CHAPTER 9
Earth Transformation Declaration

Introduction

Speakers and Participants at the May 11-13, 2007 conference on Earth Transformation: New Science and Technologies, Dolphins Consciousness and Exopolitics (Kona, Hawaii) agreed by consensus on the *Earth Transformation Declaration*. The conference was held on Hawaii 's Big Island and featured 14 international experts who approved by consensus a Declaration for launching an "Earth Transformation movement". The "Earth Transformation Declaration" comprises principles "intending to transform the Earth in a sustainable, peaceful and life affirming manner by adopting a range of environmental, scientific, spiritual and political principles and practices."

Figure 20. 2007 ET Conference Banner

A pre-conference draft had been electronically circulated to all speakers for feedback in order to develop a document for physical circulation at the conference. At the opening of the conference on Friday May 11, 2007, a draft was circulated to all participants where they could comment on each principle in written form. Participant feedback was summarized and helped guide speakers at a subsequent luncheon on the second day (Saturday) to discuss the items which had strongest support from conference participants. Speakers present at the luncheon agreed by consensus on the revisions to the Declaration based on participant feedback and speaker comments.

Conference participants were then invited to attend a special session on Saturday afternoon where they could hear the results of the participant feedback process and what was discussed at the Speaker luncheon. Based on further participant comments and suggested revisions a final version was developed. During the concluding panel session, the final version of the Hawaii Declaration on Peaceful Relations with Extraterrestrial Civilizations was formally adopted by consensus.

Following upon the success of the 2006 Hawaii Conference on Extraterrestrial Civilizations and World Peace, this was the second time consensus had been achieved on major issues concerning the development of societal relations with extraterrestrial civilizations. The consensus process was again chaired by Dr Michael Salla with assistance by the conference rapporteur, Hugh Matlock. What follows is the Declaration adopted by consensus at the 2007 Conference and subsequently circulated on the internet. [476]

Earth Transformation Declaration

We, the individuals and groups participating in or supporting the Earth Transformation Movement are a body of concerned private citizens intending to transform the Earth in a sustainable, peaceful and life affirming manner by adopting a range of environmental, scientific, spiritual and political principles and practices.

Celebrating the global spiritual awakening that is promoting health, acceptance and harmony,

Recognizing new scientific principles and the existence of new energy technologies,

Acknowledging the evidence that extraterrestrial life is observing, visiting and residing on Earth,

Noting the evidence that cetaceans possess high intelligence and communication skills,

Resolving to protect the biosphere and ensure a sustainable future,

Recalling the citizen inspired Earth Charter from 1992 promoting a "sustainable global society founded on respect for nature, universal human rights, economic justice, and a culture of peace,"

Recalling the proposed Energy Innovation Act of 2007 seeking to establish a Joint Congressional Office of Energy Innovation with a focus on "promoting and jumpstarting new and unconventional approaches to energy generation,"

Recalling the 2006 Hawaii Declaration for Peaceful Relations With Extraterrestrial Civilizations "promoting world peace and harmonious relations with extraterrestrial civilizations,"

Mindful of Hawaiian indigenous tradition and its unique spirit of Aloha,

And using a consensual decision making process among speakers, organizers, and participants at the Earth Transformation Conference in Kailua-Kona, Hawaii, May 11-13, 2007, we have agreed to:

Personal Transformation and Wellness

1. Recognize that transformation begins with the wholeness created by right relationships with oneself, that extends to other persons, other cultures, other life, our planet, and the larger whole of which all are a part.

2. Affirm faith in the inherent dignity of all people and celebrate diversity.

3. Take personal responsibility for our own transformation to whole, heart-centered, healthy human beings, fully expressing all our inherent potential.

4. Develop awareness of our interconnectedness and interdependence, embracing physical wellness and spiritual development as a means of experiencing Higher Intelligence in its various manifestations.

New Energy and Economic Transformation

5. Affirm the potential of new energy technologies to provide solutions to urgent global environmental and resource depletion issues.

6. Encourage private and public support for development, commercialization, deployment assistance and widespread adoption of these cleaner sources of energy.

7. Promote the fair and equitable distribution of new energy generation technology within nations and among nations.

8. Ensure new energy technologies provide for a transformation from a resource limited economy to a global abundance economy.

Governance and Exopolitics

9. Affirm the political sovereignty and self determination of humanity in relation to extraterrestrial civilizations, and that all sentient beings have the right to life, liberty, and the pursuit of happiness.

10. Ensure transparency and accountability in governance, inclusive participation in decision making, respect for human rights, public oversight of all government funded projects involving extraterrestrial life and technology.

11. Demand the immediate release of all evidence possessed by governments and their contractors confirming the presence of extraterrestrial life; an accounting of all agreements reached with or concerning extraterrestrial life; the establishment of truth commissions to reveal government funded actions taken concerning extraterrestrial life; and restorative justice for any injured parties.

12. Affirm the natural right of all citizens to have safe and open contact with extraterrestrial visitors, and to engage in non-official diplomacy; and affirm the heartfelt intent of humanity to live in peaceful and cooperative relationship with extraterrestrial civilizations.

Cetacean Nation and Inter-Species Harmony

13. Affirm that the Cetacea (whales and dolphins) are an ancient race of intelligent, sentient beings, who have been the friends and helpers of mankind for millennia.

14. Demand an end to whaling and irresponsible fishing practices that kill dolphins, and protect marine life from damaging sonar and other destructive technologies.

15. Recognize members of the "Cetacean Nation", comprised of dolphins, whales, and porpoises, are entitled to the same rights and protections as all people.

16. Recognize that all life is interdependent and all forms of life have inherent value, regardless of their economic worth to human beings, and so resolve to create an environment friendly to all sentient species.

Sustainability and Environmental Transformation

17. Protect and restore the integrity of Earth's ecological systems, with special attention to biological diversity, the natural processes that sustain life, and traditional sacred sites.

18. Promote re-connection to Nature through organic farming and sustainable resource management, showing reverence for the land and waters of our home planet.

19. Cooperate internationally and with extraterrestrial civilizations in promoting Earth, Cosmic and Life friendly technologies, and encouraging the right use and open availability of these technologies.

20. Adopt patterns of production, consumption, and reproduction that show respect and due care for the Earth, and that safeguard her regenerative capacities.

Adopted May 13, 2007, Kailua-Kona, Hawaii

ENDNOTES

[476] An online petition is available for viewing at:
http://www.thepetitionsite.com/takeaction/919813175

CHAPTER 10

Declaration for the Creation of a European Agency to Study UFOs and Extraterrestrial Affairs

Introduction

A committee of speakers and panelists at the July 25-26, 2009 European Exopolitics Summit drafted and agreed on a "Declaration for the Creation of a European Agency to Study UFOs and Extraterrestrial Affairs." The Declaration proposed the "creation of a European Agency or Department to investigate evidence of UFOs, extraterrestrial life and related phenomenon." A pre-conference draft had been electronically circulated to a committee of speakers and panelists for feedback in order to develop a document for circulation at the Press conference preceding the Summit. At the pre-summit Press Conference on Friday, July 24, 2009, the Declaration was formally released to the Press and to the world.

This was a unique moment in the emergence of an European exopolitics movement. Previously, exopolitics had gained much attention in North America, but relatively little in Europe. The European Exopolitics Summit, with over 1000 attendees from all over Europe, changed that. The Declaration was designed to focus European aspirations on what can be politically achieved regarding greater official study and investigations into UFOs and extraterrestrial life.

The initial draft was proposed by Dr Michael Salla and circulated to the drafting committee comprising Pepon Jover M.Sc. (Exopolitics Spain); Robert Fleischer (Exopolitics Germany); David Griffin M.Sc. (Exopolitics United Kingdom); Frederik Uldall (Exopolitics Denmark) and Paola Harris (Exopolitics Italy). The penultimate draft received additional comments by Alfred Webre, J.D. The European participants of the drafting committee ensured that various European exopolitics country groups and websites associated in the committee agreed to the Declaration before its final distribution. The Declaration was first presented to the Press Conference by Robert Fleischer, and then in the morning of the European Exopolitics Sumitt on July 25.

What follows is the Declaration adopted by consensus by the drafting committee at the 2009 European Exopolitics Summit, released at a Press Conference and Summit, and subsequently circulated on the internet. To date it has been translated into several European languages.[477]

***

Declaration for the Creation of a European Agency to Study UFOs and Extraterrestrial Affairs

We represent an increasingly growing network of concerned individuals participating in and/or supporting the European Exopolitics Summit in Barcelona Spain, July 25-26, 2009,

We are a body of concerned private citizens seeking to understand the public policy implications of evidence concerning UFOs, extraterrestrial life and related phenomena,

Recognizing UN General Assembly Decision (1978) 33/426 called for "Member States to take appropriate steps to coordinate on a national level scientific research and investigation into extraterrestrial life, including unidentified flying objects,"

Acknowledging that between 1992-1997 the Spanish Ministry of Defence declassified 75 Air Force files on UFOs from 1962 totaling 1900 pages on 97 events.

Noting that on March 22, 2007, the French Space Agency announced it was making public through its website 1600 declassified UFO files since 1954,

Acknowledging that on May 14, 2008, the United Kingdom Ministry of Defence began a 3 year programme to declassify and release to the National Archives all its UFO files, including over 12,000 sighting reports, together with policy documents formerly classified Secret UK Eyes Only".

Noting that on 21 September, 2007 the Republic of Ireland released declassified UFO files from 1947 to 1984.

Realizing that in January 2009, the Danish Air Force released on its website approximately 300 pages of reported UFO sightings from over the last 30 years,

Acknowledging that on May 11, 2004, the Mexican Department of Defense released secret UFO sighting reports to civilian UFO researchers; that on May 20, 2005, the Brazilian Air Force also released classified UFO reports to civilian researchers; that in August 2007, the Ecuadorian Air Force also released UFO files to civilian UFO researchers; and that in June 2009, the Uruguay Air Force released 2100 files to the public.

Recognizing that a high level group of former senior French military and scientific officials from the Institute for Advanced Studies for National Defence issued the COMETA Report in 1999 where the report concluded that about 5% of the UFO cases they studied were unexplainable and the best explanation for them was the extraterrestrial hypothesis;

Noting that in 1969 the U.S. National Aeronautics and Space Administration passed a Federal Regulation suspending legal rights and quarantining individuals coming into contact with extraterrestrial artifacts or life;

Recalling that UNGA Decision 33/426 was titled "Establishment of an agency or a department of the United Nations for undertaking, co-ordinating and disseminating the results of research into unidentified flying objects and related phenomena;"

propose the creation of a European Agency or Department to investigate evidence of UFOs, extraterrestrial life and related phenomenon.

The proposed Agency should:

1. collect and study into one database UFO files from different national space agencies, defense departments, and other official European entities and civilian organizations collecting UFO data;

2. cooperate with civilian organizations in the investigation and analysis of cases involving UFO sightings that may be extraterrestrial in origin;

3. sponsor scientific studies into evidence concerning UFOs, extraterrestrial life and related technologies;

4. disseminate its findings in a way that educates the general public of evidence concerning extraterrestrial life and technology;

5. provide funding for academic research into UFOs sightings and their public policy implications in cases where these are extraterrestrial in origin;

6. understand the feasibility of advanced technologies demonstrated by UFOs in resolving global environment, climate, energy, poverty, development, and health problems;

7. cooperate with business organizations in assessing the feasibility of widespread commercial applications of advanced technologies acquired through the study and investigation of UFOs and extraterrestrial life;

8. explore the feasibility of the extraterrestrial hypothesis for unexplained UFO cases;

9. sponsor studies into a proper balance between government regulatory efforts and citizen rights in open contact with representatives of extraterrestrial civilizations;

10. explore the implications of extraterrestrial life and technology for the environment, for energy consumption, and other vital areas;

11. develop protocols for peaceful and diplomatic relations with extraterrestrial life in the event of contact;

12. obtain and make available on the official European agency web site the objectives of the Agency, and any progress or other reports;

13. establish simple and reliable procedures for residents to report to European and local government authorities any sightings of, or contact with, extraterrestrial life or artifacts;

14. refer residents and visitors to properly trained European government or private professionals, as necessary, to address valid concerns resulting from sightings of, or contacts with, extraterrestrial life or artifacts.

Released at European Exopolitics Summit Press Conference on July 25, 2009.

Approved by: Exopolitics European Summit; Exopolitics Spain, Exopolitics Germany, Exopolitics United Kingdom, Exopolitics Denmark; Exopolitics Finland; Exopolitics France; Exopolitics Italy; Exopolitics Sweden.

Supporting European Exopolitics Summit Organizers, Speakers & Panelists: Pepon Jover, M.Sc., Miguel Celades, Javier Sierra, Robert Fleischer, Dr Michael Salla; Alfred Webre, J.D.; Nick Pope, Dr Steven Greer, Dr Brian O'Leary, Paola Harris, M.Ed.; Stephen Bassett; Robert Dean (CSM, ret.), David Griffin, MSc.; Frederik Uldall, M.Sc.

ENDNOTES – CHAPTER 10

[477] An online petition is available at:
http://www.thepetitionsite.com/9/declaration-for-the-creation-of-a-european-agency-to-study-ufos-and-extraterrestrial

CHAPTER 11

Galactic Freedom Day Declaration

Introduction

On 08/08/08 citizen organizations and individuals around the world joined in the inaugural 'Galactic Freedom Day' to end secret agreements concerning extraterrestrial life. A world wide positive intention experiment was conducted at 8 pm (Universal Time) 08/08/08 to put an end to secret agreements that have prevented the revolutionary technology and knowledge of extraterrestrial life entering mainstream society. A Galactic Freedom Day Declaration was written by cooperating citizen organizations clearly expressing humanity's intent to put an end to secret agreements concerning extraterrestrial life. A website was created for the Declaration together with testimonial evidence, information on sponsoring organizations and link to an online petition which by October 2009 had over two thousand signatures. What follows is the Galactic Freedom Day Declaration, list of sponsoring organizations, and the testimonial evidence cited revealing secret agreements concerning extraterrestrial life.

Figure 21. Galactic Freedom Day Banner

Galactic Freedom Day Declaration

We are an association of citizen organizations and private citizens dedicated to research, public education and political activism concerning extraterrestrial life. In circumstances where our interests are not faithfully represented by national governments in relation to extraterrestrial life, we recognize our inalienable right to exercise citizen governance. We consequently issue the following Declaration.

We recognize the reality of extraterrestrial life and its understanding and use of advanced technologies, scientific principles and universal knowledge.

We affirm the natural right of all citizens to have safe and open contact with extraterrestrial visitors, and to engage in non-official diplomacy; and affirm the heartfelt intent of humanity to live in peaceful and cooperative relationship with extraterrestrial civilizations.

We assert that national governments claiming to represent the interests of their citizenry have repeatedly failed to disclose the reality of extraterrestrial life, and the principles and knowledge such life possesses, for over sixty years.

We accept evidence from a number of sources including scientists, researchers, military personnel, corporate personnel, whistleblowers and 'experiencers' that governmental entities within the United States and other major nations have entered into secret agreements concerning extraterrestrial life and/or technology. In some cases, these agreements are with representatives of extraterrestrial civilizations, and have been elevated to treaty status.

We understand these agreements allow for the manufacture and distribution of technology and knowledge deriving from extraterrestrial civilizations. In some cases extraterrestrials are allowed to establish bases on Earth, extract a range of resources and perform invasive medical procedures on civilians.

We object that governmental-extraterrestrial agreements have not been made public or ratified in accord with constitutional procedures in the United States or other nations.

We declare these secret agreements are a violation of the sacred trust given to national governments to faithfully represent the interests of their citizens in open transparent negotiations with foreign nations including extraterrestrial civilizations.

We hereby exercise our inalienable right of citizen governance and proclaim that on 08/08/08 at 8 pm (Universal Time):

- all secret agreements between any government authorized agency, department, organization, or corporation concerning or with any extraterrestrial civilization or group are null and void;
- all future agreements between government authorized agency, department, organization, or corporation concerning or with any extraterrestrial civilization or group not publicly disclosed and openly ratified are null and void;
- all secret agreements involving corporations or groups acting independently of national governments or international organizations, and not disclosed to national governments and to the general public, are null and void.

We declare that 08/08/08 will be subsequently known as Galactic Freedom Day in recognition of our inalienable right of citizen governance.

We call upon members of the public to show their support by signing this Declaration and celebrating Galactic Freedom Day on 8/8/08, and on subsequent yearly anniversaries.

Petition Link: http://www.thepetitionsite.com/1/Galactic-Freedom-Day

2. List of Sponsors

EarthTransformation Conference , Exopolitics Institute , Exopolitics Radio , Exopolitics Toronto , Institute for Cooperation in Space , Exopolitics-UK, Exopolitics Spain , Exopolitics South Africa , Exopaedia.Org, Exopolitics Hong Kong , Phoenixlights3.com, Dolphin Connection International, Exopolitics.Org, GalacticDiplomacy.com, Extraterrestrial Phenomena Political Action Committee, Paradigm Research Group, Exopolitics World Network, Exopolitics.Com,

Interdimensional Angels, centreforgalacticdiplomacy.com ,
Prepare4Contact Forum, Alchemy2day4tomorrow

3. Testimonial Evidence

What follows is evidence in the form of testimonies of those claiming to have witnessed events or documents pointing to the existence of secret agreements with extraterrestrial civilizations.[478] As discussed in chapter two, the evidence suggests that such agreements followed meetings involving President Eisenhower in 1954 and 1955. The agreements have therefore been in place since the mid-1950s in the United States. The whistleblowers below have been divided into two categories.

A. Those for whom public documentation is available to confirm their professional credentials. Such documentation supports their claims of being at classified locations where events or documents suggesting secret agreements may have been witnessed as they claim.

B. Those for whom no reliable public documentation is available to confirm their credentials. This does not, however, dismiss the testimony of whistleblowers whose credentials have not been publicly confirmed. There is a reason to believe that in some cases documentation may have been expunged from public records as a security precaution for those employed in highly classified projects involving extraterrestrial life.

Whistleblowers with 'confirmed' credentials are the most credible sources for confirming the existence of secret agreements concerning or with extraterrestrial life.

Whistleblowers (confirmed credentials)

William Cooper [part of naval intelligence briefing team for Commander of the Pacific Fleet]

Later in 1954 the race of large nosed Gray Aliens which had been orbiting the Earth landed at Holloman Air Force Base. A basic agreement was reached. This race identified themselves as originating from a Planet around a red star in the Constellation of Orion which we called Betelgeuse. They stated that their planet was dying and that at some unknown future time they would no longer be able to survive there.[479]

Lt. Col. Philip Corso [former battalion commander & head of Foreign Technology Desk, U.S. Army]

We had negotiated a kind of surrender with them [extraterrestrials] as long as we couldn't fight them. They dictated the terms because they knew what we most feared was disclosure.[480]

Richard Doty [former Special Agent for the U.S. Air Force Office of Special Investigations]:

There is a closed circuit/videotape interview of an alien (EBE-2 ...) that was an exchanged guest here starting from 1964 until 1964. An AF Colonel did the interview. I attended that interview... From EBE-2 we learned a great deal of information about their race, culture and spacecraft. A third alien, EBE-3 was part of the same exchange program starting in 1979 until 1989.... The extraterrestrials, who are guests of the US government, reside in a number of different quarters around the US.... The National Security Agency has devised a communications system to communicate with the aliens. It's some type of electronic binary pulse. The communications takes place between the Earth and the alien ships. There are reportedly receiving points in Nevada and California. The communications are translated by a computer, which gives the landing coordinates to the National Security Agency, so we know the location of the landing and the purpose, ie.., collect resources for their spacecraft or to have verbal contact.[481]

Charles Hall [former weather analyst with U.S. Air Force stationed at Nellis Air Force Base who witnessed extraterrestrials regularly meeting with senior military leaders]

> The USAF was obviously willing to give them [extraterrestrials] as much of any food item that they requested, no questions asked. The USAF was obviously entirely willing to give them both food and non-animal based clothing items (cotton, nylon, etc) without limit for use as trading materials....The hanger appeared to have been entirely constructed by the USAF for use by the tall whites. For example, the inside of the hanger looked just like any other ordinary aircraft hanger. It included ordinary fire extinguishers, arrows marking exits, etc. In addition to writing and signs on the walls in english, it also include hieroglyphics and icons used by the aliens. The alien writing was done in pink paint against a white background.[482]

Don Philips [former U.S. Air Force and aerospace engineer]

> "We have records from 1954 that [there] were meetings between our own leaders of this country and ET's here in California. And, as I understand it from the written documentation, we were asked if we would allow them to be here and do research. I have read that our reply was well, how can we stop you? You are so advanced. And I will say by this camera and this sound, that it was President Eisenhower that had this meeting."[483]

Dan Sherman [former electronic intelligence expert with U.S. Air Force and NSA secretly trained in a highly classified program to use "intuitive communications" with extraterrestrials]

> The bitterness began a few months after I had started to receive comms from Bones [an extraterrestrial]. It hit a sharp incline when I began to receive the abduction comms and now it hit a crescendo. I was tired of being supposedly so important

because of my abilities, yet treated like an underling with no need-to-know.... Why the abduction data? Why had everything been passed in code, mostly, until now? ... I finally came to the conclusion, after reporting over 20 apparent abduction scenarios, that I wanted no part of the program any longer. Although I had no reason to believe anyone was being maliciously harmed, I did get a feeling that the abductions I was reporting were part of some sort of higher calling and the feelings of the people involved took a back seat to that calling.[484]

Clifford Stone [retired Staff Sergeant U.S. Army who secretly worked for 22 years in classified extraterrestrial projects relates a meeting with an extraterrestrial at the Pentagon]

When I got to Fort Meade where he was supposed to be [a friend at the National Security Agency], they said, well, he is going to be tied up ... This person says, by the way, have you ever been to the Pentagon? Well at this time I had never been at the Pentagon.... Why don't we go ahead and give you the twenty-five cent tour. So we went on over.... When we get out there, there are two monorails there. I mean, there are monorails under the Pentagon.... When we got out, he says, well let me show you some interesting sites down this corridor here. So we are going down the corridor and it looked like there was a door at the far end of that corridor.... Well, when you go through the door there is like a field table there. And behind the field table you had this little entity [an extraterrestrial]. The entity was a little bigger than the 3, 3 1/2 foot tall entities that are a lot of times reported. But there were two men on either side of the table slightly behind the creature. When I turned around, I looked right into the eyes of this little creature. And you know, it's like you are seeing it but everything is being pulled from your mind - he was reading my whole life.... I remember going down and grabbing a hold of my head like this and falling to the floor. The next thing I remember I wake up and I am back in my friend's office [back at Fort Mead].... I will

283

go this far to state that there is an interaction between entities and certain Government agencies within the U.S. Government.[485]

Charles Suggs [former Commander, U.S. Navy]

"Charlie's father, Navy Commander Charles Suggs accompanied Pres. Ike along with others on Feb. 20th. They met and spoke with 2 white-haired Nordics that had pale blue eyes and colorless lips. The spokesman stood a number of feet away from Ike and would not let him approach any closer. A second nordic stood on the extended ramp of a bi-convex saucer that stood on tripod landing gear on the landing strip. According to Charlie, there were B-58 Hustlers on the field even though the first one did not fly officially till 1956. These visitors said they came from another solar system. They posed detailed questions about our nuclear testing.[486]

Capt. Bill Uhouse [former US Marine Corps, USAF and aerospace engineer]

"We had meetings and I ended up in a meeting with an alien. I called him J-Rod - of course, that's what they called him.... The alien used to come in with [Dr Edward] Teller and some of the other guys, occasionally to handle questions that maybe we'd have. You know? But you have to understand that everything was specific to the group. If it wasn't specific to the group, you couldn't talk about it. It was on need-to-know basis. And [the ET] he'd talk. He would talk, but he'd sound just like as if you spoke - he'd sound just like as if you spoke... The preparation we had before meeting this alien was, basically, going through all of the different nationalities in the world.... So basically, the alien was only giving engineering advice and science advice... Sometimes you'd get into a spot where you [would] try and try and try, and it wouldn't work. And that's where he'd [the alien] come in. They would tell him to look at this and see what we did wrong.[487]

Whistleblowers (unconfirmed credentials)

Thomas Castello [alleged security officer at a secret joint U.S. extraterrestrial base at Dulce, New Mexico]

"Since I was the Senior Security Technician at that base, I had to communicate with them on a daily basis. If there were any problems that involved security or video cameras, I was the one they called. It was the reptilian "working caste" that usually did the physical labor in the lower levels at Dulce. Decisions involving that caste were usually made by the white Draco. When human workers caused problems for the working caste, the reptoids went to the white Draconian 'boss', and the Draco called me. At times, it felt like it was a never ending problem. Several human workers resented the "no nonsense" or "get back to work" attitude the working caste lives by. When needed, intervention became a vital tool. The biggest problem were human workers who foolishly wandered around near the "OFF LIMITS" areas of the "Alien Section." I guess it's human nature to be curious and to wonder what is past the barriers. Too often someone found a way to bypass the barriers and nosed around. The camera's near the entrance usually stopped them before they got themselves in serious trouble. A few times I had to formerly request the return of a human worker."[488]

(Dr) Dan Burisch [allegedly worked on classified microbiology projects at Area 51 and S-4.]

The treaties were basically inflicted on us by the Orions. As they were enforced upon us by the Orions that we needed to do what we needed to do when they figured out that we weren't able to handle the issue ourselves. They looked at their own history and said, "Huh, look at the cave men and women." OK? After we acted the way that we acted involving the Cube and all

285

of that business. They inflicted the treaty system on us and they said, "You will behave this way."[489]

(Dr) Michael Wolf

Dr. Wolf states that the most important mission objective of his Alphacom Team was resumption of negotiations with the visiting Star Nations. In the 1950s-1960s, the U.S. administration entered into agreement discussions with the Zetas (so-called Greys) from the fourth planet of the star system Zeta Reticuli, and other star peoples, but these agreements were never ratified as Constitutionally required. The Zetas shared certain of their technological advances with government scientists, apparently often while prisoner "guests" within secure underground military installations in Nevada and New Mexico.[490]

Phil Schneider (alleged civil engineer working on the construction of deep underground military bases]

Back in 1954, under the Eisenhower administration, the federal government decided to circumvent the Constitution of the United States and form a treaty with alien entities. It was called the 1954 Greada Treaty, which basically made the agreement that the aliens involved could take a few cows and test their implanting techniques on a few human beings, but that they had to give details about the people involved. Slowly, the aliens altered the bargain until they decided they wouldn't abide by it all.[491]

ENDNOTES – CHAPTER 11

[478] For a more extensive list see Michael Salla, *Exposing U.S. Government Policies on Extraterrestrial Life* (Exopolitics Institute, 2009) 9-45.
[479] Bill Cooper's Speech at MUFON 1989 Symposium Concerning MJ-12, http://www.bibliotecapleyades.net/sociopolitica/esp_sociopol_mj12_1.htm
[480] Philip Corso, *The Day After Roswell* (Pocket Books, 1997) 292
[481] Robert Collins, *Exempt from Disclosure*, 2nd Edition (Peregrine Communications, 2006) 73, 75
[482] Cited by the author in 'Tall White' Extraterrestrials, Technology Transfer and Resource Extraction from Earth - An Analysis of Correspondence with Charles Hall," http://www.exopolitics.org/Exo-Comment-25.htm
[483] "Testimony of Don Phillips," *Disclosure*, ed., Stephen Greer (Crossing Point, 2001) 379
[484] Dan Sherman, *Above Black: Project Preserve Destiny* (One Team Publishing, 1988) 134, 136
[485] "Testimony of Clifford Stone," *Disclosure*, ed., Stephen Greer (Crossing Point, 2001) 332.
[486] Personal notes supplied to the author from William Hamilton from a 1991 interview with Commander Suggs son, Sgt Charles Suggs, Jr.
[487] "Testimony of Captain Bill Uhouse," *Disclosure*, ed., Stephen Greer (Crossing Point, 2001) 386-87.
[488] Cited in Branton, The Dulce Wars: Underground Alien Bases and the Battle for Planet Earth (Inner Light, 199) ch. 11.
[489] Transcript of Project Camelot interview with Dan Burisch, Secrets of the Stargates, http://projectcamelot.org/dan_burisch_stargate_secrets_interview_transcript_2.html
[490] Richard Boylan, "Official Within MJ-12 UFO-Secrecy Management Group Reveals Insider Secrets," http://www.drboylan.com/wolfdoc2.html
[491] "A Lecture By Phil Schneider," http://www.apfn.org/apfn/phil.htm

Chapter 12

Declaration for Citizen Contact Councils

1. Introduction

The Declaration for Citizen Contact Councils emerged as a result of a collaborative effort by a number of organizations to create a model for small groups of individuals to form and deal with issues concerning extraterrestrial contact. I presented the Declaration at the 2008 Earth Transformation Conference in Kona, Hawaii and it was circulated to all participants. An internet petition was simultaneously created and all sponsoring organizations signed and promoted it.[492]

Initial inspiration for the Declaration came as a result of regular meetings held at our home where a small group of approximately 10 individuals would be led in guided meditations by Angelika Whitecliff and I on a number of issues. Sometimes the group would be directed to focus its creative visualization efforts on impending global challenges as regional wars and natural disasters; and also promoting extraterrestrial contact. The results of these group meditations were very significant in our judgment. We realized the power of positive intention when collectively focused in creative ways. We realized that we comprised a "Creation Council" and we could focus our energies on anything we desired to exert our influence. Sometimes the result would be dramatic as occurred with Hurricane Flossie which was heading directly towards the Big Island.

A state of emergency was declared for Monday, August 13, 2007 when the hurricane was expected to hit the Big Island.[493] Our small group met on the Sunday evening (August 12) before the hurricane was expected to hit. We focused our energies on the hurricane to get it to move away, and cause no damage to life and property. Different members of our group, including both of us, established direct communication with the hurricane wherein it felt gratified by the recognition we had given it. In my case, it felt as though the spirit of the hurricane recognized the presence of our consciousness, and acknowledged the love and appreciation we were directing towards it.

It appeared that the hurricane was a natural vital force that would respond to collective human intention that was based on love and appreciation. It was amazing to see the dramatic result of our group meditation on the next day (Monday) when the hurricane hardly exerted any influence at all and missed the Big Island completely. When we went down to the beaches, we were greeted by sunny skies and calm air. We had had a dramatic demonstration of the power of a "Creation Council" working together cohesively and harmoniously to influence the natural environment.

Inspired by the results of the regular "Creation Council" meetings we had been conducting at our home, we realized that a model had been found that could help others deal with global issues. Small groups of people meeting regularly and focusing their energies through positive intention on global issues was a powerful mechanism for global change. This included preparing for extraterrestrial contact. I then prepared a draft of the Declaration and circulated it to others for feedback. The goal was to inspire others to set up their own groups that could use creative visualization and positive intention experiments to impact on global issues including extraterrestrial contact.

As a result of experiences through 2007 and 2008, it became clear that we needed to stimulate others to create their own local "Creation Councils", and to also prepare for extraterrestrial contact. It was therefore decided that a Declaration for Citizen Contact Councils would help in this effort. The initial document I drafted was circulated to other exopolitical researchers for further comments and revision. These included Paola Harris, Alfred Webre, Victor Viggiani, Mike Bird, Hugh Matlock, Saleena Ki and Angelika Whitecliff. After extensive consultations, the final document was released at the concluding presentation of the 2008 Earth Transformation Conference. What follows is the Declaration.

Figure 22. 2008 ET Conference Banner

2. Declaration for Citizen Contact Councils

To: Citizens of the World

We are an association of citizen organizations and private citizens dedicated to research, public education and political activism with regard to extraterrestrial life. We are convinced that citizen groups can network together in the use of "positive intention" and 'telepathic communications' to achieve 'citizen governance' and contact with extraterrestrial life. We consequently issue the following Declaration;

We recognize the reality of extraterrestrial life; and the existence of advanced technologies, scientific principles and universal knowledge extraterrestrials offer. We affirm that the diffusion of this knowledge and technology can significantly improve the human condition.

We declare our support for the establishment of "Citizen Contact Councils" that will share the following goals:

- disclosing the reality of extraterrestrial life and exposing government policies that were secretly implemented,
- sharing the knowledge and technology provided by extraterrestrials for the benefit of humanity and the biosphere,
- representing the interests of humanity and biosphere in communications and interactions with extraterrestrials,
- promoting Open Contact with extraterrestrial civilizations, and transforming Earth into a galactic society wherein human sovereignty is respected,

291

We declare our support for "Citizen Contact Councils" using the following five principles in their operations:

- using positive intention to transform the human condition,
- establishing telepathic communications with extraterrestrial civilizations,
- building positive relationships with advanced ethical extraterrestrial civilizations,
- cooperating with advanced ethical extraterrestrials in achieving common goals,
- using consensus and empathic communications to promote group cohesion and cooperation.

We subsequently support the formation of "Citizen Contact Councils" around the world where existing 'councils' on the Big Island of Hawaii and elsewhere provide examples for the above goals and principles.

We, the undersigned, do pledge to support the creation of Citizen Contact Councils to achieve its above stated chief purpose. We call upon members of the public to show their support by distributing and/or signing this Declaration.

Declaration Sponsors: EarthTransformation.com, Exopolitics Institute, GalacticDiplomacy.com, Institute for Cooperation in Space, Exopolitics Radio, Exopolitics Toronto.

ENDNOTES – CHAPTER 12

[492] The petition is available at: http://www.petitiononline.com/D4CCC/petition.html
[493] To read about Hurrican Flossie and the Big Island, go to:
http://www.cnn.com/2007/US/08/13/hurricane.flossie.ap/index.html

CHAPTER 13

Statement of Aspirations and Code of Conduct for Extraterrestrials Interacting with Earth

Introduction

This document was produced as a result of discussion among various members of the Prepare4Contact Yahoo discussion forum over the issue of inviting extraterrestrials to show up. In response to concerns over the behavior of extraterrestrials responding to such a request, it was decided that a Code of Conduct would be designed outlining standards extraterrestrials would need to observe. Furthermore, a Statement of Aspirations was also included outlining the positive intention of humanity vis-à-vis extraterrestrials showing up and assisting human evolution.

Figure 23. Prepare4Contact Yahoo Forum Graphic

A discussion thread introducing key principles that would eventually be developed in the document below was initially circulated on November 10, 2003.[494] After extensive online discussion that resulted in numerous revisions, a final version was developed. While consensus proved elusive, the document itself was supported by a majority of members who participated in the discussions. The document was finally voted on and approved by prepare4contact forum members in a poll where 72% of voting members approved.[495] I initiated and chaired the debate process in a consultative manner with other member of the prepare4contact forum.[496]

Statement of Aspirations and Code of Conduct for Extraterrestrials Interacting with Earth

Preamble:

In a message to humanity titled "Change the World! Decide Whether We Should Show Up!" distributed throughout the internet, a group of extraterrestrial races described the dire political problems that threaten the freedom, prosperity and sovereignty of global humanity, and how they could assist by simply `showing up'. They requested permission from `individuals without distinction', as they describe those not holding significant political power, by conducting a global ballot to the question: `Do You Wish That We Show Up?' In response to that request, we `individuals without distinction' wish to declare that we have long been the visionaries, social reformers, peacemakers, healers and `contactees' in dealing with our planet's problems and communicating with extraterrestrial races. We rightfully claim our role to speak on behalf of global humanity in how extraterrestrials can assist with and transform our present global predicament.

Our planet has long been dominated by competing groups of political elites who have established predatory national policies that have threatened freedom and prosperity of all nations of our world. These predatory policies have greatly damaged social, economic and political relationships on our world, and also caused great damage to our natural environment. As a result, many of our visionaries, Edgar Cayce, Mother Shipton, Gordon Michael Scallion and Nostradamus predicted great planetary upheaval during this time of transition which we call the `end times'. Fortunately, these planetary upheavals have not occurred due to the extraordinary love, compassion, healing and forgiveness practiced by millions of `individuals without distinction' who have essentially saved our planet from global catastrophe. Unfortunately, our political elites continue in their predatory national policies and domination of our political systems, financial institutions and mass media, thereby leading to the present set of dire conditions you describe in your letter.

In exchange for the assistance extraterrestrials provide by `showing up' and thereby catalyzing solutions to the present problems affecting our planet, we will be willing to lend our assistance in their transformation as interplanetary societies that may continue to have painful histories and antagonisms. Due to the extensive diversity of our planet's population, history of violent conflict, and predatory policies of our political elites, we have developed unique qualities and strategies for promoting peace, compassion, empathy and healing in societies divided by painful histories of injustice and violence. These qualities are chiefly responsible for our triumph in preventing the predicted global catastrophe on our world, and we wish to draw the attention of extraterrestrial visitors to this. We will be able to provide expert teams of healers, peacemakers, conflict resolution experts, shamans and mystics, to advise your experts in these areas in how they can be more effective in their respective interplanetary projects.

We wish to emphasize that elected political representatives of our planet's many nations have shown little desire or ability to understand, respond to or engage in public dialogue on the extraterrestrial presence or `Message to Humanity'. The political elites of our world continue their predatory policies while exercising extensive control of our world's media, political systems and financial institutions. The extraterrestrial presence continues to be subject to a public policy of non-disclosure by responsible government and military officials; and has involved tremendous social, political and economic cost to global humanity. We declare that we `individuals without distinction' have lost faith in the ability of our government representatives to effectively deal with extraterrestrials on behalf of global humanity.

Therefore, we as a representative group of `individuals without distinction' desire to respond to the prospect of extraterrestrials showing up and/or interacting with global humanity. We declare that the following `Statement of Aspirations' and `Code of Conduct' applies to all extraterrestrials, visible or not, who show up, interact with, or desire to interact with global humanity.

Definitions

`Individuals without distinction' (IWD)- that proportion of global humanity not occupying representative public office, not having significant control of the mass media or owning appreciable financial resources.

`Contact groups' – individuals who have received the letter asking IWD if they want extraterrestrials to show up, and/or given affirmative responses and/or formed groups to discuss issues associated with the letter.

Visitors – all `non-humanoid', `synthetic humanoids' or `off-world' races that either `show up' as a result of an affirmative answer to the requested global ballot, and/or those races previously holding secret agreements with political representatives that either subsequently reveal themselves or remain hidden on Earth.

Statement of Aspirations

1. Visitors recognize and value the unique qualities of peace, compassion, hope, joy, healing and empathy `individuals without distinction' have developed as a result of living on a tremendously diverse planet with antagonistic histories, emotional traumas, legacies of violence; and predatory policies of competing political elites; and the contribution `individuals without distinction' can make as peacemakers, visionaries, and healers in interplanetary relations;

2. Visitors seeking to interact with Earth, recognize that we `individuals without distinction' have long been the visionary social reformers, peacemakers, healers, and truth seekers that have resolved

many of our planet's most intractable conflicts and promoted public awareness of the visitor's presence, and therefore deserve primacy and majority representation in formal dialogues and negotiations conducted between visitors and representatives of global humanity.

3. Visitors and `individuals without distinction' in their relation to one another, need to consider themselves as both teachers and pupils, as sisters and brothers; and not as parents, authorities, or as saviors. Visitors recognize that they and `individuals without distinction' are in a partnership where each seeks to identify, nurture and exchange their unique contributions as planetary societies for their mutual benefit in a wider interplanetary community based on the principles of individuality, free will, sovereignty, and Universal Law.

4. `Individuals without distinction' and visitors are self-empowered as a result of their interactions, and mutual advancement is obtained through communication, sharing of knowledge, and expansion in all spheres of growth for humans and visitors.

5. During the first contact event, space vehicles of visitors above Earth's population centers should appear in formations that use universal symbols of peace, love and joy. Light and holographic shows similar to fireworks displays and outdoor movies should also be extensively used to demonstrate the friendliness of the visitors, and their origins.

6. When visitors first meet large numbers of `individuals without distinction' and local officials, these meetings will use friendly and open contact scenarios that are characterized by exchanges of gifts, use of peaceful symbols and reliance on humanoid visitors that all promote confidence and trust.

7. Visitors assist global humanity for a transition period of seven years with a possible three year extension, if required, to introduce necessary reforms to prepare global humanity for full and open membership in interplanetary relations. All agreements reached between visitors and representatives of global humanity are subject to review/termination/confirmation at any time by an appropriate global planetary institution or in a global ballot of `individuals without distinction'.

8. Visitors send delegates/emissaries to visit major cities and to attend public forums where they can meet with and answer questions from the mass media and private citizens. In cases where visitors do not agree to a more public display, arrangements will be made to offer the visitors a place where they would be more comfortable.

9. Visitors assist in ensuring the effectiveness of a `Planetary Truth Commission' authorized to disclose the full extent of human rights violations stemming from all secret projects, agreements, technologies and activities that involved visitors collaboration with national military-intelligence agencies, scientific laboratories and corporations;

10. The trade and movement of renewable resources, intellectual property, or human visitors/workers to other planets, to be regulated by a duly constituted planetary authority established at the end of a transition period of seven years.

11. Establishment of an organization from contact groups authorized to monitor political representatives and executive officers of undue visitor influence, and to act as an advisory body to decision makers on the activities and influence of visitors.

Code of Conduct

12. Due to the unrepresentative and secret negotiations that have taken place in recent Earth history between government officials and visitors, visitors seeking to establish or to renew agreements with representatives of global humanity, must ensure that `contact groups' and `individuals without distinction' are respectively given major representation at all subsequent formal dialogues and negotiations;

13. All agreements reached between visitors who `show up' and members of global humanity, representative or not, will be fully disclosed and distributed through all public information channels including the mass media, non-governmental organizations dealing with extraterrestrial affairs; and a public internet site dedicated to disclosing extraterrestrial related information on a `round the clock' basis. Visitor rights will be respected by the Earth's media when providing such information.

298

14. There will be full disclosure and transparency in all visitor interventions in human affairs and the Earth's ecosystem in terms of their respective short and long-term consequences. An appropriate global institution will be created to monitor and where appropriate correct the consequences of visitor interventions or the consequences of human interventions on visitor worlds or subterranean Earth locations.

15. Visitors interacting with Earth ensure that 'secret agreements' previously made between themselves and political representatives, and all associated activities and programs, are fully disclosed to global humanity through the same communication channels as #13.

16. In all interactions between visitors and global humanity, the free will and rights of humans and visitors are at all times respected, and that all violations of these will be reported and rectified by a designated Human and Visitor Rights Office created to deal with infractions of the free will and rights of humans and/or visitors;

17. There will be full transparency and openness in all cases where visitors or their proxies, or humans or their proxies, influence or control one another by: electronic devices, mind control, etheric implants, or any other artificial methods.

18. An appropriate planetary legal institution will be responsible for creating and/or harmonizing planetary, national and local laws with the needs and rights of visitors. In interacting with political authorities at the national or sub-national levels, visitors will respect local customs and laws.

19. Visitors are required not to make any trade agreements concerning the export of Earth's non-renewable resources with any political entity, at the national, sub-national or planetary level.

20. Visitors may record information related to their experience on Earth. Visitors desiring to introduce or remove any material object from Earth must gain express permission of import/export control authorities or in compliance with regulations concerning the exchange of gifts between humans and visitors.

21. No visitor may introduce any self-replicating organism or information.

22. No visitor may initiate a chemical, biological, thermonuclear, or other chain reaction, wittingly or unwittingly.

23. Visitors recognize the principles of `freedom of speech', `freedom of religion' and `freedom of thought' in all interactions with human populations, and grant reciprocal rights to human visitors to their worlds or subterranean Earth locations.

24. Visitors interact with global humanity and the Earth only in a manner that is in harmony with the highest good of all beings.

Distributed December 9, 2003 on the discussion forum http://groups.yahoo.com/group/prepare4contact/

ENDNOTES – CHAPTER 13

[494] Available online at:
http://tech.groups.yahoo.com/group/prepare4contact/message/149
[495] 103 members voted in the poll. 75 voted yes, 8 voted no, and 20 voted uncertain. Poll results are available online at:
http://tech.groups.yahoo.com/group/prepare4contact/surveys?id=11495962
[496] The document is available online at:
http://tech.groups.yahoo.com/group/prepare4contact/message/1063

CHAPTER 14

How Celestials are Helping Humanity prepare for Extraterrestrial Contact

Introduction

The end of the Mayan Calendar came and went without the big bang many expected or hoped for. What's easy to forget is that we have begun a new cycle, according to the Mayan Calendar, and that is something to be really excited about. There's a fundamental transition that we are witnessing in slow motion as modern information technology makes possible greater knowledge of events and processes far beyond our planetary shores. The transition is "reconnection" - reconnection with the Universe. We have been living for thousands of years as a very isolated planetary culture. We really have been very insular – look at the history books. What do the history books write about? Let's think about what the ancient Greeks, the ancient Persians, the Romans, the Ottoman Empire, the Chinese and so forth wrote about. History is very limited to the recorded events of a select number of civilizations on this planet. Our history, as amply documented by Michael Cremo and Richard Thomson, authors of *Forbidden Archeology*, is much richer, and much older![497] According to Zecharia Sitchin, Cremo and Thomson our true history is Galactic, indeed it's Cosmic![498] It goes beyond the history of this planet. It's been hidden from us for a long time.

This is why this time is so exciting because we are witnessing changes in slow motion. Like many reading this book, we all want things to change quickly. We have about 50 mature adult years, or so to really contribute to life around us with our ideas and energy. We want things to happen quickly, and we want it to happen in that period when we can see them. The changes I'm speaking about are going to happen within the next few years. Within the next decade, I am very confident that we will transition from an isolated planetary culture into a galactic culture. That is really exciting for me personally as I write this book. What I'm going to explain in this chapter is a kind of a snapshot of what lies ahead. It's really exciting, and something to look forward to because we've got a lot of friends out there in the galaxy.

We have a lot of friends as I've hopefully shown in earlier chapters, but we've forgotten them. We don't know who they are so in a way I hope that this chapter helps further reintroduce some of you to our galactic friends - those who have been helping us from the sidelines, and supporting us as we move forward in a very dark period in our collective consciousness. This is an experience for humanity where we have chosen to experience a dark night of the soul – collectively! With any dark night, however, it ends eventually. We are now going to experience a wonderful awakening which involves reconnection with our Galactic family. So that's what I'm going to be doing with this penultimate chapter.

I want to begin with the question of "what would extraterrestrial life be like?" There are many approaches to answering this question, and I gave one approach in chapters three through to five about different extraterrestrial civilizations based on what whistleblowers and experiencers have told us. In this chapter, I propose another approach, one that was first proposed in 1964 by a Russian astronomer, Nikolai Kardashev, and has become most popular with natural scientists. Kardashev wanted to develop a scientific way of categorizing extraterrestrial life. So he came up with a way of categorizing extraterrestrials on how well they use energy around them.[499] So Kardashev argues that they evolve based on the ability to use energy at different macroscopic levels, so now I'll explain what that means.

A Type 0 civilization is like the Earth where we use energy in a very limited way. We use fossil fuels such as oil, coal and gas, and other limited energy sources such as Uranium. These are limited resources found around the planet that we use for energy consumption and they are non-renewable. Competition over the control of these energy sources has led to many wars and misery on our planet. The dangers of nuclear energy have even threatened our planetary survival.

A Type I civilization is able to use energy at a planetary level. It's able to tap into the energy of the ocean, or of the Earth's core, or volcanic/seismic activity. A Type I civilization can even tap into the energy grid of our planet. Our planet has an electrical energy grid as discovered by pioneers such as Nikola Tesla. There are also other ways in which energy even more subtle flows around the planet. All of these are renewable energy sources which makes them very different to the limited energy sources used by Type 0 civilizations. A Type I civilization can tap into these planetary energy sources without ever exhausting them, and use them for many purposes.

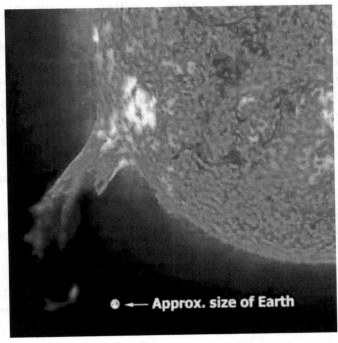

Figure 24. Size of solar CME compared to Earth. Credit: NASA

Type II civilizations can efficiently use energy from an entire sun. The sun is constantly emitting energy. We know that. We see the light, we feel the warmth. It's not just the warmth and the light. The sun is constantly emitting enormous amounts of plasma energy in all directions – 24 hours a day, seven days a week. It never rests. Some of the solar flares, Coronal Mass Ejections coming from the sun are incredible in size. In the illustration on left, we see the size of the Earth in relation to the Sun which we know is big. Look at the size of one of these Coronal Mass Ejections – it's huge compared to the Earth. If one of those ever hit the Earth directly we'd be in big trouble. So Type II civilizations can harness the energy of a sun like that.

Now we get to Type III civilizations. For many we are getting into the realm of science fiction – they can use energy from the Galactic Core, and deal with galactic wide energies such as Galactic Superwaves. Just as our sun is constantly emitting plasma energy that goes out filling our solar system – just as a Type II civilization can use that energy – a Type III civilization can utilize energy emitted from the galactic core – galactic superwaves going in all directions.

Also, Type III civilizations can create or manipulate black holes. One of the things about the creation of black holes was that Carl Sagan when he wrote his book, *Contact,* he asked a very famous astrophysicist by the name of Kip Thorne to see if it was possible for a wormhole to be created through a black hole.[500] And found that yes, it was possible provided that there was something that could keep a black hole open. He called it exotic matter. It was theoretically possible but our science was very far from being able to do anything like that. In contrast, this would be possible for a Type III civilization.

Type III civilizations can also move or engineer entire solar systems, and even create a galactic GPS using pulsars. Pulsars are like galactic beacons. In fact, one theoretical physicist, Dr Paul LaViolette, claims that pulsars are artificial beacons built by advanced extraterrestrials.[501] Pulsars have a frequency that is pretty constant so you could navigate the galaxy by pulsars. In fact, pulsars were used in creating the plagues placed on the Pioneer 10 and 11 probes so extraterrestrials could locate Earth.[502] So Type III civilizations can tap into and use Galactic wide energy.

That's where Nikoli Kardashev stopped in his typology because it was enough for scientists to wrap their minds around these kinds of advanced extraterrestrial civilizations. A civilization that could use the energy of an entire galaxy, there wouldn't be a need to think about anything more evolved than that. But of course it would evolve. Life evolves. If life evolves from Type 0 to Type I, and from Type I to Type II, and Type II to Type III wouldn't it evolve from Type III to Type IV? Of course, but what would a Type IV civilization be like?

A Type IV civilization would be able to tap into energy at a universal level. Not just the galactic core or the energy of an entire galaxy but something that is truly extra-galactic or universal in scope. As you can tap into energy at a universal level, your consciousness would evolve, naturally! So you have reached the point where your civilization's collective consciousness would be very familiar with and can easily tap into universal energy. It would be very obvious for a civilization at that level, because that's what they are tapped into, just as our planetary consciousness is really focused on fossil fuels, oil, coal, etc. Think about it. Our entire culture is fixated on it. We ask what happens when oil prices skyrocket, what happens when the oil runs out? Our whole culture is fixated on that limited energy resource because the way we use energy as a civilization is what is going to have a very large impact on our consciousness. Similarly for a Type I civilization, they use energy at a planetary level so their consciousness evolves on this basis. The same happens as civilizations go through the different levels.

So if we are talking about a Type IV civilization that uses energy at a universal level, their ethics, philosophies and politics, is going to be focused on universal consciousness, or a universal force or a universal energy. Once you have developed consciousness to that degree that you can tap into and link with the universe itself, you would be able to do incredible things compared to what we are familiar with. So are there examples of this? There are examples in our science fiction literature.

When I saw Star Wars for the first time, I was elated. I was so happy with Star Wars because for the first time it talked about something universal. It talked about "the Force" – it was great. Thank God they've finally begun talking about something universal that goes beyond technology, beyond what we can use with our technologies. That is beyond anything that our culture is identifying with. That is something that I'm sure many millions, like me, celebrated. All of a sudden it was like new idea entering into our collective consciousness. Now we can talk about the Force, something truly universal.

When Star Wars was first released, it was an example of how you can train to use this Force, trap into this universal energy that pervades all life. And the Star Wars series has been one of the very few Sci Fi movies, series or franchises that has talked about this universal energy field that we can learn to tap into with our consciousness. It was something that broke new ground, and I think is part of the reason why it's such a big favorite for so many of us who can watch it again and again; because it reminds us that yes, we have that ability! We can do that! We can tap into this universal force. We know how to do it! Sure, we've forgotten how to do it, maybe our society doesn't encourage it, but we know deep down inside that we know we can do it. That's why Star Wars was something that was pioneering.

Other sources of literature also talk about ways of tapping into this universal energy field, here we have examples of that in terms of what would a civilization be like. How would it be structured? If you have a Type IV civilization that is able to tap into this universal energy grid, or this field, what would it be like? Would it take on the parameters of a civilization that we are familiar with? We have another version of what a civilization like that would be like.

The *Keys of Enoch* is a book written by Dr J.J. Hurtak that was first published in 1973. In it, he talked about various levels of universal spiritual orders that comprise "celestial civilizations of the light."[503] The "celestials" are beings similar to the Jedi Knights in Star Wars that are able to use energy at a universal level and possess a kind of cosmic consciousness. So Hurtak was talking about these orders, these brotherhoods that exist throughout all planetary systems, throughout all galaxies. Civilizations, in this model, evolve and reach a point that they now become members of a brotherhood or sisterhood that expands throughout the universe. They comprise beings with a Type IV consciousness where they can tap into the universal energy grid. One of the orders identified by Hurtak is the universal Order of Melchizadek. It's interesting that the Old Testament refers to the Order of Melchizadek in Psalms 110. Melchizadek is someone of major importance since he was the father of Enoch, a very old pre-diluvial figure in the Hebrew scripture.

What I would like to do is focus a bit on celestials, and who these beings are that have this universal consciousness. How do they operate? What are they like? A really good introduction to celestials is a series of books by Baird Spalding, called *Masters of the Far East*. He described how 11 scientists traveled to the Himalayas in the early 20th century. Along the way they were helped by a group of beings that were described as "Ascended Masters." These Ascended Masters had all of the abilities seen in the Star Wars movies. But these Ascended Masters had these abilities fully developed. They could levitate; they could bilocate; telepathy was something they could do very easily; telekinesis – they could raise objects just as easily.

Within the *Masters of the Far East* series you read story after story of how these Ascended Masters helped that scientific mission. The mission was there for a number of years, and these celestials or "Ascended Masters" ensured that Baird Spalding's expedition could be introduced to the philosophies, to the sacred wisdom of the Far East. Spalding was certainly incredibly impressed about that and wrote his series of six books about what happened there. The interesting thing about the Ascended Masters was that they described themselves as part of a vast brotherhood, that wasn't just on the Earth, but beyond as well. Again we have that idea of a universal brotherhood.

This is something that Helena "Madam" Blavatsky also talked about. She was among the first to describe this association of Spiritual Adepts and called them the "Masters of the Hidden Brotherhood."[504] One of her close supporters and a leading theosophist from the early 20th century, Charles Leadbeater, called them the "Great White Brotherhood" in his book, *The Masters and the Path*.[505] They could do things through the power of consciousness alone – move through space-time, manipulate matter, incredible powers of telekinesis, bilocation, all of those psychic abilities. These Ascended Masters had developed these abilities to a very high level. Blavatsky and Leadbeater went into great depth into the Masters. I give this as an example of a Type IV civilization – a universal brotherhood and sisterhood comprising highly evolved males, females and androgynous beings from other worlds.

These are beings who through spiritual development, discipline, have been able to rise beyond the limitations of the body, thinking of the mind, to truly embrace and connect with a universal energy field so the power of their mind and intent was so focused that they could instantly do things. If we look at ourselves, we have very great difficulty in silencing and focusing our minds – even for ten seconds. Yet the Great White Brotherhood, or beings that have been able to go through the spiritual discipline and practices, have been able to train themselves to do that. We know it can be done. There are many examples of those that have been able to discipline their mind to do these incredible things. So we know it can be done, it's just a matter of disciplining yourself so you go through or rise beyond the point of where you are thinking about silence, to where you actually begin to be silent. That's where the power really comes in.

Leadbeater points out that the Ascended Masters are not merely from earth. He said:

> The Great White Brotherhood also includes members of the Heavenly Host (the Spiritual Hierarchy directly concerned with the evolution of our world), **Beneficent Members from other planets** that are interested in our welfare, as well as certain unascended chelas.[506]

So Leadbeater was basically putting in a very concise way what the Theosophical Society believed. The Ascended Masters, the Great White Brotherhood, The Brotherhood of Light, wasn't just limited to the Earth. This was a Universal Brotherhood/Sisterhood of celestial beings.

An example of an Ascended Master is from India - Babaji. He was described at length by Paramahamsa Yogananda who wrote the very influential autobiography, *Autobiography of a Yogi*.[507] I remember reading that about four times. It's one of those classics that you read again and again. It's like being in a desert and you find this Oasis and you think you got to drink deeply because there's a lot of desert to walk over. Yogandanda talked a lot about Ascended Masters and the beings in his particular spiritual order, Kriya Yoga. So Babaji was described as living for thousands of years in the Himalayas, and maintains a youthful appearance. That's something that's pretty important. These ascended Masters are not necessarily long bearded men with gray hair but maintain a youthful appearance for a long time. Personally I think that's important to keep in mind as we move into these possibilities of a greater connection with the Galaxy and the Universe. Even the aging process is not an iron law of the universe. Babaji and other ascended masters illustrate that.

So, to summarize so far, celestials are highly developed ethical beings that have been described in the literature in many different ways, as Angels, Ascended Masters, Elohim, etc. The important thing is that they share one key characteristic, they can tap into the universal energy grid and work with that energy in developing high states of cosmic consciousness, and manifest things in their lives and around them for the benefit of society.

I will henceforth use the term 'celestial' to refer to any life form that has achieved higher states of consciousness whereby they display a number of remarkable abilities without technological assistance.

What's the difference between celestials and extraterrestrial civilizations?

Now we get to the question of what are the key difference between celestials and extraterrestrial life? I discussed earlier extraterrestrial life and the growing scientific interest them in terms of how they would use energy at greater and greater macro levels. I pointed out that celestials are Type IV civilizations that are able to tap into a universal energy source, as opposed to Type I-III civilizations that use energy at lower macro levels on the Kardashev scale. How would this difference in energy use more clearly manifest itself in terms of behavior and the use of technology?

For one thing, celestials travel through the universe using the power of consciousness alone, and they are not confined to any one physical location. They don't need technology to move. An "Ascended Master" or celestial, can move instantaneously just by using the power of consciousness. That distinguishes them from the different extraterrestrial civilizations that we have encountered earlier in this book that would fall into the Type I or Type II categories. Basically, they need technology, spaceships, to be able to move through space and time.

Celestials have attained that advanced state of consciousness – oneness with the universe – and they don't identify themselves with one particular place in space-time. So if you think about it, because we are a Type 0 Civilization we identify ourselves primarily as American, Australian, Italian, Turkish, etc. For Type I civilizations it would be a planetary system, from a planet in the Pleiades, or Sirius star systems, and so forth as we discussed in chapters three and four. These Type IV civilizations would identify themselves with the Universe, they don't identify themselves with any particular place in space and time.

Celestials are able to travel throughout the universe through willpower alone and are not confined to any physical location. This highly advanced ability distinguishes them from extraterrestrial entities that are dependent on advanced forms of technology for space-time travel as evidenced in ubiquitous sightings of 'flying saucers' and other extraterrestrial vehicles (ETVs). This ability to travel through space-time further distinguishes celestials from paranormal entities or 'inter-dimensionals' described by John Keel and others as ghosts, fairies, goblins, etc., that are bound by spatio-temporal factors to Earth but can move between dimensions.[508]

Also, celestials have reached advanced states of consciousness wherein they have attained a level of oneness or 'cosmic consciousness' with the universe, and do not identify themselves exclusively with a stellar region, civilization, time or dimension. This ability again distinguishes them from extraterrestrial entities that exclusively identify themselves with particular stellar regions, civilizations, times or dimensions. Finally, celestials are not limited to any one physical form, and can change their form at will to suit whatever circumstances they are in. This ability again distinguishes them from extraterrestrial entities that identify with a particular physical form or genetic characteristics, and require technology to change their physical characteristics or how they are perceived by others.

Celestials have been described in a wide range of sources from religious-historical texts, and more recently contactee experiences. Celestials are described in these sources as beings that serve a higher universal will that remains hidden to ordinary humans. Celestials have been described as often intervening to assist humanity's evolution especially during periods of conflict involving extraterrestrial civilizations and advanced technologies. Celestials have been witnessed together with extraterrestrials who view the former as teachers, "Masters of Wisdom" or universal messengers whose advice is respectfully heard thought not always followed.

Extraterrestrials have been increasingly acknowledged by a number of contemporary authors as having played a leading role in the seeding of the human race and establishing technologically advanced civilizations.[509] Less well known is the role played by celestials and their precise relationship with extraterrestrials in their complex interaction with humanity's evolution. This is unfortunate since evidence suggests that celestials have played significant historical roles in humanity's evolution by ensuring that advanced technologies are wisely incorporated, and intervening in conflicts between humanity and extraterrestrial civilizations.

Understanding the historical role of celestials has become especially important in the modern era where contact between extraterrestrial civilizations and humanity has been increasingly occurring. Extraterrestrials have interacted directly with the U.S. government and in some cases have signed agreements that have *de facto* treaty status.[510] This has led to the development and incorporation of advanced extraterrestrial technologies by the military corporate sector that in a few select cases has been allowed to filter through to mainstream society.[511]

In numerous other cases of extraterrestrial contact, extraterrestrials have directly interacted with private citizens who have described experiences ranging from inspired transformative encounters to invasive violations. This suggests different types of extraterrestrials are interacting with humanity with different modalities and motivations as I discussed in chapters three through to five.[512] Evidence points to a heightened degree of human extraterrestrial contact that will culminate in open contact wherein Earth becomes an interplanetary society. This will lead to important policy choices to be made over the extent to which, humanity should interact with different extraterrestrial groups and incorporate the advanced technologies offered by them.

In the next section, I reveal the historical role played by celestials in intervening in human and extraterrestrial affairs. I will show how increased awareness of the historic presence of celestials can assist humanity in making the transition to a mature galactic culture, wherein open contact with extraterrestrial civilizations occurs. Important policy choices need to be made over which extraterrestrial groups are reliable partners to work with, and which advanced technologies ought to be incorporated into human society. Celestials can help minimize unnecessary stress and conflict in this transition, and ensure that humanity's evolution to a galactic culture is harmonious and peaceful.

The Book of Enoch and Celestials

Celestials have been described in religious-historical texts as transcendental entities that have intervened in human civilization in the form of guardians and protectors. Celestials have played leading roles in helping humanity deal with extraterrestrial entities or other life forms that have the power to significantly impact on human civilization. They appear to play critical roles in helping resolve conflicts associated with the use of advanced technologies. In some cases, celestials have directly intervened against extraterrestrial entities that have violated what appear to be universal norms such as non-intervention and the diffusion of advanced technologies to unprepared populations. In this and the next section, I examine passages from Judeo-Christian, and Vedic religious-historical traditions that describe celestials interacting with extraterrestrials and humanity.

The apocryphal *Book of Enoch* vividly illustrates the complex relationship between celestials, extraterrestrials and humanity. In the *Book of Enoch*, a group of 200 extraterrestrial entities called the 'Nephilim', or 'fallen angels', come to Earth allegedly due to their attraction to human females. The Nephilim subsequently begin to interact with humanity by interbreeding:

[1] And it came to pass when the children of men had multiplied that in those days were born unto [2] them beautiful and comely daughters. And the angels, the children of the heaven,

312

saw and lusted after them, and said to one another: 'Come, let us choose us wives from among the children of men [3] and beget us children.' And Semjaza, who was their leader, said unto them: 'I fear ye will not [4] indeed agree to do this deed, and I alone shall have to pay the penalty of a great sin.' And they all answered him and said: 'Let us all swear an oath, and all bind ourselves by mutual imprecations [5] not to abandon this plan but to do this thing.' Then sware they all together and bound themselves [6] by mutual imprecations upon it. And they were in all two hundred; who descended in the days of Jared on the summit of Mount Hermon, and they called it Mount Hermon, because they had sworn [7] and bound themselves by mutual imprecations upon it.[513]

The above passage points to extraterrestrials interbreeding with humans as a sin or violation of universal law. Presumably this stemmed from the progeny of such unions possessing genetic advantages that would inevitably lead to them becoming rulers or exerting disproportionate influence to their numbers. Furthermore, extraterrestrial technologies would likely be shared with such progeny to assist them in asserting their rule over human society.

It's important to point out that the author(s) of the *Book of Enoch* had drawn upon many elements of their account from earlier Sumerian writings concerning the Anunnaki. Apparently, the Anunnaki were a group of extraterrestrials that came to earth and claimed to have bioengineered humanity as a worker race. In the process, the Anunnaki helped the establishment of the Sumerian civilization until it was destroyed by a series of cataclysmic events involving advanced weaponry.[514] It appeared that the Anunnaki involved humanity in their fratricidal warfare that led to the destruction of a number of cities in Mesopotamia, and predictably an exodus from the affected lands. Abraham was a refugee from the city of Ur who brought with him sufficient knowledge, wealth, family members and even technology to launch the Jewish nation in Palestine.[515] The Anunnaki described in Sumerian cuneiform texts are referred to as the Nephilim in the *Book of Enoch*, the *Book of Genesis* and other Judaic texts.

The relationship between humanity and the extraterrestrials led by Semjaza is not entirely negative since the latter teaches humanity a range of technologies and esoteric knowledge essential for developing an advanced civilization. This reflected cuneiform accounts of how the Anunnaki had helped in establishing the Sumerian civilization in Mesopotamia around 3800 BCE.[516] The knowledge from the Nephilim ranged from metallic weapons, cosmetics, jewelry, divination, astronomy, weather observation, agricultural science and herbology:

> [1] And Azazel taught men to make swords, and knives, and shields, and breastplates, and made known to them the metals of the earth and the art of working them, and bracelets, and ornaments, and the use of antimony, and the beautifying of the eyelids, and all kinds of costly stones, and all [2] colouring tinctures. And there arose much godlessness, and they committed fornication, and they [3] were led astray, and became corrupt in all their ways. Semjaza taught enchantments, and root-cuttings, 'Armaros the resolving of enchantments, Baraqijal (taught) astrology, Kokabel the constellations, Ezeqeel the knowledge of the clouds, Araqiel the signs of the earth, Shamsiel the signs of the sun, and Sariel the course of the moon. And as men perished, they cried, and their cry went up to heaven . . .[517]

Whereas extraterrestrials are depicted as teachers of advanced technologies and civilization, celestials are depicted as instruments of universal will. In the process of teaching advanced technologies to humanity, the extraterrestrials have fomented much devastating warfare and suffering that has led to humanity lamenting to heaven for relief. The *Book of Enoch* describes the conflict that then occurs between the Nephilim and a group 'righteous' angelic entities or 'celestials':

> [1] And then Michael, Uriel, Raphael, and Gabriel looked down from heaven and saw much blood being [2] shed upon the earth, and all lawlessness being wrought upon the earth. And

they said one to another: 'The earth made without inhabitant cries the voice of their cryingst up to the gates of heaven. [3] And now to you, the holy ones of heaven, the souls of men make their suit, saying, "Bring our cause [4] before the Most High."' And they said to the Lord of the ages: 'Lord of lords, God of gods, King of kings, and God of the ages ... Thee. Thou seest what Azazel hath done, who hath taught all unrighteousness on earth and revealed the eternal secrets which were (preserved) in heaven, which [7] men were striving to learn: And Semjaza, to whom Thou hast given authority to bear rule over his associates. And they have gone to the daughters of men upon the earth, and have slept with the [9] women, and have defiled themselves, and revealed to them all kinds of sins. And the women have [10] borne giants, and the whole earth has thereby been filled with blood and unrighteousness. And now, behold, the souls of those who have died are crying and making their suit to the gates of heaven, and their lamentations have ascended: and cannot cease because of the lawless deeds which are [11] wrought on the earth.[518]

It appears that the celestials are concerned about the way in which advanced technologies have been disseminated to an unprepared humanity, and how human sovereignty has been usurped by the progeny of the Nephilim. A specific complaint is that extraterrestrials have "revealed the eternal secrets which were (preserved) in heaven, which men were striving to learn." This reflects a similar conflict described in Sumerian records over the extent to which humanity would be given advanced technologies and knowledge. The celestials are then depicted as carrying out universal will insofar as they intervene to end the rule of the Nephilim (also described as the 'Watchers') that have brought about an unbalanced state of affairs on the planet in terms of the level of advanced technologies and human consciousness.

Each of the celestials or archangels is given specific instructions in dealing with Nephilim/Watchers by the transcendental "Most High" described in the *Book of Enoch*. The archangel Raphael is tasked to bind and imprison one of the leading Nephilim also described as one of the fallen angels, and to heal the earth.[519] In the next set of instructions, the celestials are instructed to destroy the Nephilim by fomenting war amongst them.

> [9] ... And to Gabriel said the Lord: 'Proceed against the bastards and the reprobates, and against the children of fornication: and destroy [the children of fornication and] the children of the Watchers from amongst men [and cause them to go forth]: send them one against the other that they may destroy each other in [10] battle: for length of days shall they not have. And no request that they (i.e. their fathers) make of thee shall be granted unto their fathers on their behalf; for they hope to live an eternal life, and [11] that each one of them will live five hundred years.' [520]

In the above passage the celestials have the power to manipulate the extraterrestrials to destroy themselves, in much the same way the extraterrestrials or Nephilim have fomented war and strife among humanity. The ancient wars fought among the extraterrestrials that used advanced weapons that destroyed their cities are described by the researchers Zecharia Sitchin and Joseph Farrell.[521] Finally, the Archangel Michael is asked to capture the leader of fallen angels, Semjaza, and his cohorts, and imprison them in hidden locations throughout the Earth:

> [11]... And the Lord said unto Michael: 'Go, bind Semjaza and his associates who have united themselves with women so as to have defiled themselves [12] with them in all their uncleanness. And when their sons have slain one another, and they have seen the destruction of their beloved ones, bind them fast for seventy generations in the valleys of the earth, till the day of their judgment and of their consummation, till the judgment that is [13] for ever and ever is consummated.... Destroy all wrong from the face of the earth and let every evil work come to an end: and let the plant of righteousness and truth appear:

and it shall prove a blessing; the works of righteousness and truth' shall be planted in truth and joy for evermore. [522]

In the above passage, the celestials led by Archangel Michael are depicted as protectors of humanity, and ended what appears to have been a highly unjust and violent civilization dominated by the Nephilim and their progeny. It appears that the extraterrestrials main fault was to have tempted humanity with advanced technology and knowledge when it was not ready to responsibly integrate this. This led to an imbalance between humanity's level of technological sophistication and higher states of consciousness. The celestials therefore appear in the Book of Enoch as ultimate protectors of a humanity that is easily led astray by manipulative extraterrestrials that exploit humanity's desire for advanced technologies and knowledge. Rectifying the imbalance between advanced technology and higher states of consciousness appears to be the main goal of the celestials. A similar dynamic appears in Vedic accounts of celestials interacting with extraterrestrials and humanity.

Vedic Civilization and Celestials

Numerous Vedic texts refer to flying saucers or 'vimanas' traveling throughout earth's skies. In some cases these flying saucers were so large as to actually be cities inhabited by thousands. The inhabitants of these flying saucers, cities, etc., were given a wide array of names by Vedic authors, e.g., Asuras, Devas, Gandharvas, etc. Some appeared to be indigenous to the Earth insofar as they controlled a particular city or region, while others were visitors from another world or dimension called a 'loka'. If Vedic sources are reliable, then ancient India was an open Galactic society with a great diversity of beings originating from different worlds or 'lokas' interacting in the development of human civilization. Insofar as these beings required advanced technologies to move themselves through time and space, they can be regarded as extraterrestrials. In cases where these beings could move between worlds without technology, they can be regarded as celestials.

Vedic texts describe the conflictual relationship between the Asuras and Devas who are depicted as the primary protagonists for control over Earth's cities and other planets. The Asuras appeared intent on taking direct control over human cities and civilizations, and appear analogous to the Nephilim depicted in the Book of Enoch. The Asuras used advanced technologies to invade different planets to establish direct control though interbreeding and the introduction of advanced technologies. Their chief protagonists, the Devas, also used advanced technologies in their perennial conflict with the Asuras. In contrast to the Asuras, however, the Devas were intent on establishing what they called the Sanatana Dharma (eternal law) where righteous human rulers were in charge of Earth's different kingdoms and civilizations. The Devas did not appear interested in ruling directly the Earth, and were content in ruling over their own world or realm called Devaloka. In times when the Asuras had overrun the Earth and Devaloka itself, the Devas appealed for help from celestials. The celestials were typically the physical embodiment or incarnation of one of the three key Hindu gods, Shiva, Vishnu or Brahma or of a feminine divine being, the Devi. The Puranas give numerous accounts of how the celestials would intervene in a time of cultural degeneracy to restore of the Sanatana Dharma and help the Devas in their perennial conflict with the Asuras.

One example that highlights the perennial conflict between two groups of extraterrestrials (Asuras and Devas) with different intentions for Earth involves the celestial 'Krishna'. Just as the *Book of Enoch* described the Archangel Michael and Gabriel as stoking conflict between children of extraterrestrial factions to rid the world of degenerate civilizations, so too Krishna performed a similar function according to the Bhagavad Purana:

> When Vishnu incarnated himself as Krishna ... he came to rid the Earth of her burden of evil, in the form of millions of demons [Asuras] born into the worlds as violent kshatriyas [warriors]. He stoked the greatest war of the age between the forces of good and evil, at which Yuddhishtira's Pandava legions decimated the Kauravas and their immense host.[523]

Here the reference is to the Mahabharata wherein a great war involving advanced technologies led to the decimation of Asura dominated kingdoms in ancient India. Numerous references in the Mahabharata refer to the destructiveness of the advanced weapons used, some of which appeared to be atomic in nature as evidenced in the following passage:

> Gurkha flying in his swift and powerful Vimana hurled against the three cities of the Vrishis and Andhakas a single projectile charged with all the power of the Universe. An incandescent column of smoke and flame as bright as the thousand suns rose in all its splendor... a perpendicular explosion with its billowing smoke clouds... the cloud of smoke rising after its first explosion formed into expanding round circles like the opening of giant parasols... It was the unknown weapon, the Iron Thunderbolt, a gigantic messenger of death which reduced to ashes the entire race of the Vrishnis and Andhakas... The corpses were so burned as to be unrecognizable. The hair and nails fell out; pottery broke without apparent cause, and the birds turned white. After a few hours all foodstuffs were infected... ...to escape from this fire the soldiers threw themselves in streams to wash themselves and their equipment.[524]

The above passage almost certainly describes ancient nuclear warfare and indicates how advanced technologies were routinely used in Vedic India for destructive purposes. It appears that celestials such as Krishna intervened to bring about the end to civilizations that had not found the right balance between advanced technologies such as nuclear weapons, and higher states of consciousness.

Conclusion

We have seen that there is good reason to agree that extraterrestrial civilizations evolve in a way that would be clearly recognizable to scientists based on energy consumption. The ability to tap into different macro levels of energy - at a planetary, stellar or galactic - would indeed characterize an entire civilization's science, politics and ethics. On that score, we can agree with the work of Nikolai Kardarshev in understanding the evolution of extraterrestrial life. Yet there is no reason to agree with him that evolution stops at a galactic level of energy consumption, a Type III extraterrestrial civilization. It's logical to go further and recognize that there is also a universal energy grid that is physically present that can be tapped into. Perhaps we already partially understand such an energy grid based on the pioneering work of quantum physics that have developed concepts such as "quantum entanglement" - to explain behavior across time and space suggesting some kind of universal interconnectedness.[525]

A Type IV civilization would be as dramatically different to the preceding levels of civilization, as each of the latter to the one preceding it. So there is no reason to exclude the possibility that Type IV civilizations have evolved beyond physical technology and use consciousness instead. A Type IV extraterrestrial civilization, comprising "celestials", would work with civilizations less evolved on the Kardashev energy scale. This appears to be precisely what historical texts appear to be telling us about the history of our world.

Historical texts point to the existence of celestials who in some cases work directly with extraterrestrials. The work and philosophies of celestials appears to be focused on helping humanity align with a higher universal will and avoid the inherent dangers posed by advanced technologies or domination by extraterrestrials or their progeny. The highly advanced consciousness of the celestials distinguishes them from extraterrestrials who in some of the cases examined above defer to the celestials who are described as "Masters of Wisdom", "Elders" or "Ascended Masters." In other cases, there is outright conflict between celestials and extraterrestrials.

The celestials appear very committed to ensuring that humanity's technological progress does not outstrip its ethical development. In historic cases where this has happened with the support of some extraterrestrials, celestials have directly intervened to end such a situation. Often the results have been cataclysmic with entire civilizations being destroyed. More typically, it appears that celestials help humanity's evolution in a more gradual noninterventionist manner. In such cases, they work directly with individuals whose interest in developing higher states of consciousness makes them suitable vehicles for such contact, and disseminating the information passed on by celestials.

Currently, humanity is at the precipice of great changes due to the more than sixty years of secret government agreements with extraterrestrials willing to trade technology for Earth resources.[526] In some cases, interbreeding programs have again raised the scepter of extraterrestrial progeny gaining undue influence in human society.[527] All these technology exchange and interbreeding programs have led to a highly secretive national security system in the U.S. and other countries. Advanced technologies have been developed to an extent far in excess of humanity's ethics and collective consciousness.

Historically, this has led to the direct intervention of celestials who have attempted to rectify such an imbalance by shattering the uneasy alliances between elite groups focused on technology acquisition. The current planetary situation is also very unbalanced wherein spiritual/ethical awareness has low priority against policies emphasizing technological progress at all cost. Such a planetary situation has been shown to be historically untenable. In the next chapter, I will show how celestials are working directly with an increasing number of individuals to rectify the situation by raising the consciousness of those ready to assist the Earth's evolution by balancing technological progress with spiritual awareness. There is cause for optimism that the increasing intervention of celestials along with sympathetic extraterrestrials and humans will help address the imbalance caused by more than sixty years of secret technology acquisition programs.

ENDNOTES – CHAPTER 14

[497] For evidence of the true history of human civilization on Earth, see Michael Cremo and Richard Thomson, *Forbidden Archeology: The Hidden History of the Human Race* (Bhaktivedenta Book Club Press, 1998).

[498] See Zecharia Sitchin, *Twelfth Planet: Book I of the Earth Chronicles* (The Earth Chronicles, 1976). Michael Cremo, *Human Devolution: A Vedic Alternative to Darwin's Theory* (Torchlight Publishing, 2003); and Richard Thomson, *Alien Identities : Ancient Insights into Modern UFO Phenomena* (Govardhan Hill Pub; 2 Revised edition (September 1995).

[499] For a detailed description of the Kardashev scale go to: http://en.wikipedia.org/wiki/Kardashev_scale

[500] See http://en.wikipedia.org/wiki/Kip_Thorne

[501] Paul LaViolette, Decoding the Message of the Pulsars: Intelligent Communication from the Galaxy (Bear & Company; 2006).

[502] See http://en.wikipedia.org/wiki/Pioneer_plaque

[503] See the following interview with Hurtak in 2000 where he talks about the "celestial civilizations of the Light" http://www.mcs.ca/vitalspark/2020_schools/309enoc00.html

[504] See Helena Blavatsky, Isis Unveiled: A Master-Key to the Mysteries of Ancient and Modern Science and Theology (1877). Available online at: http://www.theosociety.org/pasadena/isis/iu-hp.htm

[505] First published in 1925. Available online at: http://www.sanctusgermanus.net/ebooks/masters_of_the_path.pdf

[506] Leadbeater, C.W. The Masters and the Path. Adyar, India: Theosophical Publishing House 1929 (Reprint: Kessinger Publishing 1997). Available online at: http://www.anandgholap.net/Masters_And_Path-CWL.htm

[507] Published by Self-Realization Fellowship, 1947. Available online at: http://www.crystalclarity.com/yogananda/index.php

[508] John Keel used the term 'ultraterrestrial to refer to paranormal entities from Earth that could move between dimensions, but not travel between planets. See Keel, *The Mothman Prophecies* (Tor Books, 2002). Similarly Jacques Vallee wrote about such paranormal entities in relationship to UFO/extraterrestrial sightings in *Passport to Magonia: On UFOs, Folklore, and Parallel Worlds* (McGRaw-Hill, 1993). For an online article summarizing Keel's view, see Ken Korczak, "Fairies and UFOs?" http://www.conspiracyarchive.com/UFOs/ufofairies.htm

[509] See Zecharia Sitchin, *The 12th Planet: Book I of the Earth Chronicles* (Avon Books, 1976).

[510] See chapter two. For an earlier version, go to Michael Salla, "Eisenhower's 1954 Meeting With Extraterrestrials: The Fiftieth Anniversary of First Contact?" (February 12, 2004) available online at: http://exopolitics.org/Study-Paper-8.htm

[511] See Philip Corso, *The Day After Roswell* (Simon and Schuster, 1997).

[512] For an earlier version, see Michael Salla, Revised. <u>A Report on the Motivations and</u>

Activities of Extraterrestrial Races – A Typology of the most Significant Extraterrestrial Races Interacting with Humanity" (January 1, 2005) available online at: http://exopolitics.org/Report-ET-Motivations.htm

513 Book of Enoch, Chapter 6:1-7, available online at: http://wesley.nnu.edu/biblical_studies/noncanon/ot/pseudo/enoch.htm

514 See Zecharia Sitchin, *The Wars of Gods and Men: Book III of the Earth Chronicles* (Avon Books, 1985).

515 There is academic debate over whether Abraham came from the ancient Sumerian city of Ur located in modern day southern Iraq, or from a Chaldean city located in the southeast of modern day Turkey. For further discussion see Wikipedia entry for "Ur Kasdim", http://en.wikipedia.org/wiki/Ur_Kasdim

516 See Zecharia Sitchin *The 12th Planet* and Samuel Noah Kramer, *History Begins at Sumer: Thirty-Nine Firsts in Recorded History*, 3rd ed. (University of Pennsylvania Press, 1988).

517 Book of Enoch, Chapter 8:1-3 available online at: http://wesley.nnu.edu/biblical_studies/noncanon/ot/pseudo/enoch.htm

518 Book of Enoch, Chapter 9 available online at: http://wesley.nnu.edu/biblical_studies/noncanon/ot/pseudo/enoch.htm

519 Book of Enoch, Chapter 10:4-7 available online at: http://wesley.nnu.edu/biblical_studies/noncanon/ot/pseudo/enoch.htm

520 Book of Enoch, Chapter 10:9-11 available online at: http://wesley.nnu.edu/biblical_studies/noncanon/ot/pseudo/enoch.htm

521 See Sitchin, *The Wars of Gods and Men*, and Farrell, *The Cosmic War: Interplanetary Warfare, Modern Physics and Ancient Texts* (Adventures Unlimited Press, 2007).

522 Book of Enoch, Chapter 10:11-16 available online at: http://wesley.nnu.edu/biblical_studies/noncanon/ot/pseudo/enoch.htm

523 Ramesh Menon, ed., *Bhagavad Purana* (Rupa and Co., 2007) 709.

524 Cited from "Ancient Technology: Nuclear Warfare in Pre-History," http://www.geocities.com/age_of_giants/ancient_technology/nuclear.html

525 See: Brian Clegg, *The God Effect: Quantum Entanglement, Science's Strangest Phenomenon*, (St Martin's Griffin; 2009).

526 See chapters two and five.

527 For description for the contemporary version of interbreeding between humanity and extraterrestrials, see David Jacobs, *The Threat: Revealing the Secret Alien Agenda* (Simon and Schuster, 1999).

Chapter 15

Celestial encounters and extraterrestrial contact

Celestials failed galactic diplomacy in preventing nuclear weapons development

There are many contactee reports describing how celestials have been intervening in the modern era to encourage political leaders to choose wisely when it came to major policy issues like nuclear weapons development. The communications of celestials with private citizens and government/military authorities are examples of galactic diplomacy that have been secretly occurring since the dawn of the atomic era. Especially so with the development of thermonuclear weapons that were first developed and tested in November, 1952 during the final few months of Truman administration.

The first contactee to report about celestial intervention and the galactic diplomacy they were conducting was George Van Tassel. Beginning in 1954, Van Tassel organized major conventions at Giant Rock, California. The biggest one ever had 11,000 people attending in 1959.[528] He also attracted very large crowds coming to his conventions in the early 1960s. It was Van Tassel's experiences with the Ashtar Command that makes him very relevant to understanding celestial interactions with humanity.

Van Tassel was the first to mention the Ashtar Command which he described as a fleet of extraterrestrial ships (he called them flying saucers) headed by a being called "Ashtar" who works directly for a celestial hierarchy. Ashtar appears to be a celestial similar to the Archangel Michael, described in the *Book of Enoch*, that directly fulfills universal divine will. Ashtar was described in one of the messages received by Van Tassel as representing the executive branch of a Galactic authority/legislature headed by the "Council of the Twelve Lords and the Council of the Seven Lights."[529] Ashtar was essentially part of a hierarchy of ascended masters/celestials. So that was very significant relationship that Van Tassel was claiming existed. It was a relationship that was directly communicated to the highest levels of government and military in the USA. This was the first recorded act of galactic diplomacy by extraterrestrial visitors with the US government.

It was in January 1952 that Van Tassel began receiving his messages. It was President Truman's final full year in office - President Eisenhower was elected later that year on November 4. George van Tassel relayed information given to him by Ashtar to the U.S. Air Force at Wright Patterson Air Force Base several months prior to the detonation of the very first Hydrogen bomb test on November 1, 1952.[530] The Ashtar Command said that it would conduct a show of force to deter US authorities from moving forward with its nuclear development program.

In his small book giving the chronology of his communication with the Ashtar Command and what he relayed to the Air Force, Van Tassel says he received the following brief message on March 7, 1952:

> Greetings from the realms of Schare. Watch your skies in your months of May to August. I am Clota, 9th projection, 2nd wave, planet patrol realms of Schare. Discontinue.[531]

On April 6, there was more information conveyed, about what was about to take place, and a warning to the US Air Force:

> Your pentagon will soon have much to muddle over. We are going to give this globe a buzz. I hope they do not intercept us from in front. [532]

Here is what Van Tassel had to say about this cryptic April 6 communication:

> This message received in April was carried out three months later in the latter part of July. 'The pentagon, can only mean Washington, D. C. There is no doubt they had "much to muddle over." The "buzz" was accomplished by the saucer beings. The statement that the saucers hoped the Air Force would not intercept them in front, indicates that the saucers also knew in advance that there would be an attempt to intercept them. Is it

coincidence that a letter mailed by me to Air Forces Intelligence Command, at the request of the Saucer beings in the July 18th message, was in their hands when the "buzz" occurred? I do not comprehend how the letter's arrival, the "buzz," the reference to the pentagon, and the expected interception, can all be coincidence. My belief is that the saucer beings timed it that way, to let the Air Force know that this information was authentic. Their return receipt showed they received the letter July 22, 1952. The "buzz" was on July 26, 27 and 28th. [533]

The "buzz" referred to the most audacious display of extraterrestrial technology ever witnessed – successive weekend flyovers over Washington DC in mid to late July, 1952. Before discussing the flyovers, I need to show you the July 18th message Van Tassel received and relayed to the US Air Force before the final flyover on July 26-28.

Hail to you beings of Shan [Earth]. I greet you in love and peace. My identity is Ashtar, commandant quadra sector, patrol station Schare, all projections, all waves. Greetings. Through the Council of the Seven Lights you have been brought here, inspired with the inner light to help your fellow man. You are mortals, and other mortals can only understand that which their fellow man can understand. The purpose of this organization is, in a sense, to save mankind from himself. Some years ago, your time, your nuclear physicists penetrated the "Book of Knowledge." They discovered how to explode the atom. Disgusting as the results have been, that this force should be used for destruction, it is not compared to that which can be. We have not been concerned with their explosion of plutonium and U235, the Uranium mother element; this atom is an inert element.

We are concerned, however, with their attempt to explode the hydrogen element. This element is life giving along with five other elements in the air you breathe, in the water you drink, in the composition of your physical self. In much of your material planet is this life giving atomic substance, hydrogen. Their efforts in the field of science have been successful to the extent that they are not content to rest on the laurels of a power beyond their use; not content with the entire destruction of an entire city at a time. They must have something more destructive. They've got it....

Our message to you is this: You shall advance to your government all information we have transmitted to you. You shall request that your government shall immediately contact all other earth nations regardless of political feelings. Many of your physicists with an inner perception development have refused to have anything to do with the explosion of the hydrogen atom. The explosion of an atom of inert substance and that of a living substance are two different things. We are not concerned with man's desire to continue war on this planet, Shan. We are concerned with their deliberate determination to extinguish humanity and turn this planet into a cinder.

... Our missions are peaceful, but this condition occurred before in this solar system and the planet Lucifer was torn to bits. We are determined that it shall not happen again. The governments on the planet Shan have conceded that we are of a higher intelligence. They must concede also that we are of a higher authority. We do not have to enter their buildings to know what they are doing. We have the formula they would like to use. It is not meant for destruction. Your purpose here has been to build a receptivity that we could communicate with your planet, for by the attraction of light substance atoms, we patrol your universe.

"To your government and to your people and through them to all governments and all peoples on the planet of Shan, accept the warning as a blessing that mankind may survive. My light, we shall remain in touch here at this cone of receptivity. My love, I am Ashtar."[534]

The message claimed that Ashtar was acting on a higher authority than human governments in his efforts to warn humanity about the dangers of thermonuclear weapons. The message's reference to the opposition of some atomic scientists to thermonuclear weapons was based on what we now know was the determined opposition by Robert Oppenheimer, "father of the atomic bomb", to the development of thermonuclear weapons.[535] Also intriguing was Ashtar's reference to the planet Lucifer that was destroyed by nuclear weapons. Was the asteroid belt the remnants of another planet in our solar system that was destroyed by thermonuclear weapons? Yes, according to Ashtar!

As Van Tassell said, this message from Ashtar was received and immediately relayed to the US Air Force on July 18, 1952. It was officially received on July 22. So what happened over the succeeding weekends from July 18 to the end of the month? This was the time of the 1952 Washington flyover which we now know was a demonstration of force by the Ashtar Command.

The 1952 Washington flyovers was a very serious historical event that is well documented. Over three successive weekends beginning on July 12, fleets of UFOs (or flying saucers as they were known at the time) flew over the restricted airspace of Washington DC. The two most publicized flyover events were on the weekends of July 19-20 and July 26-27.[536] They flew directly over the White House, the Capitol Building, and the Pentagon. The UFOs were witnessed by thousands, tracked on radar, photographed, intercepted by Air Force jets, and so on. This was startling confirmation that Van Tassel's communication from Ashtar was very serious, and the Pentagon was indeed experiencing a "buzz". So what was the official response to this startling demonstration of force by the Ashtar Command?

An order was given by President Truman to shoot the UFOs down! Here is how Grant Cameron, a prominent UFO researcher, describes what happened after the July 19-20 flyover:

"A massive build-up of sightings over the United States in 1952, especially in July, alarmed the Truman administration." It led the Truman administration to give the order that the flying saucers be shot down. On July 26, 1952, the Air Force obeyed and gave the order to "Shoot them down!" [537]

The shoot down orders were reported in the international media and created a global buzz:

> ... one such story reported that "jet pilots have been placed on a 24-hour nationwide 'alert against the flying saucers' with orders to 'shoot them down' if they ignore orders to land." An Air Force public information officer, Lt. Col. Moncel Monte, confirmed the directive stating, "The jet pilots are, and have been, under orders to investigate unidentified objects and to shoot them down if they can't talk them down." It was further stated that no pilot had been able to get close enough to take a shot at a "flying saucer", as the objects would disappear or speed away as soon as an interceptor approached, sometimes outflying their pilots by "as much as a thousand miles an hour."[538]

Thankfully, the shoot down orders were quickly reversed. According to Cameron:

> "Several prominent scientists, including Albert Einstein, protested the order to the White House and urged that the command be rescinded, not only in the interest of future intergalactic peace, but also in the interest of self-preservation: Extraterrestrials would certainly look upon an attack by the primitive jet firepower as a breach of the universal laws of hospitality. The 'shoot them down' order was consequently withdrawn on White House orders by five o'clock that afternoon." That night the saucers were back.[539]

The US Air Force subsequently held its biggest Press conference since the Second World War. Major General John Samford, Chief of Air Intelligence, claimed that the Washington UFO sightings were likely a result of a "temperature inversion." It was a lie, and ridiculed by experts. Nevertheless, the Press gave blanket coverage of the official Air Force explanation leading to the general public soon forgetting about the incident. The true significance of the Washington UFO fly over was hidden from the public ever since. Extraterrestrials working under a hierarchy of celestials called the "Seven Lights" had conducted galactic diplomacy with the Truman administration over the development of thermonuclear weapons. After communicating their opposition, and conducting a clear show of force, the extraterrestrials and the celestial hierarchy were spurned by the Truman administration. America would forge ahead in developing Hydrogen bombs.

Figure 25. Adamski photo taken in March 1951, shows a mothership and five smaller objects (scoutcraft) emerging.

Extraterrestrial concern over nuclear weapons appeared again and again in the communications relayed by other contactees in the months and years following the 1952 Washington DC UFO flyovers and Van Tassel's communications with the U.S. Air Force. Most prominent among the contactees was George Adamski.

George Adamski was first known for photographing spectacular extraterrestrial motherships and their scoutcraft. Adamski began taking his photos in 1947, and some were printed in prominent magazines of the day. They have never been shown to be hoaxed.

As I described earlier, Adamski gained public prominence due to the famous Desert Landing incident in November 1952. Six witnesses saw Adamski meeting with an extraterrestrial, Orthon, who emerged from a flying saucer.[540] That meeting happened on November 20, 1952. The date's important because this was less than three weeks after the testing of the first Hydrogen bomb by the Truman administration. This was one of the main topics of discussion according to Adamski. Orthon was relaying a warning about the dangers posed by nuclear weapons, and the threat to humanity. Here is how Adamski described their conversation:

> He made me understand that their coming was friendly. Also, as he gestured, that they were concerned with radiations going out from Earth.... I asked if this concern was due to the explosions of our bombs with their resultant vast radio-active clouds? He understood this readily and nodded his head in the affirmative. My next question was whether this was dangerous, and I pictured in my mind a scene of destruction. To this, too, he nodded his head in the affirmative... I wanted to know if this was affecting outer space ? Again a nod of affirmation....
> I persisted and wanted to know if it was dangerous to us on Earth as well as affecting things in space? He made me understand—by gesturing with his hands to indicate cloud formations from explosions—that after too many such explosions. Yes! His affirmative nod of the head was very positive and he even spoke the word 'Yes' in this instance. The cloud formations were easy to imply with the movement of his hands and arms, but to express the explosions he said, 'Boom ! Boom !' Then, further to explain himself, he touched me, then as a little weed growing close by, and next pointed to the Earth itself, and with ,a wide sweep of his hands and other gestures that too many 'Booms!' would destroy all of this.[541]

Adamski later claimed to have been taken into an extraterrestrial mothership in February 1953. In it he described meeting Orthon and a number of other extraterrestrials from planets in our solar system including Venus, Mars and Saturn. Adamski described the extraterrestrials as human looking and possessing advanced technologies. There was however, often a picture or reminder of an advanced being or 'master' that the extraterrestrials venerated as embodiments of universal wisdom. Adamski described sitting at a table with extraterrestrials on board their ship where he for the first time met one of their 'masters of wisdom':

> Now as we sat around the table, all eyes turned to the older space man as he began to speak. Although it was only later that his stature on all planets was explained to me, it was impossible not to realize that I was in the presence of a greatly evolved being, and the attitude of all present clearly indicated that they, as well as I, felt very humble before him. I learned that his age, in his present body, was close to one thousand years.[542]

Adamski clearly felt that the being possessed an extraordinarily high degree of consciousness that had great wisdom. So not only was Adamski impressed by this being, this "Master of Wisdom" or celestial, the extraterrestrials also revered him. It was beyond just one planetary culture that he was revered, but he was revered on many planets. So again that's an example of this kind of universal brotherhood that spans the Galaxy.

The celestial warned Adamski of the dangers of nuclear weapons, and this is what he said:

> Our main purpose in coming to you at this time is to warn you of the grave danger which threatens men of Earth today. Knowing more than any amongst you yet realize, we feel it our duty to enlighten you if we can. Your people may accept the knowledge we hope to give them through you and through others, or they can turn deaf ears and destroy themselves. The choice is with the Earth's inhabitants. We cannot dictate.

This is a warning about the dangers of these nuclear weapons, and about the policies we are following as a planetary culture.

Adamski described other contact experiences involving 'masters of wisdom' who were revered by the extraterrestrials on the ship, and on other worlds. His experiences help verify the existence the celestials who in some cases cooperate with extraterrestrials seen to be fulfilling a higher spiritual mission.

Something that needs to be pointed out is that Adamski claims that he regularly visited the Pentagon to brief senior military officials about his contact experiences, and the messages he was receiving. Essentially, after a contact experience, Adamski would travel to a nearby Air Force base and be flown immediately to the Pentagon. Adamski's claims are supported by several witnesses that saw documents he possessed that gave him access to military facilities. One of the witnesses was William Sherwood, who was an expert image analyst with Kodak Eastman and who analyzed Adamski's 1965 video of a flying saucer which he concluded was authentic.[543] Sherwood himself had previously worked for the U.S. Ordnance Department and possessed his own ordnance pass. Sherwood saw Adamski's Ordnance pass thereby giving credence to Adamski's claims that he secretly briefed the Pentagon about his extraterrestrial contacts.[544] Another witness who saw Adamski's ordnance pass was Madeline Rodeffer, who worked as a secretary for the U.S. Air Force.

Not only was Adamski informing the public about his incredible contact experiences and communications on the dangers posed by nuclear weapons, he was also acting as an intermediary to the Pentagon. So once again, as in the Van Tassel case, we see evidence that senior military officials were being briefed about the dangers of nuclear weapons from both extraterrestrials and celestials. Once again, the Galactic Diplomacy led by celestials was being spurned at the highest levels of the US military and government.

Celestial encounters: extraterrestrials and consciousness raising

In this section, we see the profound impact "celestials" have on the consciousness of contactees. The consciousness raising influence of celestials emerges clearly in the contactee accounts of their 'celestial encounters' – meetings with highly evolved "masters of wisdom."

Importantly, this consciousness raising process is recognized by the extraterrestrial companions of the celestials, who indeed encourage contactees to have these celestial encounters.

We begin with another prominent contactee from the Adamski era. Howard Menger first went public with his claims in 1957 at a number of radio shows and conventions. In 1959 he followed these public appearances with his first book, *From Outer Space*. In chapter six, we learned about Menger and his remarkable claims of helping extraterrestrials that were operating as agents on the Earth. There is more worth investigating in Menger's claims. When visiting one of the extraterrestrial ships, Menger claimed that he met a celestial.

The experience with the celestial came well after Menger had had many extraterrestrial contact experiences, none of which touched him as deeply as this celestial encounter. We get an idea of the profound presence and energy field of the celestial by Menger's description of him:

When it [flying saucer] landed I walked to within a hundred feet of it when two men stepped out of it and waited, one on each side of the door. I sensed something important and unusual was about to take place. I walked closer, then stopped, waiting for a feeling or sense which would indicate it was all right to proceed further. Then a magnificent sight appeared in the doorway. A tall handsome man with long blond hair over his shoulder stood towering at the entrance. He looked directly at me as he stepped out of the ship....

The sight of the man thrilled me. He was dressed in a radiant white ski-type uniform, girdled about the waist with a white belt.... Over the uniform he wore a light blue, fluorescent-like cape, fastened at the left shoulder with a gold pin in the shape of a wheel. A slight, enigmatic smile played on his lips as he looked at me, while the expression in his eyes was one of pure love and understanding. I felt like a small child, humble and loving, and I wanted to embrace him as a long lost friend and remembered loved one. I believe I had the same feelings I would have experienced had the Master Jesus just stepped out of the craft. I studied his face—it was all compassion and love....[545]

Notice that two extraterrestrials first stepped out of the craft and then stood apart by the entrance. Then the Jesus-like figure, the celestial stepped outside. Menger immediately recognized that there was something very different about him. His uniform, insignia, presence and energy field were all very different to the two extraterrestrials that flanked him. Menger didn't learn about the history of the celestial, but it was very clear that he worked very closely with extraterrestrials. Menger went on to describe the personal impact of the experience on him:

> I shall never forget this awe-inspiring experience: it is too strongly impressed in my soul by the love, compassion and wisdom of this profound teacher. That wonderful being unlocked the door to my own soul, and in a few brief moments planted the seeds of infinite knowledge in my subconscious, which over a period of months and years gradually seeps out to my conscious expression. It reminds me of the ministry of Jesus. His entire message of love and good will toward mankind was a mental capsulation to the people of his time; and it is only now that the truth of his being is gradually coming out and the understanding of his great love is emerging from the quicksand of misunderstanding, at last into the sunlight of our conscious acceptance of the Infinite Father.[546]

The celestial went on to describe how extraterrestrials have been helping humanity since the dawn of the atomic age in 1945.

> In the year of your time 1945 we concentrated a large group of servants of our Infinite Father, which you have called "angels" in your scriptures, to aid you with the help of our machines, which project thought impulses in the direction of a specified area of chaos.[547]

The basic idea being expressed here is that celestials work closely with extraterrestrials and their technology to assist humanity where needed, and to help raise humanity's collective consciousness. We see a similar dynamic with the report of a celestial encounter by another contactee from Colombia.

Enrique Castillo Rincon worked as an engineer in Bogota, Colombia when he claims he began communicating with and having physical contact with extraterrestrials from the Pleiades over a three year period, 1973-1976. Multiple witnesses saw many of the incidents described in Rincon's book that detailed his experiences and provided photographic evidence supporting some of his claims.[548] His education, profession and independent witness support give his claims much credibility.

Rincon described three times where he was taken aboard Pleiadian spacecraft and flown to various locations, and given much information about the extraterrestrials activities and agenda for humanity. In one incident, he described how he was taken by the extraterrestrials to meet with another group of 24 contactees at a remote location in the Andes. Rincon described how he and the others were given special 'ambassadorial' training to prepare humanity for the truth of extraterrestrial life. At the end of his training he describes how the group of contactees and a number of extraterrestrials were taken to meet with a "Master of Wisdom." Rincon described the appearance of the Master of Wisdom who came out of a tunnel built high in the Andes as follows:

> The instructor [an extraterrestrial] approached the entrance to a tunnel carved in the living rock and clasped his hands twice. He retired to one side, and the most incredible being made his appearance. We were astonished beyond description. That being looked exactly like Jesus, the Master. I thought immediately that the Pleiadians had brought us here with the purpose of meeting Jesus Christ, who was here again, fulfilling the prophecies...[549]

This is an example of Pleiadian extraterrestrials with advanced technologies taking someone who they recognized as having potential to embrace their message for the benefit of humanity, to a remote location in the Andes where he meets with someone who lives in a cave. Importantly, extraterrestrials also revered this cave dweller who clearly was an extraordinary individual.

The "Master of Wisdom" then dispelled Rincon's belief that he was Jesus Christ:

> I am not who you believe I am. My name is a thousand names, give me any, and That I Am. I am ancient before you, not in age, but in knowledge... My name is Age, for I am the Ages and the Time. I am Wisdom, and my name is Wisdom. I hold thirty five percent of universal wisdom."[550]

That last statement where he said, "I hold thirty five percent of universal wisdom," is very important. If a society or culture learns how to tap into the energies of a galaxy, or beyond the galaxy into the universe, then what it would value is the ability of those that have learned to be able to access universal energies to be able to channel that creatively for constructive purposes. It would probably develop a way to measure a person's ability to tap into universal energy as this being obviously was doing.

The speech by the Master of Wisdom suggested that he was a celestial who had achieved an extraordinarily high level of cosmic consciousness. This had given him the ability to transcend space and time, and made him a figure of reverence among the extraterrestrials. Rincon said that the "intelligence and love expressed by his face, projecting peace was the most incredible and marvelous that I have ever felt." [551] This strongly echoed what Menger had experienced in his own celestial encounter.

Rincon left with a number of unanswered questions from the extraterrestrials about the encounter with the celestial:

> What is the role of this unusual personality whom we met at the Vortex? Why are his words so similar to those of Jesus Christ,

being somebody else? What is his relationship with the extraterrestrials?[552]

While the extraterrestrials did not answer his questions, Rincon reached his own conclusion:

> The experience with the extraterrestrials, the instructors, and the personality with a thousand names left me in a quasi-mystic condition, which I could barely surmount…. There was no doubt, as far as I was concerned: the High Entity of the Andes was the same One that I called, and rightly so, the "Master of Wisdom."[553]

Rincon's encounter with the Master of Wisdom, demonstrated the qualitative differences in the nature of experience with celestials as opposed to extraterrestrials. While the latter can lead to very positive inspiring encounters, encounters with celestials are life transforming. This qualitative difference appears to also be recognized by extraterrestrials who give a great degree of respect and reverence to celestials. The next celestial encounter involves another South American contactee.

In chapter three I discussed the case of Luis Fernando Mostajo, who is an architect from Bolivia. His professional background, supporting witness testimony, and sincerity gives me a high degree of confidence that he is narrating actual physical events as they occurred to him. Luis Fernando claims to have had physical contacts with extraterrestrials from Venus and Ganymede (a moon of Jupiter). He says he was physically taken to Venus and Ganymede where he encountered the advanced civilizations established by extraterrestrials belonging to the Confederation of Worlds. This is what he said happened to him:

> After three years of preparation, I was in the middle of the Andes. They told me that at eight o'clock at night a ship was going to come to a valley called "Valle Potosi". This ship was going to monitor the materialization of the door through which I would be able to get in touch with them, and through which I

would arrive at a city not located on this planet, Earth, but on Venus in a valley known to them as ... the *Valley Of Silence*. This is a place where there the Academy of Spiritual Science of this civilization concentrates.[554]

He describes actually meeting with the Venusian Masters of this civilization. Luis describes being taken to visit them by a Venusian called E'tel.

He took me to the presence of three elders – the wise people of Venus. They spoke lovingly to me through the *universal language*, which is not only telepathic, but is a series of ideograms, which is what they call a *record* [represented in image on right]. We know it as the *Akashic Record*. This is something that is in the Van Allen Radiation Belt around the Earth. It is continuously recording every thought of every one of us. In its physical form, there are seven shapes. That's what the elders said.

Earth's Akashic Records are protected by an *internal government of the Earth*. This internal government of the Earth is known as the *Great White Brotherhood*. And this Great White Brotherhood was formed at the end of the destruction of the ancient Atlantis civilization. Before the disappearance of their civilization, the elders of Atlantis protected their knowledge by placing it in trusted guardianships at the various colonies that they established in different locations inside the planet. It is at these places where the *positive government of the Earth* is residing. They are waiting lovingly for humanity to mature so that they can give us this knowledge and then the *new humanity* can be guided, like a road map, so that we don't make the same mistakes again. That is how it was conveyed to me. So, near to where I used to live at Lake Titicaca, in another small lake known as Lago Winaymarka in the Aymara language, there is one of these internal places. Part of my mission is to stay in touch with them because they are human beings, teachers who, for thousands of years, have understood the purpose of the Earth and of the creation of the cosmos. [555]

It's important to point out that this civilization on Venus is not on the surface. Luis Fernando says it's an interior civilization. It's within and under the surface of Venus. Once again we have an example of "masters of wisdom" or celestials occupying leadership positions among extraterrestrials. Notice that Luis claims that a similar "internal government" exists on Earth, and that he was taken to see one of these "intraterrestrial" outposts under Lake Titicaca, Bolivia.

During one of his encounters with an extraterrestrial from Ganymede called Xenon, he was introduced to a being described as an Elder, an 'ascended master' from the Great White Brotherhood, a celestial, who resided under Lake Titicaca. Luis Fernando writes about how Xenon, introduced him to the Elder:

> Now, the priority is to start applying the teachings that I have given you for the conscious control of each of your bodies. This will allow you to access a new order of experiences that begin today with the presence of a master of Earth's White Brotherhood. He is Soromez who will join us shortly.... [556]

Luis Fernando was subsequently told more about the history of the Elders or Great White Brotherhood in terms of their alignment with higher states of consciousness or divine law:

> [T]he elders have been waiting for you since the beginning of time, because they have always been, and will always be... This is because the elders are one with the Profound and the Profound is one with them. When this planet was conceived, they were conceived along with it because they are where the work of the omnipresent creator is, in contemplation to His creative directive.... They protect your humanity with the zeal of the light in their work, with the will to serve in their surrender, and with the knowledge of life in action.... They represent in this world the active White Brotherhood, because they promote all

the positive changes directed to the development of the human race.[557]

According to Xenon, the White Brotherhood "reside in completely secluded places in the different continents of your world. These places are removed from all urban centers and are completely inaccessible, unless one has been called to them."[558] Xenon further revealed that the hidden retreats established by the While Brotherhood had been recently relocated from Tibet to the Andean mountain region of Peru and Bolivia due to the Chinese occupation. In his book, Luis Fernando describes later being taken into the underwater retreat of the Tiahuanaco Elders at Lake Titicaca.[559]

Luis described the profound nature of his celestial encounter with the Elders, as transcending everything that he had previously experienced with his extraterrestrial contacts:

> This experience was beyond the previous one I'd had, going beyond the Earth. I was able to know and integrate myself with these elders who are very, very old. They are the guardians of human history. Today they have opened the doors so that this wisdom and knowledge can reach humanity.[560]

It's important to emphasize that with the celestial encounters that Luis Fernando experienced in underground locations on Earth and Venus, in both cases extraterrestrials acted as intermediaries. They introduced Luis Fernando to the Elders/celestials that had such a profound experience on him. Once again, as in the Menger and Rincon cases, these were life changing experiences with highly evolved spiritual beings that even extraterrestrials deferred to.

Luis Fernando has led a number of seminars at a retreat he has built on the shores of Lake Titicaca one of which I attended in October 2008.[561] During the seminar we were taken by boat to an uninhabited island which he claims is physically the closest point to both the Lake Titicaca retreat of the Great White Brotherhood, and also an adjacent extraterrestrial base. In an interview I later did with Luis, I asked him "why the Lake Titicaca Lodge of the Great White Brotherhood is so close to a Galactic Confederation base." He replied:

> In Lake Titicaca you can not only find the Solar Retreat of the White Brotherhood, but also a great base of the Confederation of Worlds of the galaxy. According to the communication and information received by the extraterrestrial guides, the relevance of the ships of the Lake Titicaca, not only provides them a permanent interaction and coordination of the tasks with the Interior Government of the White City, but it will also help the strengthening of the cosmic energy in the epicenter of the same cosmic energy or feminine in this part of the planet. The energy of Love. That is why the interaction of the contact groups in Wiñaymarka, the External Retreat is permanent with the Confederation ships, having landed on more than one occasion at the Temple of Solar Initiation, radiating special energies which happened to us recently Michael, in our journey [October 18-25, 2008].[562]

Now I can summarize the most important aspects of Luis' experiences for my inquiry into celestial encounters and extraterrestrial contact. After Luis had his first experience with extraterrestrials on Earth, he is taken to an underground location on Venus where he encounters celestials who are in leadership positions for the Venusian civilization. During his meeting with extraterrestrials from Venus they said to him, "we want you to meet someone. We want to introduce you to someone. There's this being who lives right where you are, very close. He is a Master of Wisdom, and a descendent of the ancient Tiahuanaco civilization that was itself a remnant of Atlantis. He is an Ascended Master and we want to introduce you to him."

So that's what the extraterrestrials did. They introduced him to this Ascended Master or Master of Wisdom from the pre-Incan Tiahuanaco civilization. The really important thing to recognize here is that we have an example of a contact experience where the extraterrestrial tells the contactee "we want to introduce you to an Ascended Master or celestial and he is indigenous to the Earth."

Next, we look at the fascinating case of a celestial encounter by Vladimir Megre, a Russian entrepreneur. Megre revealed meeting Anastasia, a female Siberian recluse whose remarkable abilities and teachings concerning a back to nature lifestyle is having a powerfully transformative effect in Russia and beyond. Revelations of her amazing life in the Siberian 'tiaga' where she is able to live in the harshest conditions without any modern amenities, is leading to a powerful grass roots movement for small scale agriculture and spiritually reconnecting with the land. Millions in Russia and elsewhere have developed conferences and clubs where her teachings and practices are more closely studied. According to Megre, she has powerful telekinetic abilities, can telepathically communicate with animals and people, and can use remote influencing on people at great distances. Perhaps most remarkably, she is able to instantly teleport herself anywhere. Her remarkable abilities, if Megre's accounts are accurate, suggest she is a celestial since she can travel anywhere in space time without any technological assistance.

Megre's books describe several incidents where she interacts with extraterrestrials and their advanced technologies. Anastasia is particularly concerned by the possibility that extraterrestrial technology might be used as a Trojan horse to win over the loyalty of much of humanity, thereby leading ultimately to the loss of humanity's sovereignty. She is intent on demonstrating to Megre the superiority of a focused mind that can influence the environment, to the technology possessed by the extraterrestrials.

In an incident vividly described by Megre, Anastasia physically traveled to another world to persuade extraterrestrials that Earth was not worth taking over. The incident began as a remote viewing session where both Anastasia and Vladimir observed extraterrestrials planning to covertly take over the Earth by first distributing advanced technologies. According to Anastasia,

> The [extraterrestrial] visitors offer to share their technology in providing each citizen of the country with nutrient mixture and rapid construction of housing for everyone... In the apartments provided you, everything you need will react only to your voice

344

commands, identified by tones inherent in your voice.... [T]he computers in your apartments will scan your eyes, breath and other parameters to determine your physical health and prescribe the corresponding food mixture composition.[563]

Figure 26. Book cover depicting Anastasia using psychic powers

In responding to Megre's belief that such technology would be a boon to humanity, Anastasia replied:

All people on the Earth will be compelled to render daily service to those devices which outwardly serve them. All mankind will fall into a trap, surrendering their own freedom and that of their children for the sake of an artificial technological perfection.[564]

After persuading Megre about the dangers posed by advanced technology that the extraterrestrials would bring with them, Anastasia responds to Megre's request to physically travel to the planet to put a stop to their plans. He then writes:

> And all at once in front of me I saw Anastasia in the flesh.... She stood there barefoot on the floor and then all at once started walking unhurriedly over to the aliens ... They caught sight of her ... Suddenly, as if on command, they all rose and grasped hold of the medallions around their necks. All the medallions flashed with rays of light, all directed at the approaching figure of Anastasia. She stopped, lost her balanced momentarily took a small step backward, then stopped again. Giving a little stamp with her bare foot, she slowly and confidently moved forward again... The rays coming from the aliens' medallions got brighter and brighter as they joined together, concentrating on Anastasia. It looked as though it would take but a moment for them to reduce all the clothing on her to ashes. All at once she stretched her hands out in front of her. Some of the rays reflected off the palms of her hands and were extinguished. Then the others started to go out. [565]

After having rendered their medallion weapons inoperative, Megre described how Anastasia persuaded the extraterrestrials that her remarkable abilities made the Earth too difficult a place to take over.

Megre's account of Anastasia is consistent with earlier descriptions of how celestials were concerned about how advanced technologies by extraterrestrials could be used to subvert humanity. In the case of Anastasia, it appears that celestials can sometimes take preemptive action to impede take-over plans where extraterrestrials manipulate humanity's desire for labor saving technological devices.

Conclusion

In this final chapter we have discovered that contactees work directly with some of the extraterrestrial civilizations described in chapter three and four as friendly to human interests. In turn, many of these civilizations work closely with celestial beings that are a more highly evolved form of life due to their ability to tap into a universal energy grid – Type IV civilizations according to the Kardarshev scale. Celestials are helping humanity prepare for the major challenges posed by our technological development and extraterrestrial contact. Of most concern has been the development of thermonuclear weapons, a weapon designed exclusively to terrorize populations, rather than having any battlefield significance. Despite the end of the Cold War, these weapon systems remain a threat.

When contactees meet celestials/Ascended Masters they learn that most intelligent civilizations in the universe are peaceful. Celestials are part of a vast cosmic fraternity, and have an emphasis on the same values that we cherish: truth, justice, love and integrity. Extraterrrestrial civilizations recognize the suitability of these Ascended Masters to be leaders of their worlds, of their cultures, their civilizations. This has been abundantly displayed in the way the contactees have described the interaction between extraterrestrials and celestials. Most importantly, the celestial encounters reported by the contactees are the most life transformative experiences they have had. The consciousness raising impact of celestials is arguably their most important contribution to humanity at this point in our history. In conclusion, celestials are here to help our world and civilization evolve into a higher potential.

No wonder then that we have seen that authorities have scrambled really hard to suppress information through a Galactic COINTELPRO program described in chapter seven. The authorities don't want us to know about George Van Tassel's communications on behalf of the Ashtar Command and how it was responsible for the 1952 Washington UFO sightings. The authorities don't want us to know that George Adamski was genuine, and was secretly briefing military officials about the galactic diplomacy of extraterrestrials and their celestial friends. The authorities don't want us to know of the life transformative experiences of Howard Menger, Enrique Castillo Rincon, and others. Essentially, the authorities don't want us to know that celestials encounters have been happening, and that some extraterrestrial civilizations are helping humans to have such experiences.

Those public authorities leading the world wide cover-up of the existence of extraterrestrial life and technology want to spin a very different story. Their story about extraterrestrial life as illustrated by a host of recent propaganda films released by Hollywood, is based on threats and dangers from extraterrestrial visitors. In chapter five, we saw how the behavior of some extraterrestrials can, at best, be described as enigmatic. The behavior of some of the extraterrestrials visiting or based on our world does appear to be unfriendly. Yet, this is only part of a more complex story concerning the motivations of different extraterrestrial civilizations visiting and/or interacting with our world. In many ways, extraterrestrials are not too different from us. Most societies possess a criminal underclass, but these are always a small percentage of the overall citizenry who are law abiding, willing to help others in distress, and have a natural empathy for their fellow citizens. Why would extraterrestrial civilizations be any different? Our world is being thrust from a very insular shallow planetary civilization where we think it's only us, to a civilization where we recognize there's a much bigger reality happening out there.

So we are going through this great change and the scientific community is starting to come on board, thinking about the possibilities of extraterrestrial life. More scientific conferences dealing with the possibility of extraterrestrial life and its social consequences are being held. That's a very good thing. More scientists are talking about what extraterrestrials are like, using the typology developed back in the 1960s by the Russian astronomer Kardashev.

Eventually as we understand the evolution of civilizations from Type 1 to Type III, in future people will begin appreciate that there are Type IV civilizations out there, and ask, "what are they like?" Maybe an example is these Ascended Masters, Masters of Wisdom, Great White Brotherhood, or celestials. It's interesting that celestials are not only found throughout the galaxy, throughout the universe, but they are also here on our planet Earth. Sometimes we lose touch with that reality. We get focused on the possibility of life out there and forget about the incredibly evolved conscious beings that live on the Earth.

Celestials are here to help us rectify the imbalance between technology and consciousness. That's one of the topics I talked about in chapters two and five. For more than sixty years the U.S. government has been secretly liaising and developing agreements with some extraterrestrial civilizations that are very far removed from the celestial universal consciousness that I've been focusing on for the final two chapters of this book.

So what lies ahead? We will learn that the vast majority of extraterrestrial life is friendly and willing to assist in humanity's evolution in positive ways, and helping us achieve world peace. Celestials and more evolved extraterrestrials will assist humanity in transitioning from a Type 0 civilization reliant on fossil fuels into a Type 1 society using free and alternative energy sources.

Along the way, we will have to learn how to develop better tools of galactic diplomacy (aka 'exodiplomacy'), as private citizens, nations, and as a unified planet. We need to develop *principled negotiation* skills so that we can respect the vital interests of all parties impacted by visiting extraterrestrial life. We have some important tools that we can use based on earlier citizen diplomacy efforts (chapters 8-13) where groups of individuals identified the vital interests of individuals, communities and the biosphere in ground breaking documents.

We desperately need to develop transparency and discernment in how to respond to the many different extraterrestrial visitors wishing to provide us technology, and the wisdom of celestials in emphasizing consciousness raising before incorporating some of these technologies.

I sincerely hope that the information presented in this book helps us move forward in our global awakening to the reality of extraterrestrial life and its diversity. We need to make wise decisions as an emerging planetary civilization. That is especially the case when it comes to choosing who among the diversity of extraterrestrial visitors to our planet are willing to recognize our vital interests in reaching any negotiated agreements. As private citizens we need to find innovative ways of "Getting to Yes with ET;" and bring transparency to how government, military and corporate entities have conducted negotiations in the past; and what they plan to do in the future.

The path we are treading of world peace, global justice and human prosperity are all vital human interests that give us common bonds with some of our extraterrestrial visitors. Many of them have travelled further down this path than we have. We are poised to become a galactic civilization, and that means discerning our true friends as those respecting and supporting our vital interests as individuals, nations, and an emerging planetary civilization. "Galactic Diplomacy" and "Getting to Yes with ET" are ideas whose time have come.

ENDNOTES - CHAPTER 15

[528] See: http://www.lucernevalley.net/giantrock/

[529] George Van Tassel, *I Rode on a Flying Saucer* (New Age Publishing Co. 1952) 30. Available online at: www.scribd.com/doc/467760/I-Rode-A-Flying-Saucer-George-Van-Tassel

[530] The Ivy Mike test involved a thermonuclear device with destructive force of just over 10 megatons. Nearly 1000 times the destructive force of the atomic bomb dropped at Hiroshima. See: http://en.wikipedia.org/wiki/Ivy_Mike

[531] George Van Tassel, *I Rode on a Flying Saucer,* 19. Available online at: www.scribd.com/doc/467760/I-Rode-A-Flying-Saucer-George-Van-Tassel

[532] George Van Tassel, *I Rode on a Flying Saucer,* 20.

[533] George Van Tassel, *I Rode on a Flying Saucer,* 20.

[534] George Van Tassel, *I Rode on a Flying Saucer,* 30-32. Available online at: www.scribd.com/doc/467760/I-Rode-A-Flying-Saucer-George-Van-Tassel

[535] For discussion of Oppenheimer's opposition to the Hydrogen Bomb, see http://en.wikipedia.org/wiki/J._Robert_Oppenheimer#Postwar_activities

[536] See "1952 Washington DC UFO Incident," http://en.wikipedia.org/wiki/1952_Washington,_D.C._UFO_incident

[537] Cited at: http://www.presidentialufo.com/harry-s-truman/64-president-harry-s-truman

[538] Cited at: http://en.wikipedia.org/wiki/1952_Washington,_D.C._UFO_incident

[539] Cited at: http://www.presidentialufo.com/harry-s-truman/64-president-harry-s-truman

[540] Adamski's desert landing incident is described in Desmond Leslie and George Adamski, *Flying Saucers have Landed* (The British Book Center, 1954). Available online at: http://www.universe-people.com/english/svetelna_knihovna/htm/en/en_kniha_flying_saucers_have_landed.htm

[541] George Adamski, *Flying Saucers have Landed* . Available online at: http://www.universe-people.com/english/svetelna_knihovna/htm/en/en_kniha_flying_saucers_have_landed.htm

[542] George Adamski, *Inside the Space Ships* (Warner Paper backs [1955] 1974) 63.

[543] See Neil Gould, "Revisiting George Adamski's claims of Human looking Extraterrestrials," available at: http://exopoliticsjournal.com/vol-3/vol-3-2-Gould.htm

[544] See Sherwood testimony at: http://www.examiner.com/article/was-president-kennedy-given-et-ufo-message-about-cuba

[545] Howard Menger, *From Outer Space to You* (Pyramid Books, 1959) 165-67. Available online at: http://tinyurl.com/d7xfhel

[546] Howard Menger, *From Outer Space to You* (Pyramid Books, 1959) 167. Available online at: http://tinyurl.com/d7xfhel

[547] Howard Menger, *From Outer Space to You*, 169. Available online at: http://tinyurl.com/d7xfhel

[548] Enrique Castillo Rincon, *UFOs: A Great New Dawn for Humanity* (Blue Dolphin Publishing, 1997).

[549] Enrique Castillo Rincon, *UFOs: A Great New Dawn for Humanity*, 184.

[550] Enrique Castillo Rincon, *UFOs: A Great New Dawn for Humanity*, 185.

[551] Enrique Castillo Rincon, *UFOs: A Great New Dawn for Humanity*, 186.

[552] Enrique Castillo Rincon, *UFOs: A Great New Dawn for Humanity*, 186.

[553] Enrique Castillo Rincon, *UFOs: A Great New Dawn for Humanity*, 187.

[554] Luis Fernando Mostajo Maertens, "Extraterrestrial Guides: The Great White Brotherhood in the Andes & Lake Titicaca," *Exopolitics Journal* vol 2:4, available online at: http://exopoliticsjournal.com/vol-2/vol-2-4-Fernando.htm

[555] Luis Fernando Mostajo Maertens, "Extraterrestrial Guides: The Great White Brotherhood in the Andes & Lake Titicaca," *Exopolitics Journal* vol 2:4, available online at: http://exopoliticsjournal.com/vol-2/vol-2-4-Fernando.htm

[556] Luis Fernando Mostajo Maertens, *Runa Antilis: The Magical Base of Los Andes*, (Impresion Digital, N.D.) 52.

[557] Luis Fernando, *Runa Antilis: The Magical Base of Los Andes*, 51-52.

[558] Luis Fernando, *Runa Antilis: The Magical Base of Los Andes*, 53.

[559] Luis Fernando, *Runa Antilis: The Magical Base of Los Andes*.

[560] Luis Fernando Mostajo Maertens, "Extraterrestrial Guides: The Great White Brotherhood in the Andes & Lake Titicaca," *Exopolitics Journal* vol 2:4, available online at: http://exopoliticsjournal.com/vol-2/vol-2-4-Fernando.htm

[561] For information on his retreats, please visit http://retreats.earthtransformation.com/ and http://www.winaymarka.org/

[562] Michael Salla, "Sacred Encounters at Lake Titicaca – An Interview with Luis Fernando Mostojo Maertens," *UFO Digest*, December 3, 2008. http://www.ufodigest.com/news/1208/sacred-encounters3.html

[563] Vladimir Megre, *Co-Creation: Book Four* (Ringing Cedars Press, 2006) 129

[564] Vladimir Megre, *Co-Creation: Book Four*, 130.

[565] Vladimir Megre, *Co-Creation: Book Four*, 132-33.

INDEX

About the Author

Dr. Michael Salla is an internationally recognized scholar in international politics, conflict resolution and U.S. foreign policy. He has held academic appointments in the School of International Service & the Center for Global Peace, American University, Washington DC (1996-2004); the Department of Political Science, Australian National University, Canberra, Australia (1994-96); and the Elliott School of International Affairs, George Washington University, Washington D.C., (2002). He has a Ph.D in Government from the University of Queensland, Australia. During his academic career he was author/editor of four books including *The Hero's Journey Toward a Second American Century* (Greenwood Press, 2001); *Essays on Peace* (Central Queensland University Press, 1995); *Why the Cold War Ended* (Greenwood Press, 1995); *Islamic Radicalism, Muslim Nations and the West* (1993) . He has conducted research and fieldwork in ethnic conflicts involving East Timor, Kosovo, Macedonia, and Sri Lanka. He has been awarded significant financial grants from the United States Institute of Peace and the Ford Foundation for peacemaking initiatives involving mid-to-high level participants from the East Timor conflict.

Dr. Salla is more popularly known as a pioneer in the development of 'exopolitics', the study of the main actors, institutions and political processes associated with extraterrestrial life. He wrote the first published book on 'exopolitics', *Exopolitics: Political Implications of the Extraterrestrial Presence* (Dandelion Books, 2004). In 2009 he wrote his second exopolitics book, *Exposing US Government Policies on Extraterrestrial Life* (Exopolitics Institute), He is Founder of the *Exopolitics Institute*, and the *Exopolitics Journal*, and Co-Organizer of the *Earth Transformation* series of conferences in Hawaii (2006-2011). His main website is: www.exopolitics.org

CPSIA information can be obtained
at www.ICGtesting.com
Printed in the USA
FSHW022002170319
56451FS

9 780982 290217